Men's Changing Roles in the Family

Men's Changing Roles in the Family

Edited by
Robert A. Lewis and Marvin B. Sussman

The Haworth Press
New York • London

Men's Changing Roles in the Family has also been published as *Marriage & Family Review*, Volume 9, Numbers 3/4, Winter 1985/86.

The Haworth Press, Inc., 12 West 32 Street, New York, NY 10001
EUROSPAN/Haworth, 3 Henrietta Street, London WC2E 8LU England

Library of Congress Cataloging-in-Publication Data
Main entry under title:

Men's changing roles in the family.

    Bibliography: p.
    Filmography: p.
    1. Sex role—United States—Addresses, essays, lectures. 2. Men—United States—Addresses, essays, lectures. 3. Fathers—United States—Addresses, essays, lectures.
4. Family—United States—Addresses, essays, lectures.
I. Lewis, Robert A. (Robert Alan), 1932-   II. Sussman, Marvin B.
HQ1075.5U6M46   1986   305.3'1   86-256
ISBN 0-86656-501-9
ISBN 0-86656-502-7 (pbk.)

Men's Changing Roles in the Family

Marriage & Family Review
Volume 9, Numbers 3/4

CONTENTS

Men's Changing Roles
in the Family

Preface

There is a well known common sense theory of social change. It is not resonated in the social science literature as an acceptable theory with an array of assumptions, postulates, hypotheses, and theorems. Rather it is an "a hah" theory; it makes deductive or analytic sense when one observes the cyclic patterns of change. We call this "a hah" explanation of reality the pendulum theory of change. The clock is used in this analogy.

Multiple foci and conditions catalyze changes in feelings, values, and perceptions of gender roles. The history of gender relationships tracing back into primordial times with few exceptions records a superordinate—subordinate pattern of male-female connecting, with the male being superordinate and the female subordinate. In all great civilizations the original myths of creation and governance of the universe and heavens by goddesses were changed to portray control and power residing in the hands of men and men gods.

The theme of male domination encrusted in the psyche, unconscious and deep consciousness of humankind and reinforced by universal patterns of socialization and conscious behavior was called into question by the gender revolutionaries of the second half of the 20th century. The volcanic eruptions in the form of challenges in the work place, arena of social interaction, family inner space, and court systems have swept away concerns over men's roles, power, and position. The pendulum swing of the timeless clock is to women's issues; equity, self expression, equal pay and equal work, shared parenting, equal options for a fair share of community resources and power.

Buttressing these societal forces, value, and ideological changes is the evocative presentation of the yearnings for gender equity by articulate spokespersons. The critical mass of conditions, situations, and actions is viewed to be present to implant an irrevocable change in the mind, consciousness, and soul of humankind. The time is here for such seeding and growing. In the throes of major changes in gender positioning and behavior neglect of male roles, feelings,

xiii

reactive behaviors, yearnings, and perceptions will occur. Endemic to major changes is that some persons involved become "losers." Efforts are made to minimize the losses in order to sustain the loser's acceptance and internalization of the evolving changes in values and behaviors.

The focus on effecting gender equity, vis-à-vis, a swing of the pendulum from male to female issues and problems has resulted in a greater research emphasis on what is happening to women over men. This neglect is understandable. In catalyzing and invoking changes in perceptions and behaviors it is necessary to present a message, vision, and means. While presenting all sides of the story may be a logical and valid procedure it may muddle the views and acceptance of the change by those who are on the fence or who are in agreement with reservations.

The emphasis on women's over men's roles in the gender connection is justified. The time is now appropriate, however, to consider the meaning and significance of these gender changes for men; how men are reacting, perceiving, and behaving. What men do will determine the permanency of these gender changes, how deep they are rooted in the consciousness of humankind.

The pendulum is moving slowly away from a 90 degree position on the clock to a more central one, closer to 45 degrees. The evidence is a birthquake of polemics, theorizing, and research on changing men's roles with concentration on marital, family, and parenting behaviors. This book of readings reviews the evidence for men's changing roles in the family. It introduces the reader to issues, problems, and methods on the "cutting edge" of those disciplines which study men in the context of their families. Although some sociologists facetiously remark that all of family sociology is "wives' sociology," because housewives are most often interviewed, relatively little is known empirically about men in contemporary families. Very little is known about husbands and fathers from direct reports of the men themselves.

This book should reverse this situation. Most of the chapters in this book report the results of recent empirical studies of fathers and husbands. Some subjects on the cutting edge of this recent research include: (1) an examination of the effects that fathers' growing involvement with their children have on their wives and themselves (Lamb, Pleck and Levine, Chapter 6); (2) a clinical assessment of some men's angry reactions to separation and divorce and those special therapeutic goals and strategies which may help to reduce their distress (Myers, Chapter 4); (3) two separate examinations of the conflicting demands of the work world and the family upon some contemporary husbands and fathers, e.g., upon clergymen (London, Allen, and Ziegler, Chapter 13) and the negative effects of nonstandard work schedules (shiftwork, flextime, and the compressed week) upon men's family life (Staines, Chapter 5); and finally (4) an examination of some factors that make many men unhappy in patriarchal family structures (Marciano, Chapter 3).

This book also contributes toward breaking new ground and reporting on these breakthroughs by examining family roles now performed by special groups of men. Chapters report empirical findings on (1) Black fathers' roles in their children's development (McAdoo, Chapter 9), and (2) single fathers, especially single custodial fathers, and their children (Hanson, Chapter 10). Two chapters report legal changes which have recently occurred in reference to fathers' rights and obligations to their children; one is a report from Sweden where many legal innovations have arisen (Trost and Hultaker, Chapter 7); the other is focused upon legal changes in the United States (Salt, Chapter 8).

Finally, this edition reports empirical findings about men in family-like relationships. Robinson (Chapter 11) examines the evidence for the unique roles that male caregivers can offer children in day-care centers, while Farrell (Chapter 12) gives a comprehensive review of current empirical studies of men's friendships and their development.

Three other special contributions which conclude this volume: Jeter presents the honeymoon in myth and ancient times, the unconscious yearnings and pinings of men and women, bridegrooms and brides which existed in yesteryear and today and which shapes the inner psyche and outward behaviors; the bibliography on fatherhood (Hanson and Bozett, "Fatherhood: A Library") is a prodigious and useful work for the student, clinician, and academic; A "Filmography on Fathering" by Giveans is a "first." We tend to ignore the visual and favor the audible. Indeed, "a picture is worth a thousand words" and Giveans provides us with the opportunity to use this relatively unused sense. A glossary of terms included in this volume should help users comprehend the special jargons of several disciplines.

We hope that this volume will provide some new and interesting readings about contemporary husbands and fathers. It may encourage additional research and thoughtful and provocative thinking on men's changing roles in the family—an area that currently receives much attention that has been heretofore directed to other issues and problems of contemporary American families.

Robert A. Lewis
Marvin B. Sussman

Chapter 1

Men's Changing Roles
in Marriage and the Family

Robert A. Lewis

INTRODUCTION

Times are changing. Family roles are changing. But, of all family role changes perhaps the most significant changes are occurring in fathers' roles (Russell, 1983). Even in the conservative small city where I live it was not surprising to read in the local newspaper a few months ago the following announcement: "Cub scouts and their dads will compete in a cake cook-off at the Hershey Elementary School at 6:30 p.m., Nov. 22. No mothers may assist in the project . . . "

Women's work roles have been changing dramatically in the U.S.A. during the 1960's and 1970's. Perhaps less dramatic but not invisible to social scientists during the 1970's and 1980's has been the redefining of men's roles within families. Even if some men have not changed their own roles in the family, they believe that they have more role options than their fathers had (Pleck, 1976). William Goode (1982) has recently cautioned, however, against the belief that American males have ever had very strict sex-role prescriptions:

> How many men do we actually know who carry out these social prescriptions (i.e., how many are emotionally anesthetized, aggressive, physically tough and daring, unwilling or unable to give nurturance to a child)? . . . do they lose their membership cards in the male fraternity if they fail in these

Robert A. Lewis, PhD, is Head and Professor, Department of Child Development and Family Studies, Purdue University, West Lafayette, IN 47907.

1

respects? If socialization and social pressures are so all-powerful, where are all the John Wayne types in our society?" (Goode, 1982:135)

One of the purposes of this chapter and the entire book is to examine the evidence for men's changing roles in families. But, are individual men actually changing their roles, their role expectations (their attitudes) and adopting new role behaviors? Or, is that which social scientists are beginning to document and report primarily generational differences? This is one of the difficult questions which still remains to be answered by social analysts.

Media Hype

The media in the U.S. has eagerly drawn attention to some of the more apparent changes in men's family roles. At times it is difficult to distinguish between media hype and reputable change data. Also, in many areas actual change data are scant. For example, Shere Hite (1982) wrote an article, "The New, Sensitive Male: Is He Too Good to be True?" In this article she suggests that men are breaking out of their traditional socialization to become more sensitive and loving men. No empirical data, however, are given to support her contentions.

A more recent study reported in a women's magazine on the responses of some 74,000 women readers, similarly suggests that men are changing their roles. For instance, 62 percent of the women over forty and 84 percent of women under forty thought that men are just as good at child care as women are. According to the women aged 25–34, 47 percent of their husbands do grocery shopping, 51 percent cook, 51 percent clean the house and 39 percent do the laundry. And, while there were also differences between homemakers and women working outside the home, these authors conclude their article with the words: "Indeed, in the last twenty years, men and women have crossed once impenetrable boundaries into each other's territory" (Enos & Enos, 1985:183). However, in spite of the very large sample of respondents, a self-selected sample of the readership of a woman's magazine is not a representative sample. Such studies cannot document social change.

Much of the media hype seems to have been triggered a few years ago by a popular film, *Kramer vs. Kramer*; in it Dustin Hoffman was at first the unwilling recipient of the sole custody of his young son. This film was followed by another successful smash at the box office, *Tootsie*, in which Dustin Hoffman learns empathy for women by living in the clothes and eventually the personality of an actress on a television soap opera. Even more recently, a film called *Mr. Mom*, based on a role-reversal where the father becomes a househusband, was so popular among movie-goers in the U.S. that the film grossed $20.4 million in its first six weeks. Granted, American film-goers do like comedy, but what can explain the fascination which young adults and others experience in these role-reversal and role-overlap films?

A Growing Base of Data

Unmistaken to even the unsophisticated observer of our society is the fact that more men seem to be taking on roles and tasks within their homes which men in previous decades did not play—or at least, would not admit playing. Until quite recently, however, much of the data supporting these impressions was based on only personal observations, on case studies or extrapolated from cross-sectional studies.

In research with fathers and husbands during the last fifteen years I have been analyzing what men report doing within their families (Lewis, Freneau & Roberts, 1979a; Lewis & Roberts, 1979b; Lewis & Pleck, 1979; Spanier, Lewis & Cale, 1975). During these years I have become increasingly aware of men who were role-making, innovating new roles once forbidden or discouraged. Also, as a family therapist, I have observed a number of middle aged men who were thrilled with their personal developments in nurturing (giving care to) their own children, wives, kin and friends. These are men who are learning how sweet is the taste of "generativity," as described by Erik Erickson, as they learn to give more of their time and resources to others.

Case studies are another source of data. Most case studies, however, utilize soft or qualitative data, which describes rather than documents social change. Unfortunately, some of these areas (where men are experiencing and experimenting with roles traditionally played by women) are so new that not much empirical study has yet been directed to them.

One such area is that studied by Kyle Pruett, a psychiatrist at the Yale Child Study Center, who has performed case analyses of 17 New England families where there was a clear role-reversal (Pruett,

1983). In these families the mothers worked outside the home while the fathers dominated the child-care from birth. Although admittedly a small sample, Pruett reports that all infants did well, that they were achieving above average social skills, and were especially interested and comfortable with the outside external stimulation their fathers provided them. One interesting difference was the fathers' more robust style of play, e.g., carrying their infants either in a football position or tucked under their buttocks rather than at the chest/breast area. On many indicators these fathers were just as skillful and loving as the mothers. The researcher's only concern was that the parents received negative judgments from neighbors toward their role-switching. Obviously, the rest of the community was not as ready to accept the life styles they had adopted.

National polls are one source of change data which scholars usually accept as evidence for attitudinal change. Some national polls are providing a valuable data base for assessing change in men's family roles. One recent Gallup poll of a national sample of 645 new mothers reports that over 80 percent of fathers are now present in the delivery room (90 percent in metropolitan areas), compared to only 27 percent a decade ago. Eighty percent of fathers, according to the same national study, changed their baby's diapers and 43 percent gave baths to their babies. Furthermore, 25 percent of these American fathers expected to be the *primary* care-giver to their babies when their wives went back to work.

Perhaps the most valuable source of change data on fathers' and husbands' roles and behavior are national time-studies, such as time diary-studies where respondents record the activities in which they engage during various 24-hour periods for one week. As we will see in the following sections of this introductory chapter, time-studies use methodologies which are among the best means for documenting that which men actually do as husbands and fathers.

CHANGES IN MEN'S FAMILY ROLES

Changes in Role Expectations

Role expectations, i.e., attitudes, usually change prior to changes in role behaviors. Role expectations which assume equalitarianism in the husband and wife relationship have been among the more obvious to change in the U.S.A. National surveys in recent years have documented a trend in the attitudes—especially of young adults, toward the valuing of egalitarianism. In one national study of university freshmen, for instance, nearly a majority (49 percent) of the males professed a preference for an equalitarian marriage, compared to 69 percent of the females. Ten years earlier, a similar sample of university freshmen was questioned nationwide on the same topic. At the earlier time 52 percent of the males and 31 percent of the females had not wanted an equalitarian marriage. When taking into account a sizeable middle group which has no opinion, one can note a slow but perceptible change in young Americans' role expectations toward equality.

In 1983, the American life and health insurance industries conducted a telephone survey of 1,000 Americans. This poll revealed that 76 percent of young adults between the ages of 19 and 37 preferred an equalitarian marriage where both spouses share responsibilities for work, home-making and child-rearing. It is interesting, however, that 63 percent said that only economic necessity should lead a mother of pre-school children to work outside the home, whereas the majority of pre-school mothers actually do work, at least part-time, outside the home.

The movement of young adults' attitudes toward the valuing of equalitarian marriages, however, tells little about how much equality there will actually be in the marital interaction of this baby-boom cohort. Time will tell. That which can be expected is more talk about equalitarian marriages, since behavioral changes usually lag behind changes in role expectations.

Some data, however, are beginning to trickle down the channels of social research on the possible effects of equalitarian marital roles. Samuel Osherson at the Harvard Medical School and a colleague published some findings about the problems of equalitarian marriage structures, as contrasted to more traditional structures (Osherson & Dill, 1983). In this study equalitarian husbands were reported to feel that they had achieved less success at work, according to the norms of our society, than more traditional men whose wives did not work outside the home. The equalitarian husbands, however, did purport greater career flexibility, e.g., being able to pursue more self-development activities rather than just their job-related activities. The most problematic group, however, appears to be the equalitarian husbands who were also childless. They reported the lowest feelings of job success, perhaps because they were not able to draw on other rewarding experiences, such as nurturing children, which according to the researcher, might help them buffer the injuries given their self esteem on the job.

Changes in Men's Role Behaviors

Changes are more difficult to document for men's role behaviors (that which men actually do) than men's role expectations (that which men say that they should do). Data from time-diaries, however, are giving some indications that men are becoming more involved in their family roles, especially in child care.

Although changes in men's family role behaviors were rather mixed or unclear between 1955 and 1971 (See Pleck; 1983), some changes have been documented from the early 1970's. For instance, comparative analyses made of 1967–68 and 1977 time-use data from Syracuse, New York by Robert Sanik (1979) have revealed some important changes. If one controls for a number of significant variables, fathers in Syracuse at the latter time (1977) spent 25 percent more time in child care and housework than fathers spent 10 years previously. In other words, there was an increase in husbands' family work from 104 to 130 minutes a day. Although this increase may not seem very much, as Joseph Pleck has frequently asserted when reviewing these data, it depends upon whether you are optimistic or pessimistic, that is, whether you view the glass either one-fourth full or three-fourths empty. The discovery of any identifiable increase in men's involvement in the family is significant news.

Similarly, in a Panel Study of Income Dynamics two researchers in different studies have found increases from 1968 in fathers' reports of time given to housework, when other variables were controlled (Nickols, 1976; Hofferth, 1981). Robinson (1977; 1980) has also reported a six percent increase per week in urban men's family work between 1965 and 1975. Robinson (1980) cautions the reader, however, that the increase for husbands in the 1975 sample is due to a higher proportion of husbands in that sample who had characteristics associated with higher involvement in family work. Nevertheless, since the amount of time spent by the wives had actually decreased over that period, the husbands were spending a larger proportion of the couples' total time in family work in 1975 than 1965. Pleck and Rustad (1981), working from national time use data, have similarly learned that employed wives in 1976–77 spent only 12 more minutes a day in *combined* paid work and family work than their husbands spent. The best understanding of all these findings, seems to be that the husbands' proportion is apparently increasing because wives are doing less combined family and outside work, when they are employed outside the home.

These current findings are in decided contrast to earlier findings from time diary studies in the 1960's which consistently revealed little or no increase in husbands' family work when their wives were employed. For example, according to Walker (1970) husbands spent nearly the same amount of time on family tasks (1.6 hours a day) whether their wives worked or not. Yet, more recent time budget studies suggest that men with working wives are now spending significantly more time in family roles than men whose wives are homemakers (Pleck, 1983). For example, Pleck and Lang's (1978) analysis shows that men spend 2.7 hours a day in family work when wives work outside the home, compared to the 1.8 hours a man spends when his wife is not.

One of the newest studies of fathers' participation in family work also reflects the recent changes but in a slightly different form. In this study of 160 fathers and mothers of kindergarten and fourth grade boys and girls Barnett and Baruch (1984) report that the mothers' employment status (whether they worked outside the home or not) significantly predicted the proportion of the fathers' participation in child care and child play relative to the mothers'.

Another time comparison, a replication of the famous Middletown study of Muncie, Indiana, in 1924 by Robert and Helen Lynn, reveals similar change data. This replication by Theodore Caplow and Ruth Chadwick (1979) revealed a substantial increase in the number of fathers who spent more than an hour a day with their children. Whereas 10 percent of fathers spent no time with their children fifty years ago only two percent of Muncie fathers spent no time with their children in 1978. Since there have been many social changes in Muncie, Indiana, in 50 years, it is not surprising that one of the significant changes has been the increasing amount of time which fathers there now spend with their children.

In summary, although the results of time studies vary somewhat, most current time studies suggest that fathers spend an average of 15 to 25 minutes per day in more narrowly defined child-care activities, but between 2.0 to 3.6 hours a day in more broadly defined childcare. Husbands similarly spend somewhere between slightly under two hours a day to over five and one-half hours a day in family tasks (Pleck, 1983). These results differ somewhat by study, due to differences in the age of the children, the broadness or narrowness of the definition of childcare and the particular methodology which is used.

Unfortunately, the lay public remembers one piece of trivia which was given unwarranted publicity several years ago. A study by Rebelsky and Hanks (1971) reported that a nonrepresentative sample of 19 fathers spoke an average of 37.7 seconds a day to their 0–3 month old infants. Their vocalizations were timed by voice-activated microphones placed on the infants. Unfortunately, this finding has been quoted out of context and popularized to the point where its interpretations overshadow new and more adequate data on fathers' involvement with their children. Consequently, this trivia has gravely distorted Americans' perceptions of how much time fathers actually spend with their children.

CONCERNS ABOUT MEN'S CHANGING ROLES

Several chapters in this book deal with various positive concerns and implications of men's changing roles in the family. Not all outcomes, however, are positive. Personal and family costs are often involved with social change.

One of these potential implications for men's changing roles in the family has already been discussed in relation to American attitudinal changes toward a greater valuing of equalitarianism. As we noted, discrepancies between men's and women's attitudes toward marital equity can lead to both unfulfilled expectations and marital role conflict. We also raised the point that equalitarian attitudes may have some negative as well as positive outcomes for husbands in terms of lower job success, although we are not sure of the direction of causality.

Fathers' greater involvement in household tasks and child-care can also have negative outcomes, as Lamb, Pleck and Levine discuss in Chapter 6. Although fathers may have greater satisfaction in their relationships with their children when they are more involved with their children, their wives may not appreciate this involvement in all ways. Neighbors, friends and kin may disapprove of greater paternal involvement. As Lein (1979) discovered, husbands' greater involvement in household tasks is often challenged by those men's male friends who become their major impediments to making role changes.

Just as "Super Moms" face greater stressors from attempting to perform equally well the positions of mother, wife and gainfully employed woman, some fathers may also take on the impossible task of being full-time fathers, husbands and wage-earners. In addition, as even greater numbers of mothers invest their time in breadwinning roles, will the fathers become more threatened or relieved? We do not know the answer to this question.

Neither do we know answers to the question of what happens to family men when their wives earn the same or more than they do. For example, there have been no studies of marriages where wives earn more than their husbands, in spite of the fact that the U.S. Census Bureau has just reported that nearly six million American wives earned more than their husbands. This is 12.1 percent of all two parent households in the United States, certainly a small percentage but actually a large group of American couples.

In summary, men's changing roles in the family will raise new problems as well as solutions. As James Levine said at a recent "fathering forum," held at Bank Street College:

> I think we're seeing more men interested in being involved parents, but we're also hearing from fathers and mothers just how hard that is . . . It's not easy for men, or for women either, who have the responsibility for child care and also for bread-winning outside the home. (New York Times, June 13, 1983:B9)

REFERENCES

Baruch, G. K. & Barnett, R. C. (1984). Determinants of fathers' participation in family work. Working Paper No. 136, Wellesley, MA: Wellesley College Center for Research on Women.

Enos C. & Enos, S. F. (1985). The men in your life. *Ladies' Home Journal*, March, 99–101; 180–183.

Erickson, E. H. (1950). *Childhood and Society*. New York: W. W. Norton & Co.

Goode, W. J. (1982). Why men resist. In B. Thorne (Ed.) *Rethinking the Family*. New York: Longman.

Hofferth, S. (1981). *Effects of Number and Timing of Births on Family Wellbeing over the Life Cycle*. Washington, D.C.: Urban Institute.

Lein, L. (1979). Male participation in home life: Impact of social supports and breadwinner responsibility on the allocation of tasks. *The Family Coordinator*, 28, 489–495.

Lewis, R. A., Freneau, P. J. & Roberts, C. L. (1979a). Fathers and the post-parental transition. *The Family Coordinator*, 28, 514–520.

Lewis, R. A. & Roberts, C. L. (1979b). Postparental fathers in distress. *Psychiatric Opinion*, Nov./Dec., 27–30.

Lewis, R. A. & Pleck, J. H. (1979). Men's roles in the family. *The Family Coordinator, 29,* 429–646.

Nickols, S. (1976). Work and housework: Family roles in productive activity. A paper presented at the National Council on Family Relations, New York, October.

Osherson, S. & Dill, D. (1983). Varying work and family choices: The impact on men's work satisfaction. *Journal of Marriage and the Family, 45,* (2), 339–346.

Pleck, J. H. (1976). Men's new roles in the family: Housework and childcare. Unpublished paper. Wellesley, MA: Wellesley College Center for Research on Women.

Pleck, J. H. (1983). Husbands' paid work and family roles: Current Research Issues. In: Lopata, H. Z. & Pleck, J. H., eds.. *Research on the Interweave of Social Roles,* Vol. 3. Greenwich, CT: JAI Press.

Pleck, J. H. and Lang, L. (1978). Men's Family Roles: Its nature and consequences. Wellesley, MA: Wellesley College Center for Research on Women.

Pleck, J. H. & Rustad, M. (1981). Wives' employment, role demands, and adjustment: Final report. Unpublished, Wellesley College Center for Research on Women.

Rebelsky, F., & Hanks, C. (1971). Fathers' verbal interaction with infants in the first three months of life. *Child Development, 42,* 63–68.

Robinson, J. (1977). Change in American's use of time: 1965–1975. Cleveland: Communications Research Center, Cleveland State University.

Robinson, J. (1980). Housework technology and household work. In Berk, S. F., Ed., *Women and Household Labor.* Beverly Hills, CA: Sage.

Russell, Graeme (1983). *The Changing Role of Fathers?* St. Lucia: University of Queensland Press.

Sanik, M. (1979). A twofold comparison of time spent in household work in two-parent, two-child households: Urban New York State in 1967–68 and 1977, Doctoral dissertation, Cornell University, Dissertation Abstracts International 39:5334.

Spanier, G. B., Lewis, R. A. and Cole, C. L. (1975). Marital adjustment over the family life cycle: The issue of curvilinearity. *Journal of Marriage and the Family, 37,* 263–275.

Walker, K. E. (1970). Time spent by husbands in household work. *Family Economics Review, 4,* 8–11.

Chapter 2

Epilog:
Facilitating Future Change
in Men's Family Roles

Joseph H. Pleck
Michael E. Lamb
James A. Levine

Several studies (see reviews in Pleck, 1983; Pleck, in press) demonstrate increases since the mid 1960s in the average amount of time men spend in one central aspect of their family role, family work (i.e., housework and childcare). This increase is occurring at the same time that women's time in family roles is decreasing. The joint effect of these two trends is that in national time diary surveys, men's average proportion of the total family work performed by men and women rose from 20% to 30% between 1965 and 1980 (see data in Juster, in press). In the 1975 national survey analyzed by Pleck (in press), high levels of family work by husbands are associated with positive family adjustment and overall well-being. Altogether, these results argue well for future enlargements in men's family roles.

Past research has investigated several potential sources of men's low participation in family roles (especially parenting) compared to women. These factors can be grouped into two broad categories: the biological explanation and the social explanation. Biological factors which may limit men's family role continue to elicit considerable

---

Joseph H. Pleck, PhD, is Program Director, Center for Research on Women, Wellesley College, Wellesley, MA 02181. Michael E. Lamb, PhD, is Professor of Psychology, Psychiatry and Pediatrics, Department of Psychology, The University of Utah, Salt Lake City, UT 84112. James A. Levine is Director, Fatherhood Project, Banks Street College, New York, NY 10025.

11

research interest. Contemporary research and theory suggest some possible biological influences on parenting behavior, and that biological and social influences can interact. However, these influences are weak, and do not appear to set upper limits on men's family involvement (Lamb, Pleck, Charnov, and Levine, in press).

There is far greater interest in socialization and social-structural influences on men's family roles. Research suggests that men's work role by itself is not a sufficient explanation. Men's amount of time in paid work does, it is true, have a negative statistical relationship to their time in family roles. But a large husband-wife difference in levels of family work remains even when work hours are controlled for. Further, the effect of paid work hours on childcare time, a particularly important component of men's family roles, is quite weak (Pleck, in press).

Other social factors have also received attention: modeling after one's own father, social attitudes, lack of support from wives or peers, and lack of specific parenting skills. Some of these have been studied (with as yet inconclusive or inconsistent results), and others have received little or no research attention. All of these factors are probably important for at least some men. Like the work role, when any one of these social factors is studied by itself, it is likely to account for some of the existing sex difference, but a considerable difference still remains.

A complete list of these social predictors (including aspects of the work role) considered simultaneously instead of one at a time would presumably account for all the existing sex difference in family participation. But a deeper question arises: even if all the variance in men's family time could be explained through a combination of these social factors, is not the real source of men's low participation that men simply do not want to do it? It can be argued, for example, that the work role is not a major reason for low family involvement because men actually have considerable choice over the extent and intensity of their participation in paid work. To many, the work role and the other proximate social factors considered here simply reflect that men do not want to be more involved than they are.

The central issue is whether men themselves, rather than social-structural and socialization factors, are responsible for men's low family participation. In essence, does men's low participation occur because of factors which men are not accountable for, or do men ultimately bear moral responsibility for it? This question underlies much of the contemporary debate about men's family role, especially among feminists, and it cannot be answered on the basis of social scientific analysis alone. The most judicious response is that both are true to some degree.

While these social variables do not entirely explain (either statistically or philosophically) why men's family involvement is lower than women's, influencing these social factors can nonetheless increase men's involvement. For the purpose of planning interventions, the following classification of the social factors facilitating men's family involvement is useful.

Motivation: For family involvement to increase, husbands have to want to participate in family roles. Some men have high motivation at the outset of family life due to their modeling after a highly involved father, rejecting the negative model of an uninvolved father, or other family or social factors. Other men become motivated because of their wives' increasing involvement in paid work; the family simply cannot function unless the father becomes more involved. Yet other men become more motivated as part of a mid-life reevaluation, including the realization of what they missed out on earlier. New media images of men's roles and educational programs can also stimulate motivation.

Skills: Some men report that they would like to become more involved in the family (i.e., their motivation has increased), but that they literally do not know what to do or how to act, especially with children. The average man enters adult family life with less prior experience and opportunity to learn these skills than the average woman. Having specific parenting and household skills makes family participation a more self-reinforcing, satisfying experience for the husband, and gives him more self-confidence in this role.

Social Supports: High family involvement is unlikely to occur and be maintained unless significant others—spouses, relatives, friends, co-workers—approve of it and provide positive reinforcement for it. These significant others also provide advice and concrete help in the performance of family roles.

Reducing Institutional Barriers: There is clearly a social-structural dimension to the three earlier factors: social structure helps shape individuals' motivations, what skills they have opportunities to learn, and what social support networks are available to them. But institutional practices can influence men's family involvement in an even more direct way. Some men develop motivation for greater family involvement, acquire skills, and locate social supports, but then find they are constrained by institutional barriers. Recent reforms in hospital policies previously restricting fathers' presence in hospital delivery rooms, and in legal procedures limiting fathers' rights to child custody following divorce, are examples of how some institutional barriers are being reduced.

The primary institutional barriers to men's family involvement derive, of course, from the workplace. Job schedules and career tracks that are inflexible or highly demanding are particularly important, as are parental leave policies that exclude men. But also significant are the timing of career demands over the life cycle (for those husbands who have careers). The greatest work effort is required at the early stages of career development, when the demands of the family role are also at their peak. In that vast majority of families in which the husband's wage is higher than the wife's, there is also a trade-off between men's family participation and total family income. The husband doing more in the family in theory frees the wife to put more time in paid work to earn more. But since her wage is typically significantly lower than her husband's, such a choice reduces total family income. The husband-wife wage ratio can act as a powerful structural disincentive to husbands' participation.

Considering these four factors together helps make sense of some findings in past research, particularly concerning the relative importance of institutional barriers and the other factors. For example, in a study of the effect of introducing flexitime (an alternative work schedule in which workers can select their starting and ending times, within limits set by the employer) on workers' family behavior, Winett and Neale (1980) found that about half the fathers in the sample altered their schedule when flexitime was implemented, most often to arrive at work earlier and thus leave earlier. The fathers in this subgroup spent more time with their families after flexitime was introduced than before. We suggest that for the fathers who did not modify their schedules, work schedule was not a major constraint on their family involvement. Rather, they lacked the other facilitating factors—motivation, skills, and social supports (or, in some cases, their work schedule may have already been optimal). But for half the fathers, schedule flexibility clearly was a constraint: when given the opportunity, they changed their schedule in a way associated with their spending more time with their families.

As another example, a relatively small proportion of fathers take paid paternity leave when it is available to them, either in Sweden

(Lamb, 1982) or in the handful of organizations offering it in the U.S. Some fathers do not take advantage of paid paternity leave because taking one can have serious negative consequences, such as employers viewing them more negatively in terms of job advancement. But probably the reason most fathers do not take paid paternity leave is because they lack the motivation, skills, and/or social supports which facilitate father involvement. In essence, for institutional constraints to be the limiting factor, the other facilitating influences must already be in place.

These four factors differ in the social institutions through which they operate, and in the ease with which they can be altered. The emerging social ideal of the "new father" reflected in current media images, and family life education curricula which include attention to husbands' and fathers' roles, help increase motivation. Educational and social service programs about fathering (see examples in Klinman et al., 1984), as well as "support groups" for men and for fathers, provide skills and/or social supports for those men motivated to participate in them. Further implementation of alternative work schedules and gender-neutral parental leave policies will help reduce some (though not all) aspects of the constraints against men's family involvement imposed by the workplace.

The historical increase in men's actual family role participation over the last two decades suggests that men's motivation to be actively involved in family life has also been rising. Over time, there is likely to be increasing demand for and utilization of programs providing skills and social supports to men in their family role. As motivation, skills, and social supports for an expanded family role increase, the institutional barriers to men's family role will loom relatively larger in importance. As a result, there will be heightened advocacy of policies to reduce the structural barriers to men's family involvement, especially in the workplace, a phenomenon already beginning to be evident. Altering the average husband-wife wage ratio, or the timing of job demands over the life cycle, however, seem more distant prospects.

Not all programs and policies in these four areas will impact on all subgroups of men equally. Further, is it not clear that the policies and programs bearing on these factors which are realistically feasible will completely eliminate the current average sex difference in family involvement. But policies and programs influencing these four factors will promote an enlargement of the male family role, and all are worthy of support from those concerned to increase men's options to be actively involved in family life.

BIBLIOGRAPHY

Juster, F. T. (in press) A note on recent changes in time use. In F. T. Juster and F. Stafford (Eds.), *Time, Goods, and Well-Being*. Ann Arbor, MI: Institute for Social Research.

Klinman, D., Kohl, R., & The Fatherhood Project (1984) *Fatherhood USA: The First National Guide to Program, Services, and Resources for and about Fathers*. New York: Garland.

Lamb, M. E. (1982) Why Swedish fathers aren't liberated. *Psychology Today*, October 1982, 75–77.

Lamb, M. E., Pleck, J. H., Charnov, E. L., & Levine, J. A. (in press) A biosocial perspective of paternal behavior and involvement. In J. B. Lancaster et al., (Eds.), *Parenting Across the Life Span: Biosocial Perspectives*. Chicago: Aldine.

Pleck, J. H. (1983) Husbands' paid work and family roles: Current research issues. In H. Lopata & J. H. Pleck (Eds.), *Research in the Interweave of Social Roles, Vol. 3: Families and Jobs*. Greenwich, CT: JAI Press.

Pleck, J. H. (in press) *Working Wives, Working Husbands*. Beverly Hills, CA: Sage.

Winnett, R. A., & Neale, M. (1980) Results of an experimental study on flexitime and family life. *Monthly Labor Review*, *103*(11), 29–32.

Chapter 3

Why Are Men Unhappy in Patriarchy?

Teresa Donati Marciano

Patriarchy is, by definition, a system promoting the higher status and privilege of men against women. The system as it is speaks to and for dominant male groups against all women and against selected aspects of subordinate male groups. In all cultures, whatever the value on women and women's productive or reproductive capacities, men's existence and work is regarded as more honorable and more important (see Ortner, 1974).

Indeed, at any stratum of nation or culture, with actual individual exceptions, the patterned norms of existence and action are male. Even the simple sociological proposition that "leaders embody the norms" (Homans, 1950; Whyte, 1955), shows this. For if the norms are male, can a woman "embody" them, and if so, at what risk? In fact, authoritative "leadership" of the male variety is not characteristic of women's groups or the Women's Movement (see, e.g., Gilligan, 1982). Women who do operate in male structures are taught to adapt to them and are chided for failing to do so. (See accounts of this in Kanter, 1975.) Of course, they are also chided when they do adapt, but that is another issue. (See Marciano, 1981.) Women enter and leave the structured world of men, like blacks on a pass to a white district in South Africa, useful (limitedly) to work, but certainly not true peers, and not welcome into groups where deals are struck, and political-economic decisions are made.

A result of all this is that, whether or not separate realms of male and female consciousness predate patriarchy or are its outcome, the more rigid the patriarchy, the more separate the experiences of life in it for each sex (see Bernard, 1981). The categories of thought, words, and concepts, reflect the experience of males far more than

Teresa D. Marciano, PhD, is Chair and Professor, Department of Sociology/Anthropology, Fairleigh Dickinson University, Teaneck, NJ 07666.

that of females (Kramerae, 1981). The lack of "fit" between female experience and male categories of the world, is attributed to the imperfect adaptation and perception of women. Therefore, explanations abound as to why everyone, including those whose system it is not, should like, value, and adjust to it. Virginia Woolf (1957) catalogued some of the hundreds of such explanations, with delightful if sad irony.

The problem is that attempts to justify patriarchy where so many find it uncomfortable or an outright source of suffering, amounts to a "theodicy". As in religion, theodicy in any realm, by any name (e.g., Marx's "false consciousness") justifies suffering and inequality as part of a larger, divine or at least morally superior, plan.

Men should love and thrive in a system that purports to give them so much. Yet history is not static, and the men who suffer in the system, for whatever reasons, find the theodicy as lacking in comfort as do women. To the extent that men share the devaluation accorded women, by sharing the imperatives or duties or attitudes of women, they are likely to become conscious of the system's inadequacies and injustices. Or, sheer intelligence and a good distance on the immediate and historical, may point out the absurdity of what seemed to be the logical premises of patriarchy. In any case, the voices of some men have joined with women who have decried (and mocked) the system's inequalities.

But because the system is presumed to be so "natural"—with whatever logic "nature" confers upon it—one task of men who have rebelled against patriarchy has been to convince other men that one is not rejecting manhood. "Masculinity"—the social expectations placed upon biological males—is defined by the absence of "femininity" (Shively and DeCecco, 1977). Those (men) who defend a given group (women) are often accused of being one with the group defended. Men's arguments against patriarchy have tended, then, to say that the system does not make them more like women, but rather that it denies men the chance to be true men.

Yet, why should men have done this at all? Men could simply carve more comfortable niches for themselves, presumably, by operating within the system, or finding places in it where its worst effects would be avoided. Why are men unhappy in patriarchy? The rest of this paper looks at that question, and proposes not only a framework for explanation, but also an account of the role of family in resolving men's unhappiness in "their" system.

Some of the specific complaints voiced by men against patriarchy include (as a very limited list): the insufficient, often empty and alienating link between "masculinity", work, and other social hierarchies (Tolson, 1977); the rigid controls placed upon men's love and expressiveness (Balswick and Peek, 1971; Lehne, 1976); the devitalizing price of privilege, leaving men to dominate sullen, unhappy women (Goldberg, 1976); the observation (rather than complaint) that dominance has both socioeconomic and emotional costs that amount to a dialectic, with consequent tensions (Goode, 1982); the recognition that as men grow older, personal growth and satisfaction cause the adolescent sex role rigidities to give way to more recognition of interdependence and nurturance with women (Moreland, 1980; Fischer and Narus, 1981). In the last, a more "developmental" model of androgyny has been put forth to account for resolutions in the system's contradictory normative demands (for "real men") and personal human needs (love and intimacy). Women too have listed men's as well as their own objections to patriarchy, not necessarily sympathetically, but also calling the system's contradictions to account: the male provider role, placing men into money-status bondage, yet increasingly diluted by women's entry into the labor force, leaving men no comfortable legitimate new role to fill the disappearing old one (Bernard, 1981(b)); that men were driven to rebel against conformist-provider pressures to be "family men" and "mature", faithful husbands, and rebelled a decade ahead of the Second Women's Movement of the 1960s (Ehrenreich, 1983); that men have had to shape elaborate games and distortions to find a truce with each other, thence projecting their anxieties onto women (Chesler, 1978).

In the midst of these objections and observations, it is noted that patriarchy gives men many more options and life-chances than it does women: for characterological expression (Bem and Bem, 1971); occupational choices and income (Kessler-Harris, 1983; Fox and Hesse-Biber, 1984); sheer freedom of bodily and geographic movement, and absence of the fear of assault (Brownmiller, 1977 and 1984); of the lower degree of negative sanction for men who remain unmarried or, if married, to remain childless (Marciano, 1978); or if having children, to have women do the preponderance of physical work to rear them (Polatnick, 1973); or if divorced, that men escape the financial decline so likely to occur for women and children in divorce (Weitzman, 1981).

How to make sense of the apparent contradictions between the advantages of patriarchy and the discontent men feel? First, by looking how any such system is actually created and maintained, its dissonant effects for men, and the family's role, finally, in enabling men to cope with dissonance.

First to look at the system's creation and maintenance: Goode (1982) not only shows the advantages of patriarchy which are often invisible to men, but also says that men know they did not create patriarchy, and thus they do not conspire to oppress women. That absence of "conspiracy" will be stipulated for the moment. While the nature and actuality of "conspiracy" is debatable (see, e.g., Firestone, 1970), such an *effect* is systemic, i.e., built into the nature of the way the system operates and maintains itself.

But that system can be approached not from the passive-participant aspect, as in Goode, whereby we are part of a system we did not create. Rather, the system can be approached in the "social construction of reality" framework of Berger and Luckmann (1966). In that framework, we are part of a patriarchal system we indeed create; as with all systems, it is structured to make adherents of its creators.

It occurs this way: as people interact, they produce relationships, patterns of action and expectation, and things. This process is "externalization," an ongoing set of practices that produce a culture or system or set of rules for living together. Those rules provide some sort of interdependence and predictability, as opposed to a Hobbesian uncertainty or chaos. And as with Darwin, we can also begin with what is ongoing, and not consider how we all got to the point of interaction in the first place. Thus, this starts not with how patriarchy itself got started, but rather takes the production of patriarchy as a given, produced first by externalized habits and patterns of thought, action, and production.

These externalized products are institutionalized, so that as a common history is shared, it takes on an order and certainty; that very order becomes the pattern of felt expectations and obligations that are the bases of social control. As we conform to what we expect of ourselves and others, we are kept within the ongoing system, and "create" the system anew.

Over time, the social world seems to take on an independent existence and reality of its own. This is "objectivation," where we are born into a social order that seems "always" to have been there. Berger and Luckmann say (1966: 57):

It is important to keep in mind that the objectivity of the

institutional world, however massive it may appear to the individual, is a humanly produced, constructed objectivity. The process by which the externalized products of human activity attain the character of objectivity is objectivation.

This externalized, objectivated world is then incorporated into individual psyches and habits through the process of internalization. We learn to carry "society" within us. We learn to control ourselves, to conform thereby, with others there to sanction us if we deviate.

The institutions or sets of patterns in that system, come to "hang together"; they are linked by a common set of explanations or "legitimations". Each of the institutions has a set of social "meanings" attached to it. Those meanings are integrated by a larger ("second order") meaning system or legitimating system. Legitimation makes the system "plausible", explaining and justifying it to "newcomers" (i.e., those born into it or adopting it). Berger and Luckmann note (1966: 86): "Legitimation 'explains' the institutional order by ascribing cognitive validity to its objectivated meanings."

We thus learn that our social order—patriarchy in this case—is "objectively correct"; not only do we obey its precepts, but we also "know" those precepts to be "correct". They are the blueprint for the moral order in that system, for what is "right" and "wrong".

Among the legitimations of a patriarchal system are statements about why men need, and deserve to have, more than women. In addition, though inviting dissonant and dialectical responses, there are often statements that men actually do not do better than women in the system. Some version of "separate but equal" is offered to deny that anyone is really disadvantaged. In patriarchal religions, for example, this is stated as a set of different but complementary obligations for each sex, with actual equality before God. In the Parsonian reflection of patriarchal families, the complementarity of (male) "instrumental" roles and (female) "expressive" roles promote a balanced fulfillment of obligations and harmony. In both religion and family, however, "equality" lies in being judged on unequal obligation. Each sex is obliged to do certain things ascriptively—that is, expectations await us based solely on the sex in which we happen to be born. There is no equality based on demonstrated ability or felt inclination. Expectations of each sex are categorical, and individual variation is muted. Anyone uncomfortable with ascriptive expectations becomes subject to derision, ostracism, marginality, or that most powerful social control of all: self-doubt. That last is part of the internalization of the system we are "given", which is "there" when we are born, and which seems so "natural". We question ourselves instead of questioning the system's premises; thus we are deflected into thinking we must change to fit the system, rather than changing the system to accommodate its human creators.

Disadvantage in patriarchy may also be legitimated by being translated into "benefits" to women and subordinate men. Remember, the South attempted to legitimate slavery by claiming that blacks were "happy" and "cared for". Similarly, it may be acknowledged that women earn less, or are physically threatened more, but that women are "supported" by men and "protected" by them. In these legitimations, the links between sex ascription and economic or status rewards for individuals, are ignored. Thus, the feminization of poverty is ignored, or blamed on women. Those who suffer in this system are told, in effect, that they are foolish to feel their own suffering. If the system is "right", objections to it must be "wrong"; if the system is "just", then objectors, women or men, are outlaws.

Ironically, once a system is objectivated, it *has* escaped its creators, and there is for both sexes a sense that the system *is* more powerful than individuals within it. Men as well as women become "strangers" and "newcomers" who must learn the rules; once patriarchal privilege was gained, it did not stop at women, but was also exercised severely over men. But the more a system seems to exist "out there", the more likely is its artificiality to become apparent, and the more likely it will be challenged. In the Sixties, this was expressed by the injunction to "drop out of the system". It recognized that if people refuse to play by rules that create the system, it contracts or dies, or at least ceases to hold its rebels in place. (For an excellent description of how individual change shapes and mirrors social change, see Turner, 1976.)

Unhappiness with the system, expressing itself in the countercultural movements of the Sixties, was targeted differently and produced different outcomes for women and men. Given that the visible counterculture was a small fraction of the youthful population, and that both women and men were in communal, civil rights, peace, and liberation movements, there was a basic sex difference in the "center of gravity" of their campaigns. Women and feminist men found their focus in the patriarchy itself, and have continued to target it in their writings and actions. They *named* patriarchy as the source of their grievances. For young men, however, the focus of rebellion was the war in Vietnam. While most of those drafted into the war did go, the quest for draft exemption was enormous. Men filled graduate schools and teachers' ranks, doing well by their callings, but also avoiding the draft. There was no groundswell of determination to fill the jails to bursting with draft refusers, embarrassing the nation into re-examining the war. Yet there was a sense among many that to be a "warrior" was neither wonderful nor "manly", but simply a death-wish in a morally bankrupt conflict. Then and since, there was also a threat of nuclear holocaust that makes all war potentially synonymous with global suicide.

At that point, then, one major source of patriarchal aggrandizement of men—war—was already lost. And when the war ended, that common bond of young against old men, was also lost.

Meanwhile, contradictions within Hippie and other youthful ideals and movements, were not resolved by grass-roots adoption and modification into a new system. (See Howard, 1969, for a discussion of these contradictions.) Where the war was blamed on the "military-industrial complex", where the "Establishment" was the enemy of hippiedom, both movements neglected to fix on the essential patriarchy of their declared enemies.

Nor was patriarchy completely unresponsive. It repressed rebellion, certainly; but the system was forced open enough to accommodate more liberal sexual and personal expression, and somewhat more liberal educational and occupational opportunities for women and disadvantaged men. The system loosened up without basically changing. The safety-valve, the grudging concessions finally made, sufficed to hold the patriarchy in place. Women recognized this, while men did not, in terms of collective gender consciousness and action. The "problem that has no name," which Friedan (1963) described as women's malaise, *has* been named. Women have named it patriarchy. Men have not. Yet the old benefits and contradictions are still with us. The complaints by men against patriarchy are all still there.

Men are unhappy in patriarchy because, as an objectivated system, it demands that men be "in control", yet provides increasingly fewer ways to do so unopposed. Little is given to women, while less and less is given to men in terms of dominating a system that tells them they should be dominant.

The failure of patriarchy to assert men's superiority has been especially powerful at the macro-level of national and world order. Not only is war an outmoded arena, but so are politics generally for unquestioned male dominance. Nations and their politicians, male or female, are pawns in an objectivated world economy, just as individuals are in an objectivated national patriarchy. Even religion cannot provide satisfactory large-scale dominance. As religion fights a battle to maintain male "headship" of churches and families, women infiltrate just enough to make such doctrines rear-guard actions. Those macro-order institutions, then, do not either address the basic contradictions in the assumptions behind their existence.

Where, then, are the rewards that men are supposed to find in patriarchy? The micro-order could offer an alternative, within the family.

It must be said immediately, however, that this alternative does not apply to or for "every men", that it is a choice filled with its own contradictions, and as an alternative to the discomforts of the system, it is a deception. That is because it is within and is the transmittor of, the same system. Weitzman (1979), for example, shows how fathers can help their children break out of strict gender labels to individual expressions of abilities, but also that fathers are very powerful forces in conditioning children to gender expectations. Also, however unhappy the effects of patriarchy for some or many, men *and* women remain its instruments of re-creation over time. Substantial numbers of people of both sexes continue to subscribe to its premises, whether explicitly or by omitting any examination of those premises in their lives.

Yet only by looking at husbandhood and fatherhood in its patriarchal setting can one make sense of how apparent changes in men's roles in the family, still leave much dissatisfaction. It explains such simultaneous patterns as the "new fashionableness" of being a father and discussing fatherhood (see, e.g., Fein, 1978), the slow rise in joint custody of children after divorce or of father-custody, concurrent with the fact of those high divorce rates, and the financial neglect of so many children in divorce. Without denying or minimizing the real and deep devotion of men and women to each other and their children, marriage is where the strains of patriarchy literally "come home" most closely, and daily.

To see why marriage does not provide relief from men's discontent with the system, and the systemic contradictions producing that discontent, the first place to look is the setting of marriage itself in the U.S. today. That is a setting in which available marriageable men are more scarce (while marriageable women are more plentiful). It has occurred because in these past two decades there have been low sex ratios (the number of men per 100 women). Where ratios are low (e.g., where there are 101 or 103 men per 100 women), there is a "marriage squeeze" for women. This is increased by cultural factors that have men marry a bit later than women, and that enable men to choose women from their own age group and from younger age groups, widening further their range of potential mates. The number of available men for marriageable women in any adult cohort is thereby reduced. From the standpoint of simple numerical availability (and leaving love and emotions aside for now), it is easier for men to find wives than it is for women to find husbands. It is easier for men not only to find a first wife, but also to find successive wives where divorce occurs.

Paradoxically, however, conditions of low sex ratios also produce women's movements, some form(s) of collective response to the social results of their numerical disadvantage. Guttentag and Secord (1983) make a powerful argument for the relationship between sex ratios, the treatment of women in and out of marriage, and women's reactions to these changing conditions. (Though the argument here is based on Guttentag and Secord, a somewhat parallel, excellent elaboration of these linkages is presented in Heer and Grossbard-Schechtman, 1981.)

The authors take the patriarchy as a given: institutional power (political/legal, religious, and economic power at the societal level) is always preponderantly in men's hands; but dyadic power (the relative advantage or power of the man or woman in marriage) shifts with sex ratio changes. Dyadic power is greater for whichever sex is scarcer. When women are scarce they gain in dyadic (but not institutional) power; when men are scarce, they gain in both.

The scarcer sex, then, has more bargaining power with the other sex; scarcity means "not plentiful" and the scarcer-sex partner is less easily replaced. Where men are scarce, demands rise for sexual and interpersonal concessions from women, premaritally and within marriage. While this scarcity of men enables them to obtain gratifications more readily, the disadvantaged bargaining position of women leaves them feeling exploited and resentful ("powerless").

This spurs women toward alternative networks of support and intimacy, to find more egalitarian settings for emotional comfort and support. Today's Women's Movement is only the latest such reaction; it was preceded by other collective reactions by women in history where sex ratios were low.

In a modern setting, the women's reaction has been especially powerful since the democratic ideals men first put forth for each other ("all men are created equal", ignoring women and slaves) objectivated into general abstract ideals to which all claimed to aspire. The creation of a revolution so that men could fight a king, became a system in which all privilege could be challenged. The apparent advantage of men in low sex ratios, then, hold incipient a woman's reaction to that advantage. It is a contradiction, the advantage a deception, for men.

The deception of numerical advantage is exacerbated when men's desire for intimacy is added to the equation. The larger simultaneous reality of low ratios and women's Liberation "comes home" in the marital bond. Those larger conditions impinge on the couple by setting a framework for contradictory forces to work against their love. The demographic condition of low ratios, objectively and in the everyday, reduce the risk for men of breaking one marital bond and finding another woman because women are, plentifully, there to be found. At the same time the Women's Movement has made women conscious of their own needs. Divorce may show how much these needs have been unmet, bringing women to the Movement in a search to reestablish personal identity after and outside marriage. Or a woman comes to a marriage with a consciousness of equality already in place. But while women seek men with whom satisfactory relationships can be worked out to meet their needs, demographics impinge again. Men are more free to accept or reject the outcomes of more egalitarian relationships. As women press men more urgently, the tensions of negotiations are not counterbalanced by equal bargaining power; the men still have more. Since love is often stated as "pleasing the other", love itself becomes the issue. At that point, the woman who continues to press her demands, beyond the man's willingness or capacity to accede to her, risks the relationship itself. She risks more because she is more "replaceable". While the man may be passionately in love, explicitly-stated grievances and counter-grievances can as easily diminish love as enable it to become a stronger bond. The "advantages" of low sex ratios and patriarchal privilege are a "set up" that may keep privilege in place, but at the cost of the emotional pain in breaking intimate bonds.

None of this is, or looks like, "war between the sexes". Rather, it looks like concession, mutual accommodation, indulgence—in short, marital love. The power of the larger impingements upon intimacy, however, accounts for continuing inequalities in marriage. In this period of normative sexual equality, women spend on average more than 30 hours, and men average 14 hours per week, doing housework. (See summaries of time-allocation findings in Kreps and Clark, 1975, and Unger, 1979). It is not simply early socialization of the sexes that produces these discrepancies. If that were so powerful, the overwhelming majority of all women and men would reject feminist ideas at first hearing. The reality is that it is risky to be "too feminist" in marriage when sex ratios are low. (See, e.g., Bolotin, 1982, interpreted in this light.) The gains of feminism are compartmentalized, used to some extent in education and the workplace, while at home that world is left "outside". It behooves men to have economically productive wives, yet work-equality ideals advocated by men for women are also risky to men, as Goode (1982) so well stated, for those ideals might come home.

To the extent that "outside" and "inside" ideals are compartmentalized, both sexes live in "cognitive dissonance": individuals perceive the absurdity of the contradictions they experience (Festinger, 1957). While contradictory beliefs or perceptions may be part of our everyday lives, or inevitable, and accommodated by psychic and/or economic necessity (Frankl, 1965), love may be more difficult to sustain in contradiction than in congruence. Consciousness rises as contradictions are perceived. Injustices felt at work, for example, however much empathy at home from one's spouse, may increase the sense of injustices at home. The further impinging of patriarchy on intimacy here lies in the need to sustain love where that very love, in its day to day manifestations, reflects larger inequalities of which the spouses may be ever more conscious. Great lovingness between partners can cover over much or all of this; yet any weakness in the bond of love, pushed by the power of a social framework for (dis)advantage, can open the way for all other grievances to come rushing into the relationship. That is the point at which marriages change or are broken, with the numerical sex ratio advantage once more coming into play for men, but certainly not sparing them the pain and stress of break-up.

When children are born, another set of contradictions and stress is added to the struggle for enduring intimacy against patriarchy.

Men have seen in a liberated masculinity and fatherhood new opportunities for reassessment and growth (e.g., Pleck and Sawyer, 1974). More and more men have also taken direct part in the births, rearing, and nurturance of their children. Yet the presence of children will exacerbate tensions already in the marriage, since they not only require much time, effort, and energy, but also because their needs are met differentially by parents. Many writers have pointed out the effects on women's careers, and on marriages, when parenthood begins. (See, e.g., Shreve, 1982. The list of scholarly articles on the subject is very long. A good summary of children's effect on marriage is found in Glenn and McLanahan, 1982.)

Again, it is not an absence of love for children, but the often-overwhelming nature of conflicting time and economic demands, that produce negative effects of children on marriage. It is difficult to add more people to any intimate group, as the birth of children adds to the marital dyad. Two people can more readily find adult compromises with each other's needs and with dissonance, than with the further needs of dependent young. Children, while a source of love and satisfaction, will also re-focus grievances and relational inadequacies felt by each partner toward the other. The high-demand context of young families increases the vulnerability of parents to the "failures" of each toward the other.

The very enlargement of love and nurturance, then, anticipated in the birth of children, highlights the functions of an unequal system where typically neither spouse "believes in inequality", but where in fact systemic inequalities rub strongly against individual consciousness.

Where the strains of inequality and dissonance could be suppressed by two adults with personal space and free time, even the physical capacity to "run away" or "hide out" from each other for a while, disappears with the arrival of children. The love of children, which places parents in a delightful love-madness over their young, becomes a day-to-day renegotiation of who does what, and when, with its attendant strains. The love of adults cannot be replaced by the love of children. Where the spouses cannot find a new point of stability, divorce may occur. Joint custody, though on the rise, is still not a typical resolution in divorce, although its rise indicates the rising strength of commitment by men to their children. But the link between the bitterness of divorce, the psychic configurations of fatherhood among different men, their relationship to the drive for father custody or joint custody or father visitation or father financial abandonment of children, has not been examined. Logically from what has been said here, the degree of pain and bitterness between divorcing spouses would be a measure of likelihood for fathers to abandon.

The scenario of divorce is "worst case" for patriarchy. It does not consider marriages which find new points of sharing, nor unhappy marriages which find extramarital or other outlets. It simply points out the worst strains of patriarchy, resulting in the most visible pain.

If men are "set up" to ask for more, and are "advantaged" by scarcity into increased demands, while women rebel at the disadvantages of patriarchy-compounded-by-low-ratios, the outcomes are likely to be higher and higher divorce, and more and more pain. Why are men unhappy in patriarchy? Because for intimacy to prevail within it, it must first be undone in one's own life, with those costs in pain and change that mark all personal as well as social revolutions. Or else it must be lived as a lie. To live a lie, one's own life must be untrue, unreal, false. The intelligence of men increasingly recognizes that as insult.

REFERENCES

Balswick, J.D. and Peek, C.W. The inexpressive male: A tragedy of American society. The Family Coordinator, (October) 1971, 363–368.

Bem, S.L. and Bem, D.J. Training the woman to know her place: The power of a nonconscious ideology. In M.H. Garskof, (Ed), Roles Women Play. Belmont, CA: Brooks/Cole, 1971.

Berger, P.L. and Luckmann, T. The Social Construction of Reality. Garden City, NY: Doubleday, 1966.

Bernard, J. The Female World. New York: Free Press, 1981 (a)

———The good-provider role: Its rise and fall. American Psychologist, (January) 1981, 36, 1–12.

Bolotin, S. Voices from the post-feminist generation. The New York Times Magazine, Oct. 17, 1982.

Brownmiller, S. Against Our Will. New York: Simon and Schuster, 1977.

———Femininity. New York: Simon and Schuster, 1984.

Chesler, P. About Men. New York: Simon and Schuster, 1978.

Ehrenreich, B. The Hearts of Men. New York: Doubleday, 1983.

Fein, R.A. Research in fathering: Social policy and an emergent perspective. Journal of Social Issues, 1978, 34, 122–135.

Festinger, L. A Theory of Cognitive Dissonance. Stanford, CA: Stanford University Press, 1957.

Firestone, S. The Dialectic of Sex. New York: Bantam, 1970.

Fischer, J.L. and Narus, L.R., Jr. Sex-role development in late adolescence and adulthood. Sex Roles, 1981, 7, 97–106.

Fox, M.F. and Hesse-Biber, S. Women At Work. Palo Alto, CA: Mayfield Pub. Co., 1984.

Frankl, V. Man's Search For Meaning. New York: Washington Square Press, 1965.

Friedan, B. The Feminine Mystique. New York: Dell, 1963.

Gilligan, C. In A Different Voice. Cambridge, MA: Harvard University Press, 1982.

Glenn, N.D. and McLanahan, S. Children and marital happiness: A further specification of the relationship. Journal of Marriage and The Family, (February) 1982, 44, 63–72.

Goldberg, H. The Hazards of Being Male. New York: New American Library, 1976.

Goode, W.J. Why men resist. In B. Thorne and M. Yalom (Eds), Rethinking The Family. New York: Longmans, 1982.

Guttentag, M. and Secord, P. Too Many Women? Beverly Hills, CA: Sage, 1983.

Heer, D. and Grossbard-Schechtman, A. The impact of the female marriage squeeze and contraceptive revolution on sex roles and the Women's Liberation Movement in the United States. Journal of Marriage and The Family, (February) 1981, 43, 49–66.

Homans, G.C. The Human Group. New York: Harcourt, Brace, 1950.

Howard, J.R. The flowering of the hippie movement. The Annals, (March) 1969, 382, 43–55.

Kanter, R.M. Women and the structure of organizations. In M. Millman and R.M. Kanter (Eds), Another Voice. New York: Doubleday, 1975.

Kessler-Harris, A. Out To Work. New York: Oxford University Press, 1982.

Kramerae, C. Women and Men Speaking. Rowley, MA: Newberry House, 1981.

Kreps, J. and Clark, R. Sex, Age, And Work. Baltimore: Johns Hopkins Press, 1975.

Lehne, G.K. Homophobia among men. In D. David and R. Brannon (Eds), The Forty-Nine Percent Majority. Reading, MA: Addison-Wesley, 1976.

Marciano, T.D. Male pressure in the decision to remain childfree. Alternative Lifestyles, (February) 1978, 1, 95–112.

———Socialization and women. National Forum, (Fall) 1981, 24–26.

Moreland, J. Age and change in adult sex role. Sex Roles, 1980, 6, 810–817.

Ortner, S.B. Is female to male as nature is to culture? In M.Z. Rosaldo and L. Lamphere, (Eds), Woman, Culture, and Society. Stanford, CA: Stanford University Press, 1974.

Pleck, J.H. and Sawyer, J. (Eds), Men and Masculinity. Englewood Cliffs, NJ: Prentice-Hall, 1974.

Polatnick, M. Why men don't rear children: A power analysis. Berkeley Journal of Sociology, 1973, 45–86.

Shively, M.G. and De Cecco, J.P. Components of sexual identity. Journal of Homosexuality, (Fall) 1977, 3, 41–48.

Shreve, A. Careers and the lure of motherhood. New York Times Magazine, November 21, 1982.

Tolson, A. The Limits of Masculinity. New York: Harper & Row, 1977.

Turner, R.H. The real self: From institution to impulse. American Journal of Sociology, (March) 1976, 81, 989–1016.

Unger, R. Female and Male. New York: Harper & Row, 1979.

Weitzman, L.J. Sex Role Socialization. Palo Alto, CA: Mayfield, 1979.

———The economics of divorce: social and economic consequences of property, alimony and child support awards. UCLA Law Review, 1981, 28, 1181–1268.

Whyte, W.F. Streetcorner Society. Second Ed. Univ. of Chicago Press, 1955.

Woolf, V. A Room Of One's Own. New York: Harcourt Brace (1929), 1957.

Chapter 4

Angry, Abandoned Husbands: Assessment and Treatment

Michael F. Myers

The resurgence of the women's movement of the past two decades has had a major influence on the North American family. Although the divorce rate is now beginning to stabilize (Robbins, 1982), marital separation continues to be a major social phenomenon. With increasing career options for women as well as beginning societal sanctioning of autonomous strivings, increasing numbers of unhappily married women are opting to leave their marriages. Many of their husbands have a subjective sense of abandonment and are ill-prepared to cope with the "narcissistic injury" (Rice, 1977) that this type of separation entails. These men are the subject of this paper.

BACKGROUND

Over the past ten years there has been increasing research on the emotional aspects of marital separation and divorce (Weiss, 1975; Kressel, 1980; Hancock, 1980). In addition, there has been some study of gender differences in divorce (Brown & Fox, 1979) indicating higher psychiatric morbidity rates (Gove, 1972) and mortality rates (Gove, 1973) for men than for women. Bloom (1975) noted high first time psychiatric hospital admission rates for separated men—especially newly separated men. Jacobs (1982) noted the threatened loss of their relationship with their children as a common chief complaint of men in the midst of a divorce crisis.

Michael F. Myers, MD, is Clinical Associate Professor, Department of Psychiatry, The University of British Columbia, and Shaughnessy Hospital, Vancouver, BC, V6H 3N1.

31

Divorcing (Jacobs, 1983) and divorced (Hetherington, Cox M & Cox R, 1976; Keshet & Rosenthal, 1978; Greif, 1979; Wallerstein & Kelly, 1980) fathers have been studied more extensively than divorced men who are childless. This research has focussed specifically on the father's post-divorce adjustment, the father-child relationship in pre- and post-divorce situations, non-custodial fathers, and single fathers. Most data suggest that those fathers who have continued contact and involvement with their children after separation are less depressed. Furthermore, one cannot predict the nature and quality of the post-separation fathering by the relationship during the marriage (Hetherington, Cox M & Cox R, 1976; Greif, 1979; Wallerstein & Kelly, 1980): some "closely involved" fathers before separation do not maintain this behavior after separation because of inability to adapt to visitation status. Other men become more active and interested fathers only after separation.

Tepp's (1983) study of non-custodial but involved fathers three years after divorce is noteworthy. These men reported feelings of loss, dysphoria, sadness, and struggle regarding their not having custody of their children. They described feeling shut out of parenting functions, decreased feelings of being special, a sense of displacement, and a sense of confusion and difficulty about their status as parents. Anger is not mentioned as a specific emotion in these men who were examined three years after divorce which suggests that anger may be an "early" emotion which diminishes with passage of time.

The literature on divorce adjustment rarely states whether the marital separations were husband, wife, or mutually initiated. This is understandable given that most marital breakdowns are characterized by extremely complex, multi-determined, and ambiguous issues. Attempting to analyse "who left whom" as a significant variable may be not only reductionistic but also misleading or unnecessary. Nevertheless, there remains a subgroup of divorcing couples in which one party assumes the initiator role (not necessarily the one who leaves) in the separation. Halle's (1982) study of men left by their wives is one such study; she described three categories of abandoned husbands—Angry Grievers, Devoted Clingers, and Detached Avoiders—appellations which speak for themselves.

A brief review of Bowlby's attachment theory (1980) is necessary to help explain the anger in abandoned husbands. Affectional bonds or attachments between child and parent (and later between adult and adult) evolve during the course of normal development. They are not confined to childhood but continue actively throughout the life cycle. Intense emotions arise during the formation, the maintenance, the disruption, and the renewal of attachment relationships. Threat of loss precipitates anxiety and actual loss arouses sorrow; each situation is likely to give rise to anger. In adult life, the characteristic ways in which an individual's attachments are organized will be determined by the experiences he or she had with attachment figures during infancy, childhood, and adolescence.

Attachment behavior in separating adults and the "separation distress" period have been described by Weiss (1976) [who refers to and amplifies the "separation distress syndrome" published earlier by Parkes (1972)]. He notes that anger, sometimes intense, may accompany loss of attachment in separating persons. Weiss' work and that of Kressel (1980) on divorce (stages in the coping response—denial, mourning, anger, readjustment) are pertinent to this subject but their observations and concepts are not gender-specific. Likewise, we know from bereavement studies (Parkes, 1970; Glick, Weiss & Parkes, 1974) that anger is a common emotion associated with the early phases of mourning but there are few differences between widows and widowers (Glick et al. found that fewer widowers admitted to angry feelings). Dinnerstein (1976) explains male anger and dominance as a possible adult reaction to the small helpless son and large all-powerful mother dyad. Also helpful in understanding the anger in abandoned husbands are Adler's (1980) concepts of psychological inferiority and masculine protest. In the cultural context of defining masculine as valuable, strong, and victorious, these husbands feel the direct opposite.

We come now to the important and distinctive work of Pleck on the male role (1976), concepts of masculinity (1974), changing gender roles in work and family (1981a) and sex role strain (1981b). Most men are socialized to be independent, dominant, competitive, aggressive, and unemotional, i.e., instrumental. These are characteristics culturally defined as appropriate for the male sex and thereby constitute a traditional man's sex role identity. In addition, the traditional male has been socialized to be the worker and provider for his family. Major responsibility for monitoring the emotional and functional state of marriage and family has been that of the wife. In the work place men are not defined and rewarded for having a good marriage; men are indeed rewarded for being married (e.g., promotion, pay raises, etc.) but the *state* of marriage is inconsequential.

To what degree are the abandoned husband's rage, retaliatory fantasy, or propensity to violence defenses against narcissistic injury? This will vary with the level of the individual's premorbid personality integration and the peculiarities of the marriage itself, in particular unresolved power and autonomy issues. Male sex role identity theory argues that exaggerated, hypermasculine behaviours are rooted in unconscious anxiety about psychologically feminine parts of the man's personality. These feelings, i.e., of emasculation and passivity certainly occur in abandoned husbands. Pleck argues for sex role strain theory (1981b), i.e., men are homophobic and misogynistic because they are socialized to hold these values. They in part adopt exaggerated male role behaviors because of actual social rejection and ostracism they receive if they deviate from the traditional male role.

SOME CLINICAL OBSERVATIONS

The observations reported here are derived from a clinical sample of middle to upper middle class men seen in a private practice. Most of the patients were seen in the context of conjoint marital therapy before separation or later during various stages of divorce therapy. Some men were treated individually and completely independently of their wives after separation had occurred.

Sub-groups

Five sub-groups of angry abandoned husbands were delineated. They are not mutually exclusive and some men presented a mixture of sub-group features.

1. Overtly Aggressive

The predominant emotion observed in these men was anger which was clearly visible and openly acknowledged. They were completely against separation and most refused to even engage in discussing this option with their wives. All gave a history of refusing to go for marital counseling (which their wives had suggested) at an earlier time. Some of these husbands were wife batterers and their violence was the main reason for their wives' initiating divorce. Those who were not physically assaultive were psychological bullies—they controlled or intimidated their wives by threats, denigration, coercive maneuvers, and empty promises.

Some of the newly separated men who sought therapy of their own accord displayed anger extending to all women, albeit transient and intermittent. They refused to consider mediation for working out visitation and custody issues. They engaged the most notoriously aggressive divorce lawyers available. Themes of retaliation and retribution were common. Some attempted to manipulate their wives (either directly or via their therapist) into reconciliation therapy by various ploys. Some revealed (and worked through in therapy) fantasies and fears of maiming and murdering their estranged wives.

2. Passive-Aggressive

These men expressed their anger covertly and unconsciously. They resisted change by passive means. For example, they would procrastinate on many suggestions in therapy, "forget" appointments, and stubbornly refuse to negotiate on separation disputes. Some refused to leave the family home in spite of overwhelming tension and violent disagreements. They also were apt to hire a traditional lawyer, preferring an adversarial approach to mediation. In a self-seeking and revengeful way, they would fight for sole custody or contrarily, willfully refuse to see the children. In a milder form but no less traumatically they would demean their wives to their children, or would consistently be tardy in picking up and returning the children after visitation.

3. Depressed

Some of the husbands were clearly depressed—the severity of which ranged from mild to severe—including individuals with Major Affective Disorders (DSM-III, 1980). Suicidal thoughts and threats were not uncommon, as were homicidal fantasies in some individuals. Any angry husband who threatened suicide (or who had made a suicidal gesture) was carefully assessed for an underlying clinical depression and dangerously suicidal behavior. This was particularly critical when increasing risk variables were associated (advancing age, failing health, alcohol abuse, family history of affective disorder and/or suicide, etc.). Some required antidepressant medication in addition to supportive psychotherapy. Some required brief hospitalization.

4. Sexist

Men in this category had many features associated with the traditional male sex role. They worked hard, were professionally ambitious, competitive, and emotionally constricted. Most of their energy was directed outside the home and toward the acquisition of money, power, and status. They tended to take their marriages for granted, assumed all was well, and rarely had any complaints. Their wives' concerns and marital unhappiness tended to fall on deaf ears or were dismissed as silly or exaggerated. Generally, these men encouraged their wives to seek individual psychotherapy.

These men did not seek therapy—either individually or conjointly—until their marriages were virtually unbearable or their wives had left. Most were completely bewildered or were in a state of disbelief. Some illustrated an ambivalent pairing of over-idealization and devaluation of their wives. Threatened with separation (or early in the separation) they adopted lavish gift-giving behavior and redoubled courtship effort. Marital or individual therapy was an awkward, embarrassing, and frightening experience for them.

5. Passive-Dependent

These men tended to be younger abandoned husbands and had long histories of being poorly self-reliant. Their wives tended to make a lot of their decisions for them regarding work, household management, choosing recreation, buying clothes, etc. They were unassertive and unambitious in their work. Most had married at an early age without ever living apart from their parents and had unresolved separation-individuation conflicts. Some of the wives of these men actually selected and organized new living quarters for their husbands after they separated. In general, these women felt emancipated and less guilty of leaving their husbands once they got them into therapy.

Additional Characteristics

There were specific situations which require brief mention and which cut across the above sub-categories. Those men whose wives became involved with new men shortly before or after separating suffered from a more profound sense of abandonment and intensified anger. They had a subjective sense of being a "cuckold". Some men who were not fully conscious of their rage and feelings of threat developed sexual erective difficulties—either with their wives or new partners or both. Their surface behavior was a blend of sexual withdrawal and sexual redoubling. Feelings of rejection, fury, and humiliation were poignantly revealed by the statement of one man upon learning of his estranged wife's dating another man: "Couldn't she have at least waited until the body was cold?"

Two wives had become involved with other women and their husbands manifested a particular constellation of symptoms. These included feelings of disbelief, belittlement, repugnance, abasement and bewilderment. Both men were very conservative and in addition to rejection, each felt a blow to his sense of masculine self-esteem, and felt outraged at the loss of his wife to a person of "subordinate status" i.e., another woman. They were unable to appreciate the complexity and multiple determinants of this particular type of separation, assumed more than shared responsibility, blamed themselves, and reacted with guilt. One man's query smacked of simplicity: "Why else would she turn against me and my sex?"

Finally, some husbands were highly suspicious and emotionally brittle. Upon thorough and rigorous clinical assessment they were found to have primary and individual psychopathology. Some of this was causative in contributing to marital breakdown but some symptomatology was reactive and indeed exacerbated by loss and threatened loss. Diagnoses included: borderline personality, paranoid schizophrenia and alcohol-induced delusional disorder. In many of these marriages, the separation was the final act in a lengthy and chaotic union punctuated by repeated episodes of wife battering, marital rape, and delusional jealousy.

ISSUES IN TREATMENT

Women are more likely to suggest and to want separation and divorce than their husbands (Goode, 1956; Brown, 1976). Men are also prone to use denial and avoidance in dealing with marital distress (Brown & Fox, 1979). This inability to grasp the presence of marital erosion and the tendency to minimize its magnitude may be partly explained by differing societal priorities for men and women. Rossi, (1980) citing the research of Vaillant (1977) and Levinson (1978), notes that the dominant role domain in the lives of men from early adulthood into their forties is the overwhelming priority of work commitment and career progression. By the time they make the mid-life shift to the more affiliative interest of emotional accessibility to their wives and children, irreparable estrangement may have occurred.

These facts generate an important treatment consideration. The husband and wife may be at different stages of mourning; he is angry and fighting separation while she is beyond anger and desiring distance and autonomy. He wants conjoint marital therapy; she wants either individual or separation therapy. Or if already physically separated, he pushes for reconciliation therapy (aggressively and perhaps manipulatively) out of his own anxiety and attachment behavior. She pushes for space. A vicious circle ensues.

Many of these men could benefit from treatment but few directly seek help. This is in part a traditional male stance, i.e., the male's gender role socialization has been directed to self-sufficiency, independent problem-solving, and the inhibition of feelings. To seek professional help is to acknowledge vulnerability and weakness, to risk exposure or to admit failure. All too often, as clinicians, our unconscious sex role stereotyping and bias toward these men have aggravated this process. We have underestimated the magnitude of their confusion, fear, isolation, and anguish in our inability to look beyond their rage and its behavioral manifestations. Many of these husbands can be assisted into treatment with the correct approach—warm, non-threatening and invitational—with clear guidelines and responses to queries. A coercive and/or patronizing approach will fail.

There are major differences in how and in which ways men and women typically cope after separation. Commonly, the newly separated, non-custodial father feels cut off from vital social roles and a sense of social meaning or purpose (Brown & Fox, 1979). There is less day-to-day stress and responsibility, a sense of alienation, and lack of control (especially in those separations initiated by the wife). Hancock (1980) has described the loss of both social definition and the sense of belonging in all members of the separating family; this loss is particularly pungent in abandoned husbands and may in part contribute to the frantic social and sexual activity commonly seen in newly separated men. Friedman (1980) underscores the importance of the father-child relationship after divorce, particularly the benefits of the father's nurturing experience for both the father and the children. He urges mental health professionals to support these men in their fathering after divorce has occurred. His suggestions are particularly germane to father-custody and joint-custody situations.

In many centers, treatment becomes fragmented and blurred. Many professionals of diverse training and discipline may be involved before, during, and after divorce. Many marital therapists cease treatment at the point of impending or actual separation when individual concurrent or mediation work is very clearly necessary. Husbands especially flee from treatment at this point and this is precisely when a non-threatening invitational approach to individual therapy may be accepted, or at least may be considered. The therapist must be mindful of the emotional isolation (Weiss, 1974) and feelings of rootlessness (Hetherington, Cox M & Cox R, 1976) in these men. They are less likely to be in touch with possible feelings of helplessness and terror of being alone (Brown & Fox, 1979). Male sex role socialization has not prepared them to elicit help and support and to do the emotional groundwork for separation. Balswick and Peek (1971) have termed this phenomenon "male inexpressiveness".

The therapeutic approach to the self-related separated or divorced man may be quite different in that he has acknowledged his need for help in spite of the degree of ambivalence he may feel toward treatment. Tasks and goals center around ventilation of feelings (especially of anger, abandonment, hurt, failure, and guilt), regaining self-esteem (both social and sexual), understanding and working through problems of trust with women, re-establishing intimacy in new relationships, avoiding self-destructive behavior, and enhancing fathering and co-parenting skills. Accepting and overcoming feelings of loneliness, enjoying one's own company, and learning to live alone are particularly difficult for divorced men. This clinical impression is supported by empirical evidence of higher and quicker remarriage rates for men than women (Ross & Sawhill, 1975).

Countertransference issues may arise in treating the abandoned husband. These are more apt to occur with the self-referred male whose wife has never been interviewed nor treated by the therapist.

It is more difficult to remain therapeutically unbiased when one is assessing and treating only one member of a marital dyad. Another variable is therapist gender. For example, the male therapist may unconsciously overidentify with and collude with the husband's sense of outrage, indignation, and retribution such that insight-building is minimized and adversarial co-parenting may be aggravated. Conversely, the male therapist may get caught up in the patient's rage and aggression and miss the underlying hurt, loneliness, and bewilderment. The female therapist may overidentify with the husband and unconsciously overnurture and overgratify dependency needs with little direction toward his developing self-sufficiency and independence. Or conversely, she may be intimidated by his rage and lose her sense of therapeutic confidence, control, and professional objectivity.

And finally there is anecdotal and impressionistic evidence that therapists of both genders have particular difficulty in treating very regressed husbands struggling with abandonment. The emotionalism, passivity, and clinging of these men is more prone to pejorative labelling as "bad behavior" than "symptomatic behavior". Unconscious sex bias, i.e., men must be at least *moderately* strong, competitive, and in control of their feelings, in the most enlightened and androgynous of therapists may become problematic in working with this subgroup of separated husbands.

CONCLUSION

Abandoned husbands constitute a significant group of people who are in need of the services of contemporary therapists. Most are angry and are struggling with feelings of rejection, loss, loneliness, and tarnished masculinity. Patterns of traditional sex role socialization in our culture have worked against these men being able to acknowledge symptomatology and to request help. In some therapists, the same rigidity in sex role behavior has precluded accurate assessment, empathic awareness, and the ability to "reach out".

In conclusion, these husbands will be better served if therapists do at least two things. First, keep abreast of the important research on changing sex roles and incorporate this information into our therapeutic work. Second, examine and pay heed to our own personal sex role evolution as we live and work in this exciting period in history. Both tasks are essential.

REFERENCES

Adler, A: Cooperation between the sexes. Ed and trans by Heinz L Ansbacher and Rowena R Ansbacher, New York, Jason Aronson, 1980, 32.

Balswick, J and Peek, C: The inexpressive male: a tragedy of American society. The Family Coordinator, 1971, 20:363–368.

Bloom, BL: Changing patterns of psychiatric care. New York, Human Sciences Press, 1975.

Bowlby, J: Conceptual framework. In Attachment and Loss, Vol III, Loss, New York, Basic Books, 1980, 38–41.

Brown, P: Psychological distress and personal growth among women coping with marital dissolution. Dissertation Abstracts International, 1976, 37, 947-B. (University Microfilms N 76-19, 092).

Brown, P and Fox, H: Sex differences in divorce. In Gender and Disordered Behavior. Sex Differences in Psychopathology. Ed. by Gomberg, ES and Franks, V. New York, Brunner/Mazel, 1979, 101–123.

Dinnerstein, D: The mermaid and the minotaur: sexual arrangements and human malaise. New York, Harper Colophon, 1976.

Diagnostic and Statistical Manual of Mental Disorders. Third Edition. American Psychiatric Association. Washington, 1980, 205.

Friedman, HJ: The father's parenting experience in divorce. Am J Psychiatry, 1980, 137:1177–1182.

Glick, IO, Weiss, RS and Parkes, CM: The First Year of Bereavement. New York, John Wiley, Interscience, 1974.

Goode, WJ: Women in divorce. New York, The Free Press, 1956.

Gove, W: The relationship between sex roles, marital status, and mental illness. Social Forces. 1972, 51:238–244.

Gove, W: Sex, marital status, and mortality. Amer J of Sociology, 1973, 79:45–67.

Greif, JB: Fathers, children, and joint custody. Am J Orthopsychiatry, 1979, 49:311–319.

Halle E: The "abandoned husband": when wives leave. In Men In Transition: Theory and Therapy. Ed by Solomon K and Levy NB, New York, Plenum Press, 1982, 191–197.

Hancock, E: The dimensions of meaning and belonging in the process of divorce. Am J Orthopsychiatry, 1980, 50:18–27.

Hetherington, ME, Cox M, Cox R: Divorced fathers. Family Coordinator, 1976, 25:417–428.

Jacobs, JW: The effect of divorce on fathers: an overview of the literature. Am J Psychiatry, 1982, 139:1235–1241.

Jacobs, JW: Treatment of divorcing fathers: social and psychotherapeutic considerations. Am J Psychiatry, 1983, 140:1294–1299.

Keshet HF, Rosenthal KM: Fathering after marital separation. Social Work, 1978, 23:11–18.

Kressel, K: Patterns of coping in divorce and some implications for clinical practice. Family Relations, 1980, 29:234–240.

Levinson, DJ: Seasons Of A Man's Life. New York, Alfred A Knopf Inc., 1978.

Parkes, CM: The first year of bereavement. Psychiatry, 1970, 33:444–467.

Parkes, CM: Bereavement. New York, International Universities Press, 1972.

Pleck, JH and Sawyer, J: Men and Masculinity. Englewood Cliffs, N.J., Prentice-Hall, 1974.

Pleck, JH: The male sex role: definitions, problems, and sources of change. J Soc Issues, 1976, 32:155–163,

Pleck, JH: Changing patterns of work and family roles. Working paper No 81, Wellesley College, Center for Research on Women, 1981 (a).

Pleck, JH: The Male Myth. Cambridge, MIT Press, 1981 (b).

Rice, DG: Psychotherapeutic treatment of narcissistic injury in marital separation and divorce. J of Divorce, 1977, 1:119–128.

Robbins, GL: 1980 marriage rate up, divorce rate steady. Family Therapy News. American Association for Marriage and Family Therapy. January 1982, Vol 13.

Ross, H and Sawhill, I: Time of transition: the growth of families headed by women. Washington, DC, The Urban Institute, 1975.

Rossi, AS: Life span theories and women's lives. Signs: Journal of Women in Culture and Society. 1980, 6:4–32.

Tepp, AV: Divorced fathers: predictors of continued paternal involvement. Am J Psychiatry, 1983, 140:1465–1469.

Vaillant, GE: Adaptation To Life. Boston, Little, Brown, and Co., 1977.

Wallerstein, JS, Kelly, JB: Effects of divorce on the visiting father-child relationship. Am J Psychiatry, 1980, 137:1534–1539.

Weiss, RS: (ed) Loneliness. Cambridge, MIT Press, 1974.

Weiss, RS: Marital Separation. New York, Basic Books, 1975.

Weiss, RS: The emotional impact of marital separation. J Soc Issues, 1976, 32:135–145.

Chapter 5

Men's Work Schedules and Family Life

Graham L. Staines

Among all the ways that men's work and family life affect each other, the impact of men's work schedules on their family life has emerged as a topic of special concern. Much of the research on the relationship between men's work schedules and family life proceeds from the assumption that men's nonstandard work schedules are associated with reductions in the quality of their family life. Put another way, this assumption holds that the best work schedule from the standpoint of men's family life is a standard one involving regular weekday work (i.e., Monday to Friday) and regular (and nonexcessive) day hours. The review of empirical evidence that follows may be viewed as a systematic evaluation of this assumption about men, pointing out its considerable validity but also noting some important exceptions and certain limitations to its scope.

Two different approaches to measuring work schedules may be found in the research on the relationship between men's work schedules and their family life. One approach is to focus on special (or atypical) schedules and to compare their effects on men's family life with the effects of standard (or normal) schedules. Three special schedules (viz. shiftwork, the four-day week, and flextime) have received the greatest attention. The argument in favor of research designs which pit a special schedule against a standard schedule is the pragmatic one that, if such special schedules are to be introduced

Graham L. Staines, PhD, is Assistant Professor, Department of Psychology, The State University of New Jersey, Rutgers, New Brunswick, NJ 08903.

The research reported in this paper was supported by a grant (90-C-1774) from the Administration for Children, Youth and Families. I wish to thank Joseph H. Pleck for his assistance in the preparation of this manuscript. Requests for reprints should be sent to Graham L. Staines, Department of Psychology, Tillett Hall, Rutgers University, New Brunswick, NJ 08903.

or to be implemented more widely, it makes sense to determine in what ways they will improve or harm family life.

A second approach to measuring men's work schedules may be termed "dimensional". The researcher considers the various ways in which work schedules differ and then formulates a series of dimensions intended to capture many of these variations. The term "dimension" is being used here in a broad conceptual rather than in a narrow psychometric sense. Such conceptual dimensions are sometimes complex and may contain more than one component and thus more than one psychometric dimension.

Even the measure of a single dimension has certain advantages over the dichotomous measure of a special vs. standard schedule. Dimensions of schedules can be measured using scales with many (as opposed to just two) values, thus increasing the statistical power of the analysis. Given a heterogeneous sample of workers, dimensional measures typically produce less skewed (or more rectangular) distributions of scores, thus again contributing to statistical power. By comparison, only small proportions of workers in a broad cross-section work on each of the special schedules; hence each such schedule generates a highly skewed distribution in a general sample. Furthermore, dimensional measures at the interval level of measurement allow the detection of nonlinear as well as linear effects of work schedules on family life whereas the notion of nonlinear effects makes no sense in the dichotomous comparison of special and standard schedules.

Other advantages of the dimensional approach to measuring work schedules concern the availability of multiple dimensions. Whereas research on special schedules focuses on a single comparison at any one time, the dimensional approach allows the measurement of many different dimensions of work schedules within a single study. Accordingly, it allows us to determine the unique effects of any one work schedule dimension (i.e., its effect when the effects of all other dimensions are controlled statistically). The multidimensional approach also permits us to assess the total effect of all work schedule dimensions combined and, in addition, the effects of work schedules in relation to the effects of other working conditions (e.g., pay, nature of the work). Further, it enables the researcher to test for moderator effects, that is, the different ways in which one work schedule dimension may moderate the effects of other work schedule dimensions. To summarize, an applied (or policy-oriented) focus on special schedules makes sense if we wish to determine the various and resultant effects of such schedules on family life. Nonetheless, if our interest lies in a theoretical understanding of how variations in the work schedules of the general population affect family life, we should search for an underlying set of schedule dimensions.

Existing literature (Cunningham, 1982; Shamir, 1983; Staines & Pleck, 1983, 1984a, 1984b) suggests the importance of three basic conceptual dimensions of work schedules: (1) the amount of time worked, (2) the scheduling of time worked, and (3) the flexibility of schedules. The amount of time worked is typically assessed on a weekly basis. The scheduling of time subdivides into two work schedule characteristics, the pattern of days worked each week and the pattern of hours worked each day. The flexibility of schedules refers to the degree of control that workers have over the preceding two dimensions of their schedules. These three dimensions individually tap quite different (or nonredundant) issues; together they capture many of the major variations among work schedules.

This review of the literature on men's work schedules and family life attempts to integrate findings based on dichotomous measures of special schedules and measures of general schedule dimensions. In particular, the review considers the three schedule dimensions in turn (i.e., amount, scheduling, and flexibility), discussing special schedules in conjunction with the most relevant work schedule dimension. Thus, shiftwork fits neatly under the scheduling dimension, specifically within the category of pattern of hours worked. As will become evident, shiftwork is the one case where a special schedule can be converted into a dimensional measure. The four-day week also falls within the scheduling dimension. It is discussed immediately after the two work schedule characteristics that represent the scheduling dimensions (patterns of days and hours worked) because it poses a tradeoff between the number of days worked in a week and the number of hours worked in a day. The discussion of flextime comes directly after a review of the dimension of flexibility. The notions of flexibility and flextime are similar but not identical. Flexibility refers to the general level of control over the other dimensions of schedules (amount and scheduling) whereas flextime focuses exclusively and specifically on (limited) control over the starting (and ending) time of a working day. In short, much of the ensuing discussion is organized around the different measures of work schedules, especially the interweaving of special schedules and general schedule dimensions.

Measurement of the quality of family life has consistently pursued a dimensional approach. Three dimensions seem particularly relevant to the impact of men's work schedules on their family life: (1) the amount of time spent each week in various family roles including child care and housework, (2) the degree of interference between work and family life, and (3) the level of family adjustment.

AMOUNT OF TIME SPENT WORKING

Amount of time spent working represents the first of three general dimensions of schedules. A number of different approaches are available for examining workers' degree of temporal involvement in their work. Several special types of work schedules, for example, raise the issue of the amount of time spent at work: part-time employment, work sharing (or short-time), overtime, and multiple job holding (or moonlighting). The approach emphasized here is to focus simply on the number of hours a worker works each week.

Time Spent in Family Roles

The amount of time husbands spend at work might be expected to be negatively related to the time they spend in their family roles. While some research has pointed to a negative association among husbands between time spent at work and time spent on housework, in general the evidence of an association among husbands between time spent in work and family roles falls short of convincing. Walker and Woods (1976) obtained a negative relationship among husbands between hours employed and hours devoted to household tasks (no significance tests). Robinson (1977) likewise detected a negative relationship among men between work time and time on housework (cooking, laundry, marketing, etc.). Further, among men, the number of hours worked was negatively associated with time spent on general household obligations (e.g., gardening, shopping, errands) but unrelated to time spent with children (no significance tests). Based on national survey data, however, Staines and Pleck (1983) detected no relationships under multivariate control (multiple regression) between number of hours worked each week and time spent in either of two family roles (child care or housework) for husbands in two-earner families.

Attenuation of the variance of the various temporal measures would appear to explain the failure of negative relationships to emerge more consistently in the data on men. Variance in work time is attenuated because most men work full-time; variance in family role time is attenuated because most men spend so little time on child care and housework.

Interference Between Work and Family Life

The amount of time men work should generate a positive relationship with the experience of interference (or conflict) between work and family life. Empirical evidence in this case fully confirms expectation. In a study of two-earner families, Keith and Schafer (1980) found that the total hours husbands spent working each week (on the main job plus additional jobs) was the strongest significant predictor of their work/family strain. Mortimer (1980) developed an overall index of temporal requirements imposed by work, which included measures of time spent on the main job plus second jobs, as well as a question about working under the pressure of time. This index of temporal requirements was positively and significantly associated with work/family strain for her sample of married, male, college graduates, most of whom were in the early phases of professional or managerial careers.

Based on a national sample of workers, Staines and Pleck (1983) investigated the relationship among husbands in two-earner families between number of hours worked per week and several measures of work/family conflict. According to their multivariate analysis, the number of hours worked was positively and significantly associated with total work/family conflict and with one subcategory of work/family conflict (hours conflict, i.e., complaints about excessive work hours interfering with family life) but not with another subcategory of conflict (schedule conflict, i.e., mismatches between work schedules and either routine or nonroutine family events).

Family Adjustment

Time spent at work might also be thought to affect family adjustment and perhaps other qualitative aspects of family life as well, yet fewer relationships have emerged than expected. Ridley (1973) studied the relationship between the amount of time devoted to the occupational role in excess of the normal workday (a six-item scale tapping time devoted to reading, writing, talking, thinking about the job) and marital adjustment (a nine-item scale) among a sample of husbands of female school teachers. Ridley obtained no significant association between the two concepts. Mortimer (1980) detected no zero-order association between the temporal dimension of the husband's job and his marital satisfaction; however, a path-analytic model that used mediating family variables to separate direct and indirect effects did establish a significant connection between temporal requirements and marital satisfaction. Staines and Pleck (1983) analyzed the relationship between number of hours worked by two-earner husbands and an index of their family adjustment based on ratings of marital happiness, marital satisfaction, and family satisfaction. The investigators found that, when subjected to multivariate control via regression, the relationship was not significant.

Taking a different approach, Clark, Nye, and Gecas (1978) noted that husbands' self-reported work time had no effect on their competence in housekeeper, social supporter, sexual, and recreational roles, as judged by their wives. Clark and Gecas (1977) found that fathers' self-reported work time had no effect on their competence in two parental roles, child care and child socialization, again as rated by their wives.

Cross-Over Effects Involving Wives

Although the present review focuses primarily on the relationship between men's work schedules and their family life, two issues involving wives as well as husbands also deserve attention. The relationship between husbands' work schedules and their wives' family life and, similarly, the relationship between wives' work schedules and their husbands' family life both raise the interesting possibility of "cross-over" effects, that is, effects of a worker's schedule on his or her spouse's family life. There is little compelling evidence, however, of cross-over effects based on the number of hours a person works. Using a sample of two-earner couples, Staines and Pleck (1983) conducted an extensive multivariate study of cross-over effects. They found no relationship between husbands' work hours and any of six measures of wives' family life (time spent on child care and housework, three measures of work/family conflict, and level of family adjustment) and, likewise, no relationship between wives' work hours and any of six parallel measures of husbands' family life.

Results from other less elaborate studies partially agree with Staines and Pleck's negative findings. While these other studies also failed to find substantive connections between wives' number of hours and husbands' family life, they did report certain effects of husbands' hours on wives' family life that were not replicated by Staines and Pleck. We may consider the findings of these other studies for three types of measures of family life: time spent on housework, level of work/family conflict, and degree of family adjustment. Walker and Woods (1976), for example, found that as husbands' work time increased, the amount of time their wives spent on housework also increased, but the analysis was bivariate and included no significance tests. By comparison, two studies failed to detect a relationship between wives' hours of employment and their husbands' hours of housework (Meissner, Humphreys, Meis, & Scheu, 1975; Walker & Woods, 1976) and a third study, which used cross-lag analysis and panel data from six years, found only a minimal (positive) effect of wives' annual hours of employment on husbands' annual hours of housework (Nickols & Metzen, 1982).

Two studies have tested for cross-over effects using work/family conflict as the measure of the quality of family life. Keith and Schafer (1980) analyzed data on work/family role strain based on a sample of 135 two-earner families. The predictors in their multiple regressions included the respondent's total number of hours worked per week and the spouse's total number of hours worked, along with selected demographic and other variables. For both sexes, the number of hours one spouse worked was a positive predictor of that person's own work/family role strain, and, interestingly, an increase in the husband's number of work hours was associated with an elevation in the wife's level of strain—but not vice versa. Greenhaus and Kopelman (1981) reported data on a sample of male graduates from an eastern technical college. The investigators noted that for two-earner families, the wives' time involvement at work (part-time versus full-time) had no effect on the presence or intensity of their husbands' work/family conflict.

Marital adjustment provides yet another perspective on the spouse's family life. Clark et al. (1978) found that husbands' work time did not show any significant effect on their wives' marital satisfaction when husbands' income and education, wives' education and work time, and the presence of preschoolers or school-age children in the home, were controlled.

Summary

Among husbands, large amounts of time spent at work are marginally associated with less time in one family role (housework) but consistently associated with elevated levels of work/family interference. Existing studies of the relationship between the number of hours husbands work and various dimensions of their family adjustment have failed to uncover any direct associations. Nor have studies of cross-over effects based on number of hours worked produced any consistently positive findings.

SCHEDULING OF WORK TIME

Pattern of Days Worked Each Week

Scheduling of time, the second general dimension of work schedules, includes two work schedule characteristics, the first of which is the pattern of days worked. Staines and Pleck (1983, 1984a, 1984b) distinguished three different patterns: (1) a standard pattern in which workers adhere to a fixed (or nonvariable) pattern of days that excludes weekend work (nonvariable weekdays), (2) a nonstandard pattern in which workers work the same days each week but where at least one of those days is a Saturday or Sunday (nonvariable weekend days), and (3) another nonstandard pattern according to which workers do not work the same days each week (variable days). Surprisingly little research has explored the relationship between the pattern of days husbands work and their family life. Aside from some casual mention of the subject of weekend work in the literature on rotating shiftwork, only one study (Staines & Pleck, 1983) has focused specifically on the patterns of days husbands work.

Time Spent in Family Roles

Staines and Pleck (1983) reported multivariate data regarding the patterns of days worked by two-earner husbands in a national sample of workers. Compared to a regular schedule of days which excluded Saturdays and Sundays, a regular schedule that included weekend work was associated among husbands with less time in child care and housework. Working a variable pattern of days, however, was not associated with the amount of time husbands spend on either child care or housework.

Interference Between Work and Family Life

In Staines and Pleck's multivariate analyses, regular weekend work on the part of two-earner husbands did not produce a significant association with any of the three measures of work/ family conflict: total conflict, hours conflict (i.e., excessive hours) or schedule conflict. Nor did a significant relationship emerge among such husbands between working a variable pattern of days and any measure of work/family conflict. Nonetheless, a multivariate study by Shamir (1983), which included data on both sexes but did not report separately on either sex, found a positive relationship between number of weekends or holidays worked in the last month and level of work/nonwork conflict.

Family Adjustment

Regular weekend work performed by two-earner husbands bore no relationship to their level of family adjustment in Staines and Pleck's multivariate analyses. Working a variable schedule of days likewise failed to generate a relationship with adjustment.

Cross-over Effects Involving Wives

Staines and Pleck (1983) studied cross-over effects within a sample of two-earner couples, and found two such effects involving the pattern of days worked. First, having a wife who worked a variable number of days each week reduced a husband's time in housework. Interestingly, this same characteristic had a nonsignificant, negative effect on the wife's own housework time. Second, a husband's regular weekend work was associated with a significant elevation in his wife's reports of schedule conflict (though not his own). The latter cross-over effect may be interpretable in light of the effects of weekend work on husbands' and wives' time use. A husband's weekend work significantly reduced his time in child care and housework, since he could use weekends to "catch up" on these activities. In this circumstance, the wife's conflicts were increased. By contrast, a wife's weekend work led to only small, nonsignificant decreases in her own time in family roles and to little change in her husband's. Thus the husband's conflict was not elevated.

Summary

One major departure from a husband's regular schedule of days (regular weekend work) tends to be associated with less time in family roles, but other evidence of links between a husband's nonstandard pattern of days and his family life is generally lacking. Among dual-earner couples, certain links exist between an individual's pattern of days worked and his or her spouse's family life.

Pattern of Hours Worked Each Day (Shift)

The pattern of hours worked, the second work schedule characteristic within the overall dimension of scheduling of time, is typically represented by a worker's shift. By distinguishing among different shifts, we can convert a dichotomous measure of a special schedule (shiftwork vs. regular day work) into a dimensional measure with several categories.

Time Spent in Family Roles

Until quite recently, no published studies offered hard evidence as to whether shiftwork is associated with any change in the actual amount of time workers spend in family roles and, if so, in which direction. Two recent studies, however, have made more concerted efforts to quantify the connection between shiftwork and time spent in family roles, but the first of the two studies exhibited a number of limitations. Jamal and Jamal (1982) collected data from (mostly male) production workers in a manufacturing organization but, among the deficiencies in this study's research design, was its failure to differentiate among different family roles (e.g., child care, housework, and time with spouse).

Staines and Pleck (1983) distinguished among three types of husbands' work shifts (day, nonday, and variable). They examined the relationships for two-earner husbands between working on shifts and spending time in two family roles (child care and housework). Multiple regression analyses showed no effect of any shift on time with one's children but they did show that working a nonday shift had a significantly positive effect on housework time. In sum, Staines and Pleck's data on shiftwork and time in family roles produced an unexpected finding. Shiftwork did not reduce the amount of time husbands spent in the two family roles measured; instead it appeared to *increase* the time they devoted to housework.

Staines and Pleck speculated as to why shiftworkers reported spending more time on housework than did other workers. They pointed out that this extra time on housework may have derived in part from the fact that people who work at night (i.e., those on night and rotating shifts) have been shown in other studies to sleep from one to two hours fewer per night than daytime workers. In addition, housework includes many solitary activities whose scheduling is highly flexible; thus, workers whose shifts precluded their spending time in regularly scheduled family activities may have viewed housework as the family role to which they could most reasonably allocate their available time.

Interference Between Work and Family Life

The bulk of the evidence linking husbands' shiftwork to family life concerns whether their shiftwork is associated with elevated levels of work/family interference. A study by Mott, Mann, McLoughlin, and Warwick (1965), one of the more extensive investigations of shiftwork, illustrates how problems of research design and analysis strategy can limit the utility of empirical findings. Using a sample of white, male, blue-collar workers in continuous-process industries in the east-central part of the United States, the researchers collected data through questionnaires from day workers and shiftworkers and also from the wives of shiftworkers. The first problem with their study is that workers on nonday shifts (afternoon, night, rotating) were asked to compare their current shift with a steady day schedule in terms of difficulty in engaging in various marital and parental activities. Mott et al.'s data thus included no analytic comparisons between the work/family interference reported by shiftworkers and day workers, only the judgments of shiftworkers comparing interference under the two types of schedules (and finding it greater under conditions of shiftwork). Second, in their analytic comparisons of levels of work/family interference among the three nonday shifts, Mott et al. performed one-way analyses of variance and omnibus F tests but included no pairwise t tests. As a result, it is unclear which pairs of shifts were significantly different.

Of some interest, however, are Mott et al.'s (1965) findings comparing work/family conflict for the three nonday shifts. According to the data on husbands, rotating shifts consistently created high levels of interference with various components of the marital role (e.g., assisting wives with housework, providing diversion and relaxation, sexual relations, and decision making). Afternoon and night shifts generated roughly equal but lower levels of interference with marital activities. Data on interference with the parental role presented a different pattern. Among fathers on shiftwork, the afternoon shift reportedly interfered much more than did the other two shifts with a variety of parental activities (e.g., companionship with children, teaching useful skills, control and discipline).

Several other studies of employed men, nonetheless, did include relevant comparisons between the levels of work/family interference reported by shift and day workers. Young and Willmott (1973) asked husbands in a London sample whether their work interfered with their family life. A majority of the shiftworkers (52%) replied affirmatively, compared to only a third of the weekend workers (34%) and a quarter of the other workers (27%) (chi-square significant). House (1980) studied the effects of shiftwork among a population of nonmanagerial factory workers. However, his index of job/nonjob conflict included three items, only one of which asked about work/family strain. Based on an analysis sample of white males, House reported a significantly positive relationship between shiftwork (generally the 3 p.m.–11 p.m. shift) and non/nonjob conflict, even after the imposition of multivariate controls.

A third study offers extensive evidence linking shifts and work/family conflict. Tasto, Colligan, Skjei, and Polly (1978) analyzed data from food processors (71% male). Shiftworkers reported significantly more interference than other workers between their work hours and their sexual activities. Night shiftworkers reported the most interference, followed in order by rotators, afternoon shiftworkers, and workers on day shift. Tasto et al. also employed a more indirect measure of work/family conflict, satisfaction with the amount of time able to be spent with various family members. Each shift of food processors reported significantly less satisfaction with the amount of time spent with their spouses than did those working on daytime schedules; and rotators and night shiftworkers were more dissatisfied on this item than afternoon shiftworkers, who were in turn more dissatisfied than day shiftworkers. Similarly, all other food-processor shift categories were significantly more dissatisfied than were day shiftworkers with the amount of time they had available to spend with their children. Afternoon and rotating shift food processors were the least satisfied.

Using data from the two-earner husbands in their nationally representative sample, Staines and Pleck (1983) examined the relationship between shiftwork and three measures of work/family conflict: total conflict, hours conflict, and schedule conflict. In their multivariate analysis they found working a nonday shift to be positively associated with total conflict and schedule conflict but unrelated to hours conflict. Husbands working a variable shift, on the other hand, registered higher levels of hours conflict.

Staines and Pleck commented on their finding that the major nonday shifts tend to be associated with both *more* time spent on housework and *more* work/family conflict, especially of the schedule variety. They viewed their data on shiftwork and family life as pointing up the important distinction between amount of time in family roles and scheduling of that time. Contrary to popular conception, shiftwork does not detract from the amount of time workers spend in family roles; in fact, shiftworkers spend more time than other workers on housework. The problems that shiftwork poses for family life concern the scheduling of available time. Apparently, the time that shiftworkers have available for family roles comes at the wrong period of the day; that is, schedules of family members fail to mesh, hence workers' reports of schedule conflict.

Family Adjustment

As part of their study, Mott et al. (1965) evaluated the connection between husbands' shiftwork and marital adjustment. In this section of the analysis, fortunately, the statistical comparisons involving husbands included the day shift along with the earlier three nonday shifts, although again the bivariate statistical testing included F tests but not t tests. According to the data on three indices of marital adjustment (viz. marital happiness, avoidance of friction, coordination of family activities), adjustment among husbands was highest for those on the day shift. Differences among the three nonday shifts lacked consistency across indices of adjustment, but Mott et al. did not test the significance of these differences.

Staines and Pleck's (1983) study also included an analysis of the relationship between shiftwork and an index of family adjustment (based on ratings of marital happiness, marital satisfaction, and family satisfaction). Under multivariate control, neither nonday nor variable shifts had a significant effect on family adjustment. In short, according to the two available studies, whatever links exist between husbands' shiftwork and family adjustment appear to occur only in bivariate analyses and do not survive the statistical rigor of multivariate analysis.

Cross-over Effects Involving Wives

Although several studies have investigated whether husbands' shiftwork affects wives' family life or wives' shiftwork affects husbands' family life (i.e., cross-over effects), serious problems of research design frequently complicate the interpretation of the data. One study that survives several of the standard methodological objections is Mott et al.'s (1965) comparison of the work/family interference reported by the wives of men on nonday shifts. The investigators observed that shift interference with the marital role was notably low among wives of men on afternoon (as opposed to night or rotating) shifts, whereas it was notably high among husbands on rotating shifts (no pairwise t tests). Moreover, husbands' shift schedule was unrelated to the ease or difficulty with which wives performed the parental role even though the afternoon shift was accompanied by special problems for the parental role among husbands. In addition, Mott et al. found that comparisons among the wives of the three groups of shiftworkers yielded no significant differences on any of the three indices of marital adjustment.

Staines and Pleck (1983) also tested for cross-over effects of shiftwork but their analyses differed from Mott et al.'s in several respects. Whereas Mott et al. studied the effect of a husband's shiftwork on the family life of his (typically) nonemployed wife, Staines and Pleck examined the effects of each partner's shift on his or her spouse's family life among a sample of two-earner couples; and whereas Mott et al. compared the effects of different nonday shifts (afternoon, night, rotating), Staines and Pleck compared day shifts with both fixed nonday shifts (afternoon and night combined) and variable shifts (rotating and other combined). Based on six measures of family life, Staines and Pleck detected one significant cross-over effect. A wife's nondaytime schedule (afternoon and night shifts combined) significantly increased her husband's experience of schedule conflict. Wives were not equally sensitive to shiftwork by their husbands. Staines and Pleck pointed to a possible reason why a husband's schedule conflict responded to his wife's shiftwork. They noted that a wife's shiftwork tended to increase her husband's time in child care and, although this increment was not statistically significant, it appeared to be an additional family responsibility that caused the husband to experience more conflict. By comparison, when a husband worked a nondaytime shift, he increased his housework, thus taking over some of his wife's traditional family responsibility. Therefore, a wife's conflict was not significantly increased by her husband's shiftwork.

Summary

Few people have attempted to justify the adoption of shift-work on the basis of its positive effects on working men and certainly not in terms of its impact on their family life. Current research reveals that, although husbands' shiftwork is associated with more time spent in one family role (housework), it is also associated with increased levels of interference between work and family life. Multivariate analyses do not indicate any association between shiftwork and time spent in a second family role (child care) or between shiftwork and level of family adjustment. Among dual-earner families, one cross-over effect of shiftwork does emerge: When a wife works on a fixed non-day shift, her husband's work/family schedule conflict is likely to increase.

The Four-Day Week: A Special Schedule

The four-day, 40-hour (or 4/40) workweek, also known as the compressed workweek, stands apart from the traditional five-day, 40-hour (or 5/40) workweek. It requires workers to accept a longer workday in exchange for working fewer days per week. The issue raised by the four-day week clearly concerns the scheduling (as opposed to the amount or flexibility) of work time but it is not captured by the earlier categories for patterns of days per week and hours per day. The four-day week thus illustrates a variation from the standard schedule that cannot easily be represented by the three general dimensions of schedules.

Time Spent in Family Roles

By far the most intensive study of the effects of the four-day week on family life was Maklan's (1977a; 1977b) investigation of a sample of male, blue-collar workers in Michigan and Minnesota. The study compared the responses of workers on four-day work weeks with those of workers on five-day schedules. Maklan noted that four-day workers spent a great deal more time with their children when compared to five-day workers (no significance tests). In the case of house work, he observed minimal differences between the four- and five-day workers regarding hours spent on traditionally female house work (grocery shopping, cooking, washing dishes, and laundry). As for more traditionally male household chores (home repairs, maintenance of heat and water systems, and shopping for goods and services other than groceries), four-day workers contributed substantially more time.

Family Adjustment

Maklan hypothesized that, owing to their greater flexibility in organizing family-related activities, four-day workers would express greater satisfaction with their conjugal and parental role performances and with their marriages in general than would a comparable group of five-day workers. Maklan found, however, virtually no differences between the two groups in mean satisfaction scores on the three dependent variables. Yet this did not mean that the four-day work schedule proved unrelated to adjustment in the family setting. Whereas, on average, four-day and five-day men expressed equal satisfaction, there were marked differences in the distributions of their responses on the measures of satisfaction with conjugal role performance and with marriage. Five-day workers indicated feeling moderately satisfied with conjugal role performance and marriage. Four-day workers, on the other hand, gave significantly more extreme responses.

Summary

The effects of the compressed workweek on men's family life have not been extensively studied. According to the best available investigation (Maklan, 1977a; 1977b), the 4/40 schedule is positively related to the amount of time husbands devote to child care and to traditionally male home chores, but compacted schedules do not differ from standard schedules in terms of mean levels of family adjustment. Unfortunately, Maklan's analysis included no explicit measures of work/family interference. It bears emphasis that the current literature tells us little about any cross-over effects of the 4/40 schedule.

FLEXIBILITY OF SCHEDULES

Schedule Control

Flexibility, the third dimension of work schedules, refers to a worker's level of control over the amount and scheduling of work time. Less research attention has been given to the general dimension of flexibility than to the preceding dimensions. From a micro-perspective, Cunningham (1982) has discussed the flexibility of the scheduling of particular work (and, likewise, nonwork) activities. From the opposite (or macro) perspective, Best (1978) has discussed the flexibility of lifetime scheduling (i.e., the timing of education, work and leisure over the total lifetime). Only one team of investigators has pursued the middle ground and systematically investigated the flexibility of the scheduling of the workweek. Staines and Pleck (1984a, 1984b) constructed an index of flexibility of schedule based on items about the worker's ability to change the patterns of days and hours worked.

Staines and Pleck's (1984b) hypothesis about the flexibility of schedules differed from their hypotheses about the earlier two dimensions of work time (amount and scheduling). Whereas the researchers searched for only the direct (or main) effects of amount and scheduling of work time on family life, they examined both the main effects and the moderator effects of schedule flexibility. They expected flexibility to have positive main effects on family life. They further expected flexibility to moderate the relationships between the earlier two schedule dimensions and family life. In other words, they reasoned that flexibility of schedule should act as a buffer against the effects of stressful schedules; excessive amounts of work and nonstandard scheduling of work time should have less harmful effects on family life under conditions of high (as opposed to low) flexibility.

According to Staines and Pleck's (1984a) multiple regression data for the two sexes combined, schedule flexibility had significant main effects on only two of the six measures of family life: a negative effect on total work/family conflict and a positive effect on family adjustment. The investigators did not, however, report any findings for men and women separately. Using the procedure of moderated regression, Staines and Pleck (1984b) tested for interactions between schedule flexibility and the other measures of work schedules. Their data for the combined-sex sample established that flexibility moderated the effects of the scheduling of work time on family life but not the effects of the amount of time worked. In other words, flexibility appeared to buffer the negative effects of nonstandard patterns of days and hours on the quality of family life but not the negative effects of working long hours. When the researchers examined whether the moderator effects applied equally to men and women, they found that women exhibited the buffering effects more frequently and strongly than did men. Put another way, flexibility provided men's family life with less protection against the stresses of nonstandard patterns of days and hours than it afforded women's family life.

In sum, schedule flexibility is positively related to the quality of family life in two distinct ways: it has a direct relationship to certain measures of family life although this has not been established separately for men and women, and it reduces negative relationships between stressful schedules and family life albeit less so for men than for women.

Flextime: A Special Schedule

Researchers may have given little attention to flexibility as a general dimension but the overall notion of flexibility has not been ignored. Instead, researchers have concerned themselves with a special schedule, flextime, that does involve issues of flexibility. Flextime actually covers a variety of schedule arrangements in which workers exercise some control over the hours they work. Typically, a core period of time in the middle of the day is mandatory for all workers, but certain variations in starting (and hence finishing) times are permitted. Flextime, in short, offers workers a limited amount of flexibility regarding one work schedule characteristic within the scheduling dimension (pattern of hours worked).

Time Spent in Family Roles

Winett, Neale, and Williams (1982; also Winett & Neale, 1980) conducted quasi-experimental studies of the effects of fixed flextime on family life at two agencies of the federal government. Using a nonequivalent control group design at each agency, the investigators collected time budget and attitudinal data from workers who opted for a flextime program (which permitted them to change their daily schedule by about an hour) and also from those who remained on regular hours because of commuter arrangements, spouse's work hours, or personal preference. The quasi-experiments included workers in secretarial and administrative positions at each agency, all of whom had at least one child under 13. Participants were drawn from both sexes. Reported for the two sexes combined rather than separately, the data for both agencies indicated modest gains in the amount of time spent with the family among the workers on flextime but not among the other workers.

Bohen and Viveros-Long (1981) compared reports of family life from personnel at two federal agencies, one on fixed flextime and one on standard hours. At each agency, the survey sample included slightly more men than women. Workers in the survey estimated how much time they typically spent on two family roles (child care and housework) during workdays and off days, thus making possible a computation of estimated average weekly hours spent on each role. The type of work schedule did not make a significant difference in the time workers allocated to child care. Yet, both male and female workers on flextime spent significantly more time on housework (two and three hours more per week, respectively) than did workers on standard hours.

Interference Between Work and Family Life

Winett et al. (1982; Winett & Neale, 1980) reported analyses relevant to the subject of work/family interference although they did not present their findings separately for men and women. Their questionnaire included items concerning the difficulty of coordinating aspects of family life, particularly with respect to hours of work (for example, spending time with one's children). Although pre-flextime scores of the flextime and control groups did not differ significantly at either government agency, the introduction of flextime made a difference at both agencies. Workers on flexible hours found it significantly easier to coordinate work schedules with afternoon and evening time with their children, time with their spouse during the week, and time on shopping and chores. Bohen and Viveros-Long (1981) compared data on personnel from the two government agencies in their study, using two indices of work/family stress. For the total sample and for both the male and female subsamples, people on flextime reported significantly less stress on the two indices than did those on standard time.

Unlike some of the other nontraditional work schedules, the effect of flextime on family adjustment or the cross-over effects of one person's flextime on his or her spouse's experience of family life have never received serious study.

Summary

Flextime appears to increase family time by small amounts. In one investigation, both male and female workers on flextime spent more time on housework than did other workers. Flextime has also been shown to be related to lower work/family conflict among both sexes. Nonetheless, the associations between flextime and two other factors—family adjustment and cross-over effects involving spouses—lie outside the scope of available information.

In sum, flexibility, the third dimension of work schedules, manifests itself in various ways. When flexibility is measured by a general index its main effects on family life for the two sexes combined consist of a negative association with work/family conflict and a positive association with family adjustment. When (as in the case of flextime) flexibility takes the form of partial control over the starting time of a day's work, it exhibits a negative relationship with conflict for both men and women and, again for both sexes, a positive relationship with time spent in family roles, but the relationship of flextime to family adjustment has not yet been determined. The general dimension of flexibility also has certain moderator effects, a phenomenon that has no parallel in the case of flextime.

CONCLUSIONS

As noted earlier, a good deal of research on men's work schedules and family life proceeds from the assumption that men's nonstandard work schedules are associated with reductions in the quality of their family life. The foregoing review of empirical research finds much to support this prevailing assumption but also locates evidence that suggests a need to qualify it. In line with the assumption among husbands, excessive amounts of time spent working are somewhat associated with less time devoted to housework and consistently associated with more interference between work and family life. Also in line with the assumption, one major departure from a husband's regular pattern of days worked each week (weekend work) is associated with less time spent in family roles. Again consistent with the assumption, husbands' nonstandard patterns of hours each day (i.e., shiftwork) are linked to higher levels of work/family conflict. In addition, limited evidence exists that husbands' nonstandard work schedules are associated with some reductions in the quality of their wives' family life and, conversely, that wives' nonstandard work schedules are associated with some reductions in the quality of their husbands' family life.

Evidence inconsistent with the assumption about husbands' nonstandard work schedules begins with shiftwork. Although married male shiftworkers report more conflict than those not on shifts, they also report spending more time on housework. Moreover, the compressed workweek, another example of nonstandard scheduling, is associated among husbands with more time invested in family roles. Further, all manifestations of the dimension of flexibility represent departures from standard schedules and all are positively associated with measures of the quality of family life. High overall flexibility of schedule, for example, is linked to low work/family conflict and high family adjustment although these two relationships have not yet been demonstrated for husbands and wives separately. Flexibility also moderates the negative effects of various nonstandard schedules on family life for both sexes but less so for husbands than for wives. Flextime is likewise associated among husbands with lower work/family conflict and is also accompanied by increments in the time husbands spend on housework.

In short, nonstandard (large) amounts of time worked are consistently associated with decrements in the quality of husbands' family life; nonstandard scheduling of work time (i.e., nonstandard patterns of days and hours) is generally but not always associated with poorer family life among husbands; and schedule flexibility, a nonstandard characteristic of work schedules, has consistently positive links with husbands' family life. Put another way, among the various fixed schedules that may be imposed on employed husbands, a standard pattern of week days and daytime hours offers more to family life than most (though not necessarily all) other schedules; however, once schedule flexibility and personal choice become possible, husbands will often find that a fixed standard schedule is not in the best interests of their family life.

Future research on the relationship between men's work schedules and family life need not restrict itself to the empirical questions that have already been investigated. Instead, it may in addition address a variety of new and provocative issues: the impact on family life of husbands' second jobs, the interactive effects of the amount and scheduling of husbands' work time, the impact of husbands' schedules on other measures of family life (e.g., time spent in the marital role, family decision-making power, the father-child relationship, and children's development), the relative impact of work schedules and other working conditions on husbands' family life, and systematic differences between husbands in one-earner and two-earner families. Clearly, this area of scientific inquiry faces no shortage of intellectual challenges.

REFERENCES

Best, F. (1978). Preferences on worklife scheduling and work-leisure tradeoffs. *Monthly Labor Review, 101*(6), 31–37.

Bohen, H. H., & Viveros-Long, A. (1981). *Balancing jobs and family life: Do flexible work schedules help?* Philadelphia: Temple University Press.

Clark, R. A., & Gecas, V. (1977). The employed father in America: A role competition analysis. Paper presented at the Pacific Sociological Association.

Clark, R. A., Nye, F. I., & Gecas, V. (1978). Husbands' work involvement and marital role performance. *Journal of Marriage and the Family, 40,* 9–21.

Cunningham, J. B. (1982). Compressed shift schedules: Altering the relationship between work and non-work. *Public Administration Review, 42*(5), 438–447.

Greenhaus, J. H., & Kopelman, R. E. (1981). Conflict between work and nonwork roles: Implications for the career planning process. *Human Resources Planning, 4,* 1–10.

House, J. S. (1980). *Occupational stress and the mental and physical health of factory workers.* Research Report Series. Ann Arbor, MI: Institute for Social Research.

Jamal, M., & Jamal, S. M. (1982). Work and nonwork experiences of employees on fixed and rotating shifts: An empirical assessment. *Journal of Vocational Behavior, 20,* 282–293.

Keith, P. M., & Schafer, R. B. (1980). Role strain and depression in two-job families. *Family Relations, 29,* 483–488.

Maklan, D. M. (1977a). *The four-day workweek: Blue-collar adjustment to a nonconventional arrangement of work and leisure time.* New York: Praeger Publishers.

Maklan, D. M. (1977b). How blue-collar workers on 4-day workweeks use their time. *Monthly Labor Review, 100*(8), 18–26.

Meissner, M., Humphreys, E. W., Meis, S. M., & Scheu, W. J. (1975). No exit for wives: Sexual division of labour and the cumulation of household demands. *Canadian Review of Sociology and Anthropology, 12,* 424–439.

Mortimer, J. T. (1980). Occupation-family linkages as perceived by men in the early stages of professional and managerial careers. In H. Z. Lopata (Ed.), *Research in the interweave of social roles, Vol. 1: Women and men.* Greenwich, CT: JAI Press.

Mott, P. E., Mann, F. C., McLoughlin, Q., & Warwick, D. P. (1965). *Shift work: The social, psychological, and physical consequences.* Ann Arbor, MI: The University of Michigan Press.

Nickols, S. Y., & Metzen, E. J. (1982). Impact of wife's employment upon husband's housework. *Journal of Family Issues, 3*(2), 199–216.

Ridley, C. A. (1973). Exploring the impact of work satisfaction and involvement on marital interaction when both partners are employed. *Journal of Marriage and the Family, 35,* 229–237.

Robinson, J. P. (1977). *How Americans use time: A social-psychological analysis of everyday behavior.* New York: Praeger.

Shamir, B. (1983). Some antecedents of work-nonwork conflict. *Journal of Vocational Behavior, 23,* 98–111.

Staines, G. L., & Pleck, J. H. (1983). *The impact of work schedules on the family.* Ann Arbor, MI: Institute for Social Research.

Staines, G. L., & Pleck, J. H. (1984a). Nonstandard work schedules and family life. *Journal of Applied Psychology, 69,* 515–523.

Staines, G. L., & Pleck, J. H. (1984b). Work schedule flexibility and family life. Unpublished paper, Rutgers University.

Tasto, D. L., Colligan, M. J., Skjei, E. W., & Polly, S. J. (1978). *Health consequences of shift work.* SRI Project URU–4426.

Walker, K., & Woods, M. (1976). *Time Use: A measure of household production of family goods and services.* Washington, DC: American Home Economics Association.

Winett, R. A., & Neale, M. S. (1980). Results of experimental study on flexitime and family life. *Monthly Labor Review, 103*(11), 29–32.

Winett, R., Neale, M., & Williams, K. (1982). The effects of flexible work schedules on urban families with young children: Quasi-experimental, ecological studies. *American Journal of Community Psychology, 10,* 49–64.

Young, M., & Willmott, P. (1973). *The symmetrical family.* New York: Pantheon.

Chapter 6

Effects of Paternal Involvement on Fathers and Mothers

Michael E. Lamb
Joseph H. Pleck
James A. Levine

In the last two decades, average levels of paternal involvement in childcare have increased significantly (Lamb, Pleck, Charnov, & Levine, in press), albeit more slowly than many in the media would have us believe. Most professional discussions of these secular changes have focused on the effects of increased paternal involvement on *children*. In this brief chapter, we discuss the likely effects of increased paternal involvement on mothers and fathers.

WHAT'S IN IT FOR THE MOTHERS?

Many discussions of paternal involvement argue that paternal participation either is increasing or must increase in the future because this is necessary to ensure the satisfaction of mothers (e.g., L. Hoffman, 1983). These arguments often lay great stress on the well-known fact that an increasing number of women, including mothers, are now permanent participants in the paid labor force. By 1978, 50% of the women in the US and 44% of the married women with husbands present were in the paid labor force, and this figure is expected to reach 57% by 1995 (Glick, 1979). Employment rates

Michael E. Lamb, PhD, is Professor of Psychology, Psychiatry and Pediatrics, Department of Psychology, The University of Utah, Salt Lake City, UT 84112. Joseph H. Pleck, PhD, is Program Director, Center for Research on Women, Wellesley College, Wellesley, MA 02181. James A. Levine is Director, Fatherhood Project, Banks Street College, New York, NY 10025.

are not substantially lower for married mothers in intact families than for women in general: In 1979, 52% of the married mothers of school-aged children and 36% of the married mothers of infants and preschool-aged children were employed (Glick & Norton, 1979). For obvious economic reasons, employment rates are even higher among single mothers and Black mothers, both single and married (Glick & Norton, 1979). In other words, *most* American children now grow up in families in which both parents, or the single resident parent, are employed outside the home.

Considerations of equity have been used to justify the need for increased paternal involvement in dual-earner families. Commentators such as Lois Hoffman (1977) and Lamb and Bronson (1980) have argued that levels of paternal involvement should increase as a result of increasing rates of maternal employment because it is unfair for employed women to be burdened with the demands of two roles—those of breadwinning and homemaking/parenting—while their husbands must deal with only one—that of breadwinning. This argument implies that role strain will be reduced, and marital satisfaction enhanced, when fathers are more involved. Both Hoffman and Lamb and Bronson expect this to be desirable not only for the women themselves, but also for their children, since contented parents tend to be better parents. Unfortunately, while arguments such as these have a common-sense plausibility, the empirical evidence suggests that they are not generally true.

Do Mothers—Especially Employed Mothers— Want More Help From Their Spouses?

There has been substantial controversy about whether or not maternal employment does lead to increased paternal participation in home and child care (Hoffman, 1983 *vs.* Pleck, 1983). However, all agree that the *relative* involvement of men is certainly higher simply because their wives have much less time to devote to child care, and that women seem to feel overloaded when employed (Pleck, 1983). Because we do not have any longitudinal data available, however, we do not know whether maternal employment, actually affects levels of paternal participation, whether paternal participation potentiates maternal employment as Sagi (1982) suggests, or whether some third factor (e.g., "liberal" attitudes) affects both paternal participation and maternal employment. In the present context, we need simply note that whereas the life satisfaction of women *may be* enhanced by increased paternal participation, there is little evidence that appreciable changes in paternal participation have taken place in response to increases in women's total (family plus paid) workload (Pleck, 1983). Furthermore, the argument that employed women would be substantially more satisfied if their husbands played a greater role in family and child care is weakened by evidence indicating that many women do not want their husbands to be more involved in childcare, and that the rates are not appreciably higher for employed than for unemployed women (Lamb et al., in press). If these expressed desires can be taken at face value, increased paternal participation may not have a desirable effect on life satisfaction in many families.

In fact, Baruch and Barnett (1983) found that women whose husbands did more child care were less satisfied with their own role-pattern than were women whose husbands participated less. Of course, we do not know whether the low satisfaction precipitated increased paternal participation, rather than having been caused by it, as the data are all correlational. However, Bailyn (1974) found that, whether employed or not, women were more satisfied when their spouses were "family-oriented".

If it is true that many women do not want their partners to become more involved in family work and childcare, the question is: "Why?" The answer may lie in traditional patterns of female power and privilege. Some women may fear losing their traditional power and domination over home activities if they allow men to relieve them of even part of the home and family work which has always been their responsibility (Polatnik, 1974).

Does Role Overload Affect the Mental Health of Women?

Although there is only equivocal evidence that role overload (total of paid and family work demands) affects the mental health of women (Hauenstein, Kasl, & Harburg, 1977; Pearlin, 1975; Radloff, 1975), there does appear to be a relationship between the amount of family work for which women are responsible and the marital adjustment they report. In a sample of dual-worker British families, Bailyn (1970) found that lowered marital happiness occurred when women had higher family workloads. A similar relationship was not found by Gross and Arvey (1977) but unfortunately the latter researchers used relative rather than absolute measures of family work. A large US survey conducted in

1973 reported that for employed wives with children, wives' marital happiness increases in proportion to increases in their husbands' absolute involvement in home and child care (Staines, Pleck, Sheppard, & O'Connor, 1978). The relationship was not significant for unemployed women and their husbands. Analyses of data gathered in two surveys conducted in 1975–76 reveal somewhat different results. In one study absolute measures of work load were involved, and the results showed that increased family work had different effects on the reported marital satisfaction of men and women. Men who engaged in more family work reported better family adjustment, whereas when women did more, worsened family adjustment was reported. In the other study, workloads were measured in relative terms, and here time in family work had positive effects for both men and women. Unfortunately, the analyses reported did not indicate whether increased involvement by fathers increased mothers' satisfaction, which is our major concern here. However, it is significant that when employed mothers reportedly wanted their husbands to be more involved than they were, family adjustment and well-being were substantially lower. In other words, increased paternal involvement seemed likely to have desirable consequences when it was valued by mothers, whereas the failure of fathers to be more involved only had adverse consequences when it was desired by the women concerned.

Apparently, therefore, the effects of increased paternal participation vary depending on the attitudes of the women concerned. Whatever burdens accrue to women who are both breadwinners and primary housekeepers and caretakers may be offset by the increased satisfaction obtained from employment or pursuit of a career. Further, individuals who find both parenthood and employment gratifying may maximize their total satisfaction by pursuing both, even if this increases their total workload (Baruch & Barnett, 1979; Owen, Chase-Lansdale, & Lamb, 1982; Stewart, 1978; Verbrugge, 1980).

These results point to need for recognition of the variability among families. There appears to be a substantial minority of families in which increased paternal involvement would alleviate a source of stress and dissatisfaction, and there appears to be another, perhaps larger group of families in which this would not occur. Perhaps this is because many women are employed seasonally or part-time and because the amount of work involved in home and child care has decreased as smaller families and labor-saving devices have become more common. In any event, the implication is that equity is not sufficient grounds for urging increased paternal involvement, because these considerations do not apply to many families. However, since at least some families would benefit in this way, there is reason for broadening the options that would allow some families to adjust levels of paternal involvement to suit their individual preferences.

Does Paternal Participation Enhance Wive's Satisfaction?

It also seems possible that extensive paternal involvement would facilitate career advancement in their wives and thus contribute to an enhancement in their overall satisfaction. Both scholarly and popular analyses have repeatedly noted that women with young children are considered employment risks because of the work-family conflicts that are likely to arise. These prejudices are likely to remain as long as women employees alone take time off to care for sick children, to attend parent-teacher conferences, and to supervise children released from school for holidays, for example. If male employees requested time off for these reasons, too, it might go a long way toward relieving the skepticism and prejudices concerning female employees in general, whether or not the individuals themselves had ever allowed work-family conflicts to interfere with their performance as employees. From this perspective, increased paternal participation may have important implications for the attainment of equal employment opportunities. At the very least, it may permit individual dual-career or dual-worker families to share and thus limit the adverse effects of work-family conflicts on either career.

As Russell's (1982, 1983) study of highly involved Australian fathers revealed, however, there are some potential costs. Many of the wives in his study expressed dissatisfaction about the quality of the fathers' home and child care performance, and this in turn was a source of marital friction. Since most of the families did not choose their nontraditional lifestyle, but had it thrust on them by economic circumstances, one wonders whether similar concerns would arise in families where the unusual distribution of responsibilities was chosen on ideological grounds. Interestingly, Baruch and Barnett (1984) found that women were more dissatisfied when their husbands were highly involved than when their husbands were less involved.

As mentioned earlier, many women claim not to want their husbands to be more involved in home and child care (Pleck, 1983). Presumably, what motivates this is not simply a love of household and childcare chores, but a concern about marital power relationships and the assumed association between relative involvement in caretaking and relative affective importance to children. Although multiple interpretations are possible, these findings may reveal a concern on the part of many women that increased paternal participation would involve a loss of domination in the family arena and would bring about a dilution of exclusive mother-child relationships. These concerns are reasonable ones; it is hard to believe that mothers would feel the same sense of crucial importance to their children's development when childrearing was shared with another person with equal or greater investment and commitment. As long as motherhood remains a central aspect of self-definition for many women and as long as prospects for fulfillment in the employment arena remain uncertain, many are likely to fear the abdication or partial abdication of responsibility for parental care. Those who do so may experience ambivalence, regret, and guilt. Further, mothers will no longer be able to count on obtaining custody of their children after divorce, because fathers who have been more involved in child care may have established close relationships to their children, and may thus legitimately claim full or joint custody for themselves.

Summary

Increased paternal participation evidently will not bring equivalent and unambiguously positive effects for all women. While the sharing of responsibilities that have hitherto been the exclusive province of wives and mothers may relieve the total work overload of employed mothers and may facilitate their increased commitment to work roles, this will be achieved only at the expense of the exclusive, close relationships to children that mothers have traditionally enjoyed, and at the expense of the mothers' traditional domination of the home. Given the extent of "socialization for motherhood" which most women experience, it is unlikely that these costs will be insignificant to many women. This underscores that increased paternal involvement necessarily involves major changes in family responsibilities and roles and more specifically requires that women share power in the one arena in which their domination has hitherto been sacrosanct. In exchange for this, they obtain greater flexibility to pursue success and fulfillment in the occupational sphere, although attainment of either success or fulfillment is quite uncertain. At the very least, therefore, many women are likely to feel ambivalent about increased paternal involvement because increased involvement, while enhancing the women's opportunities and flexibility, also threatens their prerogatives in the one area where their domination and power have been assured. Whether a reallocation of parental responsibilities is desirable in any individual case depends on the relative evaluation of the costs and benefits, and this in turn will be influenced by the family circumstances as well as the attitudes and aspirations of the two parents. Further, even when the benefits exceed the costs, some disadvantages and some misgivings are inevitable. Evaluation of the costs and benefits depends on the individuals' evaluations of the relative importance of factors such as career, motherhood, etc. Since this evaluation will vary from one family to the next, we believe that it is flexibility, rather than prescribed levels of paternal involvement—whether high or low—which is desirable.

WHAT'S IN IT FOR FATHERS?

However beneficial for mothers (i.e., wives/partners) and children, fathers are unlikely to change their lifestyles radically so as to become more involved in childcare unless they feel that the changes are desirable and beneficial for themselves. In this section we consider what fathers stand to gain or lose from assuming a more extensive direct involvement in the lives and rearing of their children. Essentially, the issue here has to do with the choice between career and paternal involvement and this choice depends on the relative evaluation of the two.

Traditionally, fulfillment for men has been defined mainly in terms of occupational and economic success (e.g., Cazenave, 1979; Benson, 1969; Pleck, 1983). Within the family, a "good" father is one who is a reliable economic provider, and one who buffers other members of the family (especially mothers) from concerns about economic stresses. Of course, to the extent that their jobs permit them to play a more active role in the family—doing things with their wives and children—men have usually been lauded for direct involvement. However, economic provision has always been the *sine qua non* of the paternal role. Furthermore, although national statistics show that an increasing number of couples are now delaying childbearing, most young families still have their children at a time when the career-oriented male is trying to establish himself and "get-ahead", and when the seniority and job security of all working males remain tenuous. As mentioned in the preceding chapter, these circumstances exert a powerful brake on paternal involvement as there is little doubt that fathers devote time to childrearing at the expense of the time devoted to work. In many studies of role-sharing or role-reversing families, fathers have reported that their occupational advancement was adversely affected, or that a lack of concern with this made the changed lifestyle possible (e.g., Radin, 1982; Russell, 1982, 1983). In addition, many of Russell's highly involved fathers only adopted their roles when unemployment or underemployment made it a viable option. Even if they are able to maintain their productivity and professional skills while devoting additional time to their families, highly-involved fathers are likely to be perceived as less committed or less serious by colleagues and superiors, and thus their professional status and future prospects are deleteriously affected. As long as these factors are of central importance to some men's evaluations of their success, increased paternal involvement would seem to be an unattractive proposition.

Thus far, there is no empirical evidence available concerning the effects of increased paternal participation on career advancement and income. Concerns about adverse effects of this sort appear to constitute one of the barriers to increased paternal involvement, and the fears certainly appear well-founded (Lamb et al., in press). The experiences of employed mothers indicate that when family responsibilities impede the ability to work long uninterrupted hours or go on business-related trips, the opportunities and promotions go to others, even when the individual is performing well within the range of contracted responsibilities. Bailyn's (1974) data suggest that the same is true for fathers, since family-oriented "accommodators" seemed to be confined to lower status positions than their non-accommodative peers. Increased paternal participation precludes overtime and moon-lighting as means of supplementing family income. Furthermore, professional responsibilities are often at their maximum at precisely the time that family work-loads are heaviest, which maximizes the cost of increased paternal involvement to career-committed men. As Veroff and Feld (1970) point out: "at this point in the life cycle, work represents their attempt to solidify their career for the sake of their family's security. They are torn between their desire to establish a close relationship with their children and their desire to establish financial security for the family" (p. 180). The situation is also complicated by the fact that male employees continue to earn much more than female employees; this means that the reduced earnings of a father are offset only by disproportionate increases in the outside workload of their partners. Taken together, these considerations suggest that increased paternal participation may often entail a decrease in the family's present and future earning power. As long as this remains the case, increased paternal participation will be economically intolerable for many families. It will not become an acceptable option for many unless there is a radical change in the relative evaluation of career advancement and family involvement as determinants of individual male fulfillment.

Why Might Some Men Want to Become More Involved?

There is some reason to believe that young men today are less willing than their fathers or grandfathers to define personal success solely in terms of occupational and economic success. Many men today (such as those interviewed by Rubin, 1982), report dissatisfaction with the relationships they had with their fathers. This leads us to expect that these men will strive to be more involved than their fathers were, and indeed this is what some attitude surveys seem to suggest. In an admittedly unrepresentative sample of *Esquire* readers, Gail Sheehy (1979) found that many young men considered satisfying personal relationships—especially those with spouses and children—to be of great importance. Many commented that, if it was necessary to retard their occupational progress in order to have sufficient time for family relationships, they would be willing to do this, because fulfillment for them required some measure of success in close relationships as well as occupational achievement. These data thus suggest that at least some men are redefining "success" in a way which might make increased paternal involvement attractive.

Further evidence that fathers may be willing to increase their involvement in child care and family roles more generally comes from a national survey reported by Pleck (1983). Pleck reported that the majority of fathers have a greater interest in, and derive more satisfaction from, their families than from their paid work. Of course, it is not clear from these data just what aspects of their family roles are most satisfying, and it cannot simply be assumed that these fathers are expressing a desire to become primary or even co-equal participants in child care. For example, a traditional man may express his commitment to family in the form of increased effort at the work place, since increased earnings enhance the quality of life he makes possible for his family. The evidence suggests that average levels of paternal involvement have risen, but very little, in the last two decades (Lamb et al., in press). One reason for this may be that the effects of involvement on the quality of father-child relationships are more complex than many initially hoped.

Do Closer Relationships Follow When Fathers Are More Involved?

For this changing definition of male fulfillment to produce increased paternal involvement, increased involvement would have to facilitate closer, richer personal relationships and/or be intrinsically enjoyable. There is some reason to believe the first proposition to be true although we should view the data cautiously, since we do not have adequate data to conclude that involvement produced sensitivity and competence rather than that the more competent and sensitive fathers chose to become more involved. In a longitudinal study focused on the relationships among maternal and paternal attitudes about work, parenting, and child-rearing, for example, Owen, Chase-Lansdale, and Lamb (1982) found that men who valued parenthood highly were more involved in child care and found parenthood more satisfying than did those for whom parenthood was less intrinsically important. Similar relationships were found by Frodi, Lamb, Hwang, Frodi, Forsstrom, and Corry (1982) in a study of Swedish mothers and fathers. Further, Russell (1982, 1983) and Kelly (1981) in Australia, Radin (1982) and Hood and Golden (1979) in the United States, Gronseth (1978) in Norway, Frodi et al. (1982) in Sweden, and Sagi (1982) in Israel all found that highly involved fathers spoke favorably of their family arrangements. When dissatisfaction was mentioned, it was usually expressed by men who were not as involved in childcare as they would have liked. In each study, a common reason for the positive evaluation by highly involved fathers was that it allowed the fathers to become closer to their children, observe and participate in their development more closely, and feel more intrinsically important to their children. Thus the evidence provides some support for the assumption that increased paternal involvement presages closer, richer, relationships with one's children—at least when the men concerned opted for increased involvement when they wanted it and circumstances made it possible.

What Are the Other Possible Rewards of Increased Paternal Involvement?

There is another way in which increased paternal involvement can be rewarding. As Goldberg (1977) and Lamb and Easterbrooks (1981) have argued, parents' sense of accomplishment and fulfillment is enhanced when they feel that they are competent and effective caretakers. One factor affecting caretaking competence is experience. For many traditional fathers, early uninvolvement by fathers allows mothers to develop their skills while fathers remain unskilled. Later, the perception that mothers are more competent serves to limit fathers' involvement because they feel incompetent. The perception of personal incompetence serves to limit further involvement and thus fathers do not have the practice and experiences that would give them the self confidence needed to make active parenting a rewarding experience. By contrast, fathers who are involved in childcare rapidly realize that they can be just as competent and effective as their spouses, and thus fathering becomes an increasingly rewarding and enjoyable experience.

Consistent with these notions, two-thirds of the role-sharing Norwegian fathers included in Gronseth's (1978) small study (N = 16) reported that they understood their children better as a result of being home with them. Similarly, a quarter of the highly-participant Australian fathers studied by Russell (1982) reported that their increased participation led them to a better understanding of their children and their everyday needs. Interestingly, they explicitly identified sole responsibility, rather than amount of time together, as the critical factor. Furthermore, the fathers reported that their increased competence and sensitivity made them feel more self confident and more effective as parents. Finally, in Sagi's (1982) analysis of variously involved Israeli fathers, nurturance was highly correlated with the degree of paternal involvement. The only discordant findings were reported by Radin and Sagi (1982) and

Radin (1982) in a study of highly involved American fathers whose behavior was no more sensitive or nurturant than the behavior of traditional fathers. It is not clear whether these discordant results reflect a cultural difference (all the other studies were conducted outside the US), or a difference in methodology, since only Radin and Sagi (1982) assessed nurturance on the basis of unobtrusive behavioral observations. In all other studies, however, highest satisfaction was reported by those fathers who were highly involved in childcare, while dissatisfaction with their current roles was limited to those fathers who were relatively uninvolved. It was the lack of sufficient contact with their children that seemed to result in dissatisfaction (e.g., Sagi, 1982).

How Does Increased Paternal Involvement Affect the Father's Personality and Feelings About Himself?

Although there is reason to claim that increased paternal involvement can be rewarding for fathers, it is important not to romanticize fathering or exaggerate the joys of parenting. In addition to the undeniable economic costs mentioned earlier, there are also personal and emotional costs the extent of which may vary depending on the reasons why fathers have chosen to be unusually involved in childcare. In other words, the costs and benefits will differ depending on whether fathers are involved because they cannot find paid work, because they are committed to sexual equity, because they enjoy children, or because their wives insist on greater paternal involvement.

In the only long-term follow-up of men who had been primary caretakers, Russell (1982, 1983) found that many of the families later returned to more traditional divisions of family roles. In retrospect, many of the men who had been primary caretakers had a fairly negative perception of their experiences, and these perceptions were frequently shared by their wives. The men's complaints sound familiar to those who have been monitoring the concerns of traditional mothers: they felt deprived of adult contacts and they found their lives boring and repetitive. In addition, many reported that neighbors, family, and friends were consistently unsupportive and rather critical of the unusual divisions of family responsibilities. For their part, the mothers felt distanced from their children. Both parents in the role-reversing or role-sharing families felt that their lives were chaotic and rushed—a familiar complaint among dual-career families. Consequently, when the fathers were able to obtain well-paying jobs, they returned to paid work and reverted to more traditional roles within the family. In many of Russell's families, the nontraditional lifestyle was originally precipitated by economic circumstances (i.e., the fathers' inability to find jobs) rather than ideological commitment and we do not know whether the same negative evaluations would have been reached by fathers who had chosen increased involvement for ideological reasons. Furthermore, although dual-career families inevitably experience more chaos, overextension, and stress than traditional single career families, the question is whether that chaos is likely to be more or less when both parents share in breadwinning and parenting instead of having mothers fill these two roles while their traditional partners devote themselves exclusively to breadwinning. Interestingly, Gronseth's (1978) Norwegian subjects reported far more positive effects on the marital relationship than did Russell's (1982, 1983) Australian respondents. Perhaps this was because *none* of Gronseth's subjects worked full time, whereas in Russell's study at least one, and often (50%) both, of the parents in each couple were employed full-time. Role overload would thus be more predictable in Russell's study.

Another source of marital conflict reported by Russell (1982), De Frain (1979), and Lein (1979) had to do with the mothers' dissatisfaction with the quality of the fathers' childcare and house-work. According to Russell, one reason for this was that the mothers felt threatened by their husbands' participation in traditionally female domains. In 30% of Russell's families, however, the increased conflict occurred mainly during a brief adjustment period beginning right after the nontraditional roles were adopted.

Bailyn's (1974) study of highly-educated businessmen showed that the family-oriented accommodators had more negative self concepts—such as reduced self esteem, and less confidence in their creativity or problem-solving ability—than did men who were more single-mindedly committed to their jobs. The accommodators were also more professionally passive and less successful professionally. They also tended to be in less prestigious jobs within their organizations, although it was not clear whether this was a cause or an effect of the family-oriented accommodative strategies.

Another adverse consequence of increased paternal involvement was described by Russell (1982, 1983) and Kelly (1981) in studies of Australian families. In both studies, highly participant fathers had more conflicts with their children than did less involved fathers.

Similarly, Radin and Sagi (1982) found that highly involved fathers were perceived as more punitive by their children. As Russell (1982) suggests, these findings mean that highly participant fathers had more realistic (i.e., less romanticized) relationships with their children, which was seen as a positive consequence of paternal participation by mothers, but not by fathers!

Summary

Increased paternal involvement promises both advantages and disadvantages to fathers themselves. Among the costs are the likelihood of diminished earnings and career prospects as well as retarded promotion, marital friction, dissatisfaction with the boring tedium of day-to-day parenthood, and social isolation from disapproving friends, relatives, and colleagues. Among the advantages or benefits are the potential for personal fulfillment through closer, richer relationships with one's children, along with the opportunity to witness and influence their development more thoroughly. As in the case of mothers, the relative evaluation of the costs and benefits must depend on the individual's values and aspirations as well as both economic and social circumstances. Thus many men and many couples may find increased paternal involvement an undesirable option, just as their values and circumstances may make increased paternal involvement desirable for other couples. The fact is, however, that the number of men currently willing to sacrifice their careers and wage-earning roles in order to achieve greater involvement with their children is apparently very small.

CONCLUSION

The evidence reviewed in this chapter is sketchy, inconclusive, and at times contradictory. This makes it difficult to make clearcut defensible conclusions. Attempts to assess the effects of increased paternal involvement are hampered by the fact that all available data are derived from comparisons of families in which fathers are and are not currently involved: we do not know whether paternal involvement "caused" the differences between the groups, or whether some other factors may be more crucial. Until we have longitudinal studies, in which changes in interaction and satisfaction are tracked in relation to changes in paternal involvement, we really cannot specify the effects of increased paternal involvement.

As far as mothers are concerned, increased paternal involvement should reduce the total (combined family and paid) work load of employed women, although the empirical evidence suggest that maternal employment has not in the past substantially affected paternal involvement in housework or child care and that, on average, many employed women today do not have a larger total workload than their husbands do. On the negative side, increased paternal involvement will diminish, and perhaps eliminate, maternal domination in the childrearing domain, and at least some women may resent this both because of its effect on the balance of marital power as well as because it may dilute the exclusive intensity of mother-child relationships. To the extent that fathers have less experience with home or child care skills, mothers may find these responsibilities being fulfilled by others less vigorously (or at least differently) than they would like. Agreeing to share family work may facilitate women's advancement in the employment sector but there is always the risk that if the latter sector proves disappointing, some women will find themselves without any arena in which they dominate.

For men, finally, the advantages of increased involvement in child care may consist primarily of closer, richer, and more realistic relationships with their children, coupled perhaps with the fulfillment of the desire to express nurturant feelings and behavior. The costs are the possible retardation of career advancement, in terms of both money and status. As in the case of women, the relinquishment of domination in one arena brings the attendant risk of ending up between a rock and the proverbial hard place.

Individual characteristics and circumstances obviously determine whether the net costs exceed the benefits—at least in the eyes of the particular parents concerned. Effects on the children may well vary depending on the parents' evaluation of the changes, because if there is one general truism in developmental psychology, it is that contented, adjusted parents tend to have contented, adjusted children. Stated another way, we have to consider the effects of changing family roles on all family members even if our real interest is only in the psychological status of only one member. Since parents are most likely to be satisfied and contented when they feel fulfilled and actualized, the flexibility to divide family and breadwinning responsibilities in accordance with their individual preferences is of maximum importance.

The fact that increased paternal involvement may have both beneficial and detrimental consequences for mothers and fathers precludes us from concluding that changes in paternal involvement would necessarily be *either* "good" or "bad" in themselves. Clearly, each couple must weigh the potential costs and benefits in the light of their own values, attitudes, and aspirations. Each decision about the distribution of childcare, household, and paid work must represent an individual couple's appraisal of what arrangement appears best in the light of personal considerations and socioeconomic circumstances.

REFERENCES

Bailyn, L. (1970) Career and family orientations of husbands and wives in relation to marital happiness. *Human Relations, 23*, 97–113.

Bailyn, L. (1974) Accommodation as career strategy: Implications for the realm of work. Working Paper 728–74, Sloan School of Management, Massachusetts Institute of Technology.

Baruch, G. K., & Barnett, R. C. (1979) Fathers' participation in the care of their preschool children. Unpublished manuscript, Wellesley College.

Baruch, G. K., & Barnett, R. C. (1984) Consequences of fathers' participation in family work: Parents' role-strain and well-being. Unpublished manuscript, Wellesley College.

Baumrind, D. (1971) Current patterns of parental authority. *Developmental Psychology Monographs, 1*, whole number 2.

Cazenave, N. (1979) Middle-income black fathers: An analysis of the provider role. *Family Coordinator, 28*, 583–593.

DeFrain, J. (1979) Androgynous parents tell who they are and what they need. *Family Coordinator, 28*, 237–243.

Frodi, A. M., Lamb, M. E., Frodi, M., Hwang, C.-P., Forsstrom, B., & Corry, T. (1981) Stability and change in parental attitudes following an infant's birth into traditional and nontraditional Swedish families. *Scandinavian Journal of Psychology.*

Glick, P. C. (1979) Future American families. *COFU Memo, 2*(3), 2–5.

Glick, P. C., & Norton, A. J. (1979) Marrying, divorcing, and living together in the U.S. today. *Population Bulletin, 32*, whole number 5.

Goldberg, S. (1977) Social competence in infancy: A model of parent-infant interaction. *Merrill-Palmer Quarterly, 23*, 163–177.

Gronseth, E. (1975) Work-sharing families: Adaptations of pioneering families with husband and wife in part-time employment. Paper presented to the International Society for the Study of Behavioral Development, Surrey (England), July.

Gross, R. H., & Arvey, R. D. (1977) Marital satisfaction, job satisfaction, and task distribution in the homemaker job. *Journal of Vocational Behavior, 11*, 1–13.

Hauenstein, L., Kasl, S., & Harburg, E. (1977) Work status, work satisfaction, and blood pressure among married black and white women. *Psychology of Women Quarterly, 1*, 334–350.

Hoffman, L. W. (1977) Changes in family roles, socialization and sex differences. *American Psychologist, 32*, 644–657.

Hoffman, L. W. (1983) Increased fathering: Effects on the mother. In M. E. Lamb & A. Sagi (Eds.), *Fatherhood and Family Policy*. Hillsdale, NJ: Lawrence Erlbaum Associates.

Hood, J., & Golden, S. (1979) Beating time/making time: The impact of work scheduling on men's family roles. *Family Coordinator, 28,* 575–582.

Kelly, S. (1981) Changing parent-child relationships: An outcome of mother returning to college. Unpublished manuscript, University of Melbourne (Australia).

Lamb, M. E., & Bronson, S. K. (1980) Fathers in the context of family influences: Past, present, and future. *School Psychology Digest, 9,* 336–353.

Lamb, M. E., & Easterbrooks, M. A. (1981) Individual differences in parental sensitivity: Origins, components, and consequences. In M. E. Lamb & L. R. Sherrod (Eds.), *Infant social cognition: Empirical and theoretical considerations*. Hillsdale, N.J.: Lawrence Erlbaum Associates.

Lamb, M. E., Pleck, J. H., Charnov, E. L., & Levine, J. A. (in press) A biosocial perspective on paternal behavior and involvement. In J. B. Lancaster, A. Rossi, J. Altmann, & L. R. Sherrod (Eds.), *Parenting across the lifespan: Biosocial perspectives*. Chicago: Aldine.

Lein, L. (1979) Male participation in home life: Impact of social supports and breadwinner responsibility on the allocation of tasks. *Family Coordinator, 28,* 489–496.

Owen, M. T., Chase-Lansdale, P. L., & Lamb, M. E. (1982) Mothers' and fathers' attitudes, maternal employment, and the security of infant-parent attachment. Unpublished manuscript.

Pearlin, L. (1975) Sex roles and depression. In N. Datan (Ed.), *Lifespan developmental psychology: Normative life crises*. New York: Academic.

Pleck, J. H. (1983) Husbands' paid work and family roles: Current research issues. In H. Lopata & J. H. Pleck (Eds.), *Research in the interweave of social roles*, (Vol. 3), *Families and jobs*. Greenwich, CT.: JAI Press.

Polatnik, N. (1974) Why men don't rear children: A power analysis. *Berkeley Journal of Sociology, 18,* 45–86.

Radin, N. (1982) Primary caregiving and role-sharing fathers. In M. E. Lamb (Ed.), *Nontraditional families: Parenting and child development*. Hillsdale, NJ: Lawrence Erlbaum Associates.

Radin, N., & Sagi, A. (1982) Childrearing fathers in intact families in Israel and the U.S.A. *Merrill-Palmer Quarterly, 28,* 111–136.

Radloff, L. (1975) Sex differences in depression: The effects of occupation and marital status. *Sex Roles, 1,* 149–165.

Russell, G. (1982) Shared-caregiving families: An Australian study. In M. E. Lamb (Ed.), *Nontraditional families: Parenting and child development*. Hillsdale, N. J.: Lawrence Erlbaum Associates.

Russell, G. (1983) *The changing role of fathers?* St. Lucia, Queensland: University of Queensland Press.

Sagi, A. (1982) Antecedents and consequences of various degrees of paternal involvement in child rearing: The Israeli project. In M. E. Lamb (Ed.), *Nontraditional families: Parenting and child development*. Hillsdale, N. J.: Lawrence Erlbaum Associates.

Sheehy, G. (1979) Introducing the postponing generation. *Esquire, 92* (4), 25–33.

Staines, G., Pleck, J. H., Sheppard, L., & O'Connor, P. (1978) Wives' employment status and marital adjustment: Yet another look. *Psychology of Women Quarterly, 3,* 90–120.

Stewart, A. (1978) Role combination and psychological health in women. Paper presented in the Eastern Psychological Association, New York, March.

Verbrugge, L. (1980) Women's social roles and health. Paper presented at Women: A developmental perspective: A conference on research. National Institute of Child Health and Human Development, Bethesda, MD., November.

Veroff, J., & Feld, S. (1970) *Marriage and work in America*. New York: Van Nostrand Rinehold.

Chapter 7

Legal Changes and the Role of Fathers: Swedish Experiences

Jan E. Trost
Orjan Hultaker

The functional perspective of Parsons and Bales (1955) has stressed the necessity of role differentiation within the family where one of the spouses functions as the instrumental leader and the other as the expressive leader. A functional prerequisite is that one of them (the father) fulfills the role of provider or breadwinner and that the other one (the mother) is the emotional center interacting with all family members.

Many objections can be raised, and have been raised, against this view. Although they are not a functional necessity, the roles of women and men are culturally and differentially patterned in e.g., the U.S.A. as well as in Western Europe. Suffice to mention as examples the varying percentages of gainfully employed men and women, or the predominant pattern of expectations that demand women to take care of small children. Nevertheless, the patterns differ to some extent between cultures, although there are many similarities in the sex role expectations and sex role behaviors.

This chapter analyzes the role of fathers in Sweden. Emphasis will be on legal determinants of the role and in particular on the way in which legal changes affects the social position of children. Custody of children will be the issue of pivotal interest, and custody will be analyzed in terms of an interplay between parental wishes and societal norms.

Jan E. Trost, PhD, is Visiting Professor, The Kinsey Institute for Research in Sex, Gender, and Reproduction, Indiana University, Bloomington, IN 47405. Orjan Hultaker, PhD, is Professor, Sociologiska Institutionen, Uppsala Universetet, 751 20 Uppsala, Sweden.

Legal changes have seldom any immediate effects on people's behavior, attitudes, or thinking, but laws are indicators of changes in society. Nevertheless, laws sometimes and to some extent have directed or affected the behavior of role occupants as well as the behavior of persons and groups interacting with them. Often role occupants are perceived according to the paradigm offered by the legal system.

DIFFERENT ROLE SETS

Maternal and paternal roles do not only vary in content, and they are also bounded differently to other positions within the family. They belong to different role sets (Merton, 1957).

The female role in families with small children is certainly different from the female role in families without children. Using, for a moment, the paradigm of Parsons and Bales (1955), we could claim that the role of women is the same expressive role regardless of whether they have children or not. Nevertheless the content as well as the amount of expectations will differ considerably: the expectations of women depend on whether they are mothers or not. The male role as provider is different since potential children only change the role quantitatively, not qualitatively; the number of family members affects the quantity of money needed in the family, but not the type of money.

Thus, somewhat simplified, the traditional expressive maternal role requires interaction with each single member of the family whereas the traditional instrumental paternal provider role only requires interaction with the entire family as an undifferentiated collectivity. This does not, however, prohibit fathers from interacting with their children, but it mainly means that they are acting outside the traditional instrumental provider roles in their interactions; they are fulfilling expressive roles.

CHILD SUPPORT

Mothers more often than fathers, traditionally still are awarded legal custody of their children after divorce in many countries, in e.g., the U.S.A. (Weitzman and Dixon, 1979) and Sweden (Trost, 1984). Fathers become even more specialized in their instrumental role as breadwinners since their only remaining obligation is the duty to pay child support. Of course, the Swedish law does not differentiate between the sexes (since 1920), it only states that the non-custodial parent is obliged to pay child support regardless of sex. When legal joint custody is the case, the parent who does not have the physical custody is obliged to pay child support— regardless of sex. Reality, however, shows that fathers are awarded sole custody of only 10–15 percent of the children, and the majority of these children are teenagers (Trost, 1984). This situation is similar to that of children born by unmarried mothers; their fathers are normally not custodians and must pay child support at least until the child is 18 years old.

Swedish legislation expects that both custodial and non-custodial parents should support their children with amounts that depend on their financial resources; the sex of the support payer should not affect the amount to be paid. Nevertheless, Swedish courts are affected by the sex of the payer; a mother who is not awarded custody has to pay only about half as much as a father has to pay under similar economic conditions (Trost, 1975).

Decisions about child support are formally taken by courts, but almost all parents decide in consultation with e.g., their legal advisor, and their decisions are mostly confirmed by the court. Most couples and legal advisors are guided by traditions in these respects, so there is no reason to believe that the situation of today is drastically different from the situation a few years ago.

The amount to be paid by the non-custodial parent may differ from what is received by the custodian since the state often pays part of the child support. That is, every child of divorced parents has a right to a minimum support whether or not the non-custodial parent is able to pay. Parents who do not pay what they should (which often is less than the amount guaranteed to the child) will have debts, not to their children but to the state. The state pays for the children to the custodians, and the non-custodians in these cases have to reimburse the state if they can; if they do not, society might make attachments of wages.

Moreover, if, e.g., a father failed to pay child support in due time, he will thereafter not be allowed to "interact" directly with his ex-wife by sending the money directly to her. He will automatically have to pay to the state which in turn pays to the mother in order to secure that the child will get what it should (local authorities can decide, with the consent of the mother, that the father once again should be allowed to pay her directly).

In 1981 more than 12 per cent of all Swedish children younger than 18 years received child support paid by the government (SOU 1983). Almost 60 per cent of these children had divorced parents while about 40 per cent were born to unmarried parents. More than 60 per cent of these children had parents who paid at least some of the child support through official authorities.

Ericsson (1977 and 1980) has studied the social and economic situation of fathers who should pay child support. She found that these men often had economic difficulties which sometimes were so severe that they interfered with and hampered an ordinary social life. Some of the fathers had experienced downward social mobility, and they lacked both jobs and homes; some of them belonged to the group of outcasts of society.

They had accumulated debts to the state, and the demands for reimbursements were too high to allow a minimum standard of living. However, change in laws in 1979 decreased demands on reimbursements which allowed for a more decent living also for non-custodial parents.

Thus, Swedish practice that concerns child support accentuates the different role sets of fathers and mothers. The differences in marriages are accounted for by the fact that mothers traditionally are responsible for the social and emotional interaction with their off-spring, whereas fathers mostly act as breadwinners. Children are generally part of both parents' role sets, but the amount of direct person to person interaction between the child and its mother and father, respectively, is so unequal that it indicates a qualitative and not only a quantitative difference.

Traditional patterns of interaction change slowly, and they still are recognized in at least some sections of society because the decisions to give custody to mothers constitute an overwhelming majority of all cases where parents do not cohabit. Children, to a certain extent, do not belong to the role set of their fathers after divorce, and neither do children born outside of marriage. There is no need for person to person or face to face interaction in order for fathers to fulfill their instrumental role: to pay their child support. Moreover, the support is often mediated by a third party—i.e., the state bureaucracy.

CHILD CUSTODY

Child custody is closely related to the ''marital'' status of the child's parents, and there are in Sweden six different types of status affecting custody. Transitions from one status to another sometimes necessitate new decisions about custody. The six types of status are:

1. the parents are married
2. the parents are not married; they cohabit under marriage-like conditions
3. the parents have never been married or cohabiting
4. the parents have been cohabiting but have separated
5. the parents are divorced
6. one of the parents has died.

1. The first situation (i.e., that the parents are married) is not very problematic since the father and the mother have a joint custody, automatically.

2. Unmarried mothers have been awarded custody over their children traditionally and automatically in Sweden as well as in many other countries. Custody remains with the mother if she does not marry the child's father, in which case the parents automatically are awarded joint custody. Whether the child's parents were cohabiting under marriage-like conditions or not, or whether they had been doing so, did not effect the custody: it automatically went to the mother.

Nevertheless, this legal situation has been considered as somewhat unsatisfactory because of the increasing prevalence of unmarried mothers who, officially classified as singles, in fact cohabit with the fathers of their children. According to anthropological definitions of families (e.g., Murdock, 1948), Sweden has two types of families: one where the parents are legally married (first status) and one where the parents are not married but cohabiting under marriage-like conditions (second status). Both types of families have gained social acceptance by the general public and society although until 1977 fathers were not legally accepted as custodians of their children unless they were married (cf. Trost, 1979).

Such a situation was not supposed to be in accordance with the best interest of the child, so a government bill was brought before the Swedish Parliament in 1976. The bill proposed a possibility for cohabiting parents to be awarded joint custody of their children. The bill was passed and unmarried parents have been awarded joint custody since 1977.

Joint custody for cohabiting parents was introduced in order to make life easier for children and not primarily to enhance the position of fathers. As a by-product, the new rights of fathers have an effect on the fathers' own position within the family. Moreover, fathers still have an inferior position compared to that of mothers in families with parents cohabiting but not married. This fact can be exemplified by the process through which cohabiting parents can be awarded joint custody.

The parents automatically will be awarded joint custody if they are married, but this is not the case for parents who cohabit. Custody is automatically awarded to mothers alone if they are not married, and legal joint custody can be awarded only by decision in court or (since 1983) by announcing their wish to a regional administrative authority.

The power of mothers still is greater than that of fathers; a father cannot be awarded any part of the legal custody without the mother's consent. The father can get new rights through the new law but only if the mother assists him. She has partial control over him as this concept is defined by Thibaut and Kelly (1959:100 ff).

3. The possibility of joint legal custody for unmarried parents does not only affect parents who cohabit without being married. The same rights are given to parents who do not form a common family but who live in separate dwellings.

Thus, unmarried parents have the same right to joint custody whether they are cohabiting or not, and the same procedure is required as when cohabiting parents are awarded joint legal custody. The mother has partial control over the father's right to custody also when they never have cohabited.

4. There is no legal or official awareness of the dissolution of unmarried cohabitation. Thus, there are no special rules requiring changes in legal custody after separation of cohabiting parents, but custody continues as during the cohabitation period. A mother continues as the sole custodian after separation if she alone had legal custody when cohabiting with her child's father. Parents who had applied for and who were awarded legal joint custody during the cohabitation period, will also continue in the same way as earlier, i.e., they will continue to have joint legal custody.

There is nothing in the separation *per se* which causes a change in the legal arrangements of child custody. Parents have to go to court in order to get a change from legal joint custody to a situation where the mother is the sole legal custodian. Legally everything continues as before; if not, at least one of the parents takes an initiative for changing the arrangements. A legal continuity may, however, hide important changes since it may be difficult to continue with joint physical custody when the parents have moved apart. There are social and practical difficulties similar to those of parents who never cohabited.

5. It is quite different when parents legally divorce after marriage, because there has to be a decision made or confirmed by the court. Joint legal custody has come to an end in most countries and the child's mother (in a clear majority of the cases) or the child's father will be awarded sole custody. There is, however, a possibility that the divorcees want joint custody. In Norway, many of the states in the U.S.A., and in Sweden between 1977 and 1983, parents can apply for joint legal custody.

It is interesting to note that in the U.S.A. and Norway, there has to be a decision about custody of children after legal divorce but not as a consequence of separation between unmarried cohabiting parents. The practical reasons have been indicated earlier; it is sufficient to add that the legal system builds upon the old idea that it is necessary to reconsider the matter of custody after a divorce. In Sweden since 1983, however, the courts need not decide about the custody after divorce unless one or both of the parents so requires; if neither of them requires sole custody, they are automatically awarded joint legal custody. This fact is of interest to those analyzing consequences of divorce since custody of children is often one of the causes for problems and fights during the process of divorce.

Social reality, however, is more complicated, since joint legal custody can be somewhat of a social, although not a legal, fiction when parents do not cohabit. To form joint decisions about a child's well-being requires those who are supposed to make the decision to meet in order to decide, which is a difficult meeting to arrange when mothers and fathers live in different homes. A probable solution is that the one of the parents who lives together with the child will function as the sole custodian except for some important and not very frequent decisions.

One of the parents (usually the mother) will live together with her child, and their complementary roles will be expressive in kind. The other one of the parents (usually the father) will live in a separate home, and the interaction between him and his child will mostly be instrumental.

We have calculated some data from a Swedish study of parents who divorced in 1978; data were collected two to three years after the divorce (cf. Trost and Hultaker 1982). These data show that, when the parents are awarded joint legal custody, 36 percent of the children alternate between the parents, 46 percent live with their mother, and 18 percent live with their father.

The alternative for the child can be to move between the parents who have joint legal custody and to live every second week, month, or other time period, with each of them. This, however, might not be a true joint custody since most of the decisions etc. are not taken jointly but alternate between the parents. These types of solutions are not usually stable arrangements; in the long run often problems will arise when parents are not living in the same area of a town or a city; the child may for instance have difficulties establishing good social relations with his or her peers.

Moreover, there may be a lack of continuity in custody which will hinder effective learning of relevant norms. This in turn may make a child socially and emotionally insecure. The further apart the parents live, the more severe will these difficulties probably become.

Joint custody may have positive effects on the role of fathers, and it may enhance their importance to their children even though the fathers sometimes cannot take part in the daily custody. Legal custody stresses the importance of the expressive role of fathers, and they are no longer seen only as breadwinners and payers of child support. Nevertheless, the stability of the role may be in doubt except under very favorable conditions.

6. The situation after the death of one of the parents is somewhat different from the situation at other types of parental status. If the parents have a joint legal custody, the death of one of them has (in Sweden) the automatic effect that the surviving parent is awarded sole custody regardless of whether the parents were married, cohabiting, divorced, separated after cohabitation, or never married nor cohabiting. In cases of sole custody, the surviving parents have the right to be awarded sole custody, if it is not evident that he/she is not fit.

Table 1 shows the most frequent types of custody for each of the six kinds of parental status. It is seen that mothers are sole custodians in three out of five types of parental status. Moreover, mothers are most commonly the custodians following separations after cohabitation since it is most common that mothers are sole custodians during cohabitation; there is no automatic change of custody after such separations.

Table 1: Modes of child custody and alternative options for six types of parental status.

Parental status	Type of legal custody	
	Most frequent	Alternative
Married	Joint	--
Unmarried cohabitation	Mother	Joint
Unmarried not cohabiting	Mother	Joint
Divorced	Mother	Joint or Father
Separated after cohabitation	No change	Change
One parent dead	The survivor	Grandparent, fostercare

The position of the father is not regulated by the legal system except for married parents, but there is an alternative legal role pattern open to parents who themselves ask for it. The role of fathers may be extended from the instrumental provider role into one with at least some expressive functions if fathers and mothers agree to it; both can block the extension.

DECISIONS ABOUT CUSTODY AFTER DIVORCE OR SEPARATION

The change from mothers as sole custodians to joint custodians has meant a diminishing degree of role specialization. One intention, besides the best interest of the child, of the legislator has been to simplify for the fathers to perform more expressive functions.

As can be seen from several social indicators, the change in the role of mothers has gone on for a longer period, than the change in the role of fathers. One indicator is the increased frequency of female employment, especially the increased employment of mothers with small children (Hultaker, 1980; Trost and Hultaker, 1979). Another indicator is the fact that almost no woman any longer gets alimony from her ex-husband after divorce; those who receive alimony will quite often do so only during a very short period (Trost, 1975). It is believed that women should support themselves, and this belief also affects their interaction with their children.

The equalization of paternal and maternal roles has had very little effect on decisions about custody of children except in cases where the parents have agreed upon a joint physical custody after divorce or separation. Mothers have very seldomly declared their wish not to have custody of their children while fathers often have not demanded any right to custody.

The normative expectations of society at large and of most subgroups have demanded mothers to take care of their children, society has perceived this demand as obligatory. To deviate from the norms of custody has meant a neglect of what society regards as the most important part of the female role—women so doing would have been looked upon as being "bad mothers."

Fathers have traditionally been in quite a different situation; they have not been regarded as "bad fathers" when they did not fight for custody of their children. There were no norms forcing them to fight, but they may instead have been accepted as "good fathers" because they wanted their children to be under the mothers' custody, which was thought to be in the best interest for all children.

Traditional role differentiation eliminates many potential fights and quarrels about custody. The situation might change, however; more and more fathers might fight for custody at time of divorce or separation. Moreover, mothers might refuse to accept custody of their children. This change may be an effect of the maternal and paternal roles changing toward more equity in instrumental as well as in expressive functions.

The behavior of fathers and mothers during a divorce process will become more variable and more directed by the true wishes of the ex-spouses; norms will become more permissive to individual wishes, and they will allow alternative behaviors for both fathers and mothers at time of divorce. There may be no predominant pattern of interaction like the traditional norms that prescribe mothers to fight for their children (if necessary) and fathers to surrender. Moreover, the lessening of normative pressure means there will be fewer internalized norms regarding custody of children.

Table 2 presents an interaction pattern between the wishes of mothers and fathers after divorce or separation. It shows nine different patterns which are defined by three possible alternative wishes of fathers as well as of mothers: both have the alternative to be positive (i.e., wanting custody), to be neutral (i.e., being indifferent or ambiguous to having custody) or to be negative (i.e., not wanting to have custody).

Table 2: Attitudes of parents towards having custody of their children after divorce or separation.

| | | | Mother | |
		Positive	Neutral	Negative
	Positive	1	2	3
Father	Neutral	4	5	6
	Negative	7	8	9

The first cell shows the situation when both fathers and mothers want to have custody of their children. Traditionally, both mothers and fathers have believed it to be impossible for fathers to get custody in courts when both parents wish to take care of their child. There have been few fights and custody has generally been awarded to mothers.

We presume fights to be more common in the future since fathers will more often believe in their chances to be awarded custody of their children. Fathers will have fulfilled expressive functions during marriage and cohabitation, and they may be aware of the weakening of norms which deny them the right to custody.

Joint custody after divorce presents one possible solution for the problem. It is to the child's benefit when joint custody prevents the parents from using the child as a weapon. There is, however, a risk that this solution will be used to suppress the fathers more than the mothers.

In a study made before joint legal custody was permitted in Sweden it is shown that five to ten percent of divorced parents' children aged 0–6 years were awarded to the fathers' custody and the rest to the mothers' (Trost, 1975). In a study made some years after joint custody was legally accepted it is shown that no children of that age were awarded sole custody to their fathers; about 30 percent of the children aged 0–6 years were awarded to joint legal custody (Trost, 1984). This implies that all fathers have "lost" their sole custody and relatively few of the mothers have "lost" their sole custody. One interpretation, among others, is that the fathers who have "lost" have been suppressed while the mothers have "gained." They can be assumed to have gained twofold by gaining power when the fathers "lost" and by forcing more fathers to take more of their responsibility, which means that some fathers have "lost" their sole custody, while others have "gained" through joint legal custody.

The second and third cells show the situation where a father wants to have custody of his child but his ex-wife is less eager to have it; in the second cell she is indifferent or ambiguous while in the third cell she is negative. Mothers in this situation have not in the past been "allowed" to hand over custody to fathers because such an action would prove themselves to be "bad mothers." The norms have forced them to fight for custody, and these norms have often been internalized, albeit at odds with the true wishes of the mothers.

Both mothers and fathers would benefit from a new situation with weakened norms since both of the ex-spouses would have better chances to fulfill their personal wishes. Moreover, their children would also be in a better position because they would *ceteris paribus* benefit from being with the parent who really wants to have them. Here, too, joint custody can help the mothers to more easily avoid the social pressure.

The fourth and seventh cells show situations where a mother is positive to having custody of her child and the father is less willing to accept custody; he is neutral in the fourth cell and negative in the seventh. These two situations have in the past posed no problems. Mothers have traditionally received custody, and this custom will probably continue into the future.

All the cells analyzed so far have shown at least one of the parents as actively wanting to have custody of the child. The remaining cells are more problematic; all four indicate that neither fathers nor mothers actively want to have their children. The fifth cell shows both parents to be indifferent or neutral, which is a difficult situation not only to the parents but also to their children.

Joint custody may be a solution at least in the short run; it could give the parents an impression of distributive justice especially if the children alternate between living with the father and the mother. Nevertheless, the situation is less stable than one with joint custody when both parents want to have custody of their children. The situation may easily change to one in which one of the parents becomes more positive or more negative than the other one who demands new arrangements of custody. One reason for such a change might be that a father or a mother gets married or starts cohabiting.

The ninth cell is similar to the fifth, but the difference between the. two is that both parents actively want to avoid custody of their children. Joint custody is more problematic in this situation than when both parents are indifferent, and it is hardly probable that it will work satisfactorily. The parent who would be a custodian against his or her own wishes will be in a difficult situation, and the same is true for the children; they will be as bad off with their mother as with their father.

Traditional norms, however, have given some stability to situations in the fifth and the ninth cells. Norms have demanded mothers to accept custody of their children, and they have not openly been allowed to expel their children. Although children were not wanted, they were at least not openly admitted to be a burden. Norms told mothers that they ought to accept, want, and like the custody, and mothers were better off when they acted in accordance with the norms than when they acted contrary to the norms. Thus, mothers benefitted from accepting custody even when they in fact wanted to get rid of the burden because by accepting custody they themselves proved to be "good mothers."

There remains no such benefit when the traditional norms have been weakened; parents may quarrel about whether the father or the mother shall have to accept the burden of custody, and children will be in a much more difficult situation than children whose parents quarrel about whom is to be awarded the advantage of custody as in the first cell.

The sixth and the eighth cells are also problematic because no one really wants to have the child; one of the parents is neutral and the other one is negative. The best solution for children as well as for their parents would be to give custody to the one of the parents who is neutral. Traditional norms have stated that mothers should accept custody whether they were the neutral or the negative; mothers needed to accept their duty in order to prove themselves as women and as "good mothers."

Wishes or norms acting as guides make no difference in the eighth cell; mothers will be awarded custody anyway. It will, however, make a difference in the sixth cell because traditional norms "force" mothers to accept custody even though a decision based on wishes gives custody to the fathers who are at least not negative.

We might expect that in the future the personal wishes and attitudes of fathers and mothers will have greater importance on the decision about custody of children after divorce. This trend follows from the change in roles during marriage and cohabitation and from the weakened importance of norms governing maternal behavior during the divorce process.

The children will sometimes benefit from this new situation but will sometimes lose, while those children lacking active support more often will lose. It is shown that joint custody sometimes may be a solution, although not always.

CONCLUDING REMARKS

Traditional role differentiation within families has meant that mothers specialize in expressive and fathers in instrumental functions. Moreover, parents have had different role sets since the expressive role demands individual interaction with each of the family members, whereas the instrumental role only requires interaction with the family as a collectivity.

The same pattern of roles have traditionally been found after divorce; the ex-wife is awarded custody of the children and the ex-husband is presumed to pay child support (and sometimes alimony). The arrangements of payment have further emphasized the limited role set of fathers to instrumental functions.

Nevertheless, traditional role arrangements are by no means structural prerequisites because the roles are changing, although slowly. Mothers are fulfilling more instrumental functions within families and fathers are getting more expressive responsibilities; however, maternal roles are changing faster than paternal roles.

These changes within the existing families affect role behavior after divorce and separation; the decreasing differentiation within marriages will make for more equal rights and duties also after divorce. An example of this change is the fact that alimony almost has ceased to be a social institution in Sweden.

Another example, this trend is the change of traditional norms governing role behavior at time of divorce. Women no longer need to prove themselves as "good mothers" by demanding custody even when such an arrangement is against their true wishes. Fathers will no longer see their position as inferior to that of their ex-wives in cases where fathers want to have custody of their children.

Times might come when fathers and mothers will meet as equal parties during the divorce process, and both will have the same rights to receive as well as to avoid custody of their common children. Joint custody, however, is a social institution which recently has been extended as an option also to parents who are neither married nor cohabiting. This change, a sign of the changing sex roles, makes for more equity in the interaction between parents; both mothers and fathers will have to fulfill expressive and instrumental functions regardless of whether they are cohabiting or not.

Nevertheless, let us once more stress the fact that much of the traditional role specialization still exists in Sweden. It might even be said that traditional norms are governing most of the role behavior in families whether they have experienced divorce and separation. There are, however, some indicators of a normative change and it is important to study them in order to understand the future.

We are quite certain that the normative changes are good both for women and men; both will in the future have better possibilities to fulfill their own wishes, provided that they do not want the guidance of norms directing their behavior.

The changes will, however, also affect small children, and it is more difficult to predict the consequences for them. Children who live in families with both a mother and a father will certainly gain, *ceteris paribus*; the lessening of role differentiation will mean an increase in resources at the disposal of children. Both mothers and fathers can fulfill expressive as well as instrumental functions. The only danger is if both parents specialize in the same type of behavior as when both mainly are interested in the provider role.

The changes in norms governing custody after divorce and separation is rather difficult to evaluate, but joint custody may be a solution in many situations although not always a stable solution. In the end probably, there will be a stable state in which one of the parents will be the physical custodian while the other one will be rather marginal, even though enhanced compared to traditional sole custody.

Most difficult will be situations where neither mothers nor fathers want to have custody of their children; there will no longer be any norms forcing one of them to accept custody. Although difficult, the situation will probably not be very frequent. It might be much more common for parents to fight in order to get custody than fight to avoid custody. The reason is that fathers have learned to fulfill an expressive role. Difficulties will occur when mothers have become increasingly specialized in instrumental roles and when fathers have not learned to fulfill expressive functions; these spouses might be prone to divorce and eagerly avoid a custody that would hamper their careers or other interests.

Finally, a decision about custody or child support should not be viewed as *the* decision. It should be viewed as one decision out of a series of potential future decisions or re-decisions. If the decision is viewed as *the* decision there is a great risk for failures and negative effects upon the children as well as upon the parents. Re-decisions are expected to be reasonable in almost all cases; changes in the situation of the two parents and the child may occur and this change will call for new decision making processes.

REFERENCES

Ericsson, Margareta (1977). Den ekonomiska situationen for foraldrar med bidragsskyldighet mot barn, Uppsala.

Ericsson, Margareta (1980). Some Empirical and Theoretical Reflections on the Conditions of the Non-Guardian, in J. Comp. Fam. Studies, 11, 87–114.

Hultaker, Orjan E. (1981). Maternal Employment, J. Comp. Fam. Studies, 12, 95–111.

Merton, Robert K. (1957). Social Theory and Social Structure, Free Press.

Murdock, Georg P. (1948). Social Structure, New York.

Parsons, Talcott & R. F. Bales (1955). Family Socialization and Interaction Process, Free Press.

SOU (1983). Bidragsforskott, SOU 1983:51, Stockholm.

Thibaut, John W. & Harold H. Kelly (1959). The Social Psychology of Groups, John Wiley & Sons.

Trost, Jan (1975). Vardnad och underhall, i SOU 1975:25: Tre Sociologiska Rapporter, 33–120, Stockholm.

Trost, Jan & Orjan E. Hultaker (1979). Metodavsnitt, in SOU 1979:89.

Trost, Jan (1979). Unmarried Cohabitation, International Library.

Trost, Jan (1984). Divorcees, Children, and the Public, key paper presented at the 22nd International Seminar of the Committee on Family Research, Melbourne, Australia, August 19–24, 1984.

Weitzman, Leonore J. and Ruth B. Dixon (1978). Child Custody Awards: Legal Standards and Empirical Patterns for Child Custody, Support, and Visitation after Divorce, UCD Law Review, 12, 471–521.

Chapter 8

The Legal Rights of Fathers in the U.S.

Robert E. Salt

It is ironic considering the amount of power American men allegedly possess, to see the discriminatory practices against men in American family law. For centuries, fathers dominated their families in Western Europe and then in the United States. The twentieth century, though, has seen American males relegated to second class citizens when it comes to disputes over their children. Despite the gains achieved by men during the past fifteen years, fathers are still discriminated against in almost all areas of family law: paternity cases, rights of unwed fathers, custody decisions and support allocations.

What makes this situation so interesting is that for all of written history men have enjoyed most of the power and responsibility in society. This responsibility ranged from running governments to running families. In this century however many American men have been excluded from having any power or responsibility in family law disputes.

Society seems to have assumed that men are irresponsible, unconcerned, unnecessary and incompetent when it comes to family issues. Although changes have been well documented about men's recent family attitudes and participation, stereotypes die hard. Those individuals in the legislatures, administrations and courts who set family law and policies through their actions and decisions still seem to base their ideas on this concept of the irresponsible man.

Before proceeding, let it be said that the author is not claiming that men should be superior or that men haven't done much to create the stereotype already mentioned. It is claimed though that the

Robert E. Salt is a Doctoral Student, Department of Child Development and Family Studies, Purdue University, West Lafayette, IN 47907.

101

inequality in family law (which this paper will attempt to prove) is illegal under the U.S. constitution and unfair to men, and to women and children growing up in these times of social change. In a chicken and egg argument it can't be argued that the laws haven't been at least partly based on men's supposed irresponsibility. But how much of men's lack of participation has been based on the laws and customs that made it difficult for men to *try* to participate?

This essay will discuss four aspects of family law: paternity cases, rights of unwed fathers, child custody and support. Beforehand, however, a few general comments need to be made about family law in America.

Due to the complex structure of the U.S. political system, it is difficult to make definitive statements about just what the law is. Family law is created by state laws and federal laws, state courts and federal courts, state bureaucracies and federal bureaucracies. Adding another dimension of variation is the vast power of judicial discretion enjoyed by district court judges. Individual decisions are highly influenced by judges' own interpretations of the law and of the specifics of each case. This is especially true in cases involving family matters. This system inherently produces a lack of homogeneity of laws and court decisions. As a result there are some statutes and court decisions that are fair to fathers and those that are not.

Although not all have been eliminated, many laws that had discriminated against fathers have recently been overruled. Based on the 14th amendment's Equal Protection clause the supreme court has ruled that "classification by gender must serve important governmental objectives and must be substantially related to achievement of those objectives" (Craig v. Boren, 429 US 190, 1976).[1] Most laws in the past 15 years have not been found to pass this test for treating mothers and fathers differently.

The area then in which discrimination against fathers is still most prevalent is in individual court cases. These are cases between fathers and mothers, the state, potential adoptive parents, and other interested third parties. It is in these cases that fathers suffer the most. Judges all too often disregard the fathers' claims in favor of the mother or other interested party. Much of the focus of this paper then will be on recent court cases that have defined the legal rights of fathers. It is in the district courts where the present battles are being fought, and where change is the slowest.

PATERNITY

When the terms "maternity" and "paternity" are brought up, two very different ideas are conceptualized. For most, maternity is a concept connected to thoughts of warmth and child birth. Paternity however has a connotation of an illicit act perpetrated by an irresponsible man who is served with a lawsuit to make him pay for his indiscretions. The legal rights of those men charged in paternity suits seem to be based in this negative image. Men charged in paternity suits have found it extremely difficult to get fair treatment in the courts. As with all issues in this paper this is changing, but slowly.

The courts, in an effort to protect the reputation of the mother, have made it impossible for the alleged father to offer evidence of the mother's sexual involvement with other men during the time period of conception (Dorn v. Lawrence 31 NY, 2d. 145). This denies men the defense that they were not the only person capable of being the father of the child. This is an important issue since courts have not yet taken full advantage of the blood testing techniques.

Blood Tests

H.L.A. Testing is a blood grouping test which has been found to be 99 percent accurate in demonstrating cases where paternity is excluded. State courts have overlooked blood test evidence in paternity cases as recently as 1974 when the North Carolina Supreme Court upheld such a decision (see Krause, 1982).

Recently, the Supreme Court has ruled that an indigent man was denied due process when the state refused to pay for the blood grouping test (Little v. Streater, 452 US, 1 1981). This should provide a message to the states that blood tests are important protections in the rights of men alleged to be fathers. The high level of accuracy of these tests should also be seen as a protection of the rights of the child to have his proper father determined in court.

Recent court cases have said that the right of privacy does not permit men to refuse a blood test in paternity cases. As recently as Dec. 1983 a Wisconsin Court of Appeals ruled that the trial judge had the authority to hold a man in contempt of court for refusing such a test (in re D.A.A.P. Wisconsin Court of Appeals, 12/27/83).

The current trend is toward the use of blood grouping tests as primary evidence to determine paternity. Its use has been recommended widely by both men and women (Katz & Inker, 1979; Krause, 1982; Seider, 1980). Krause (1982) has urged that state lawmakers review their current statutes with reference to this issue and update them wherever necessary.

Standing to Originate a Paternity Suit

Surprising to the laymen is the situation in U.S. law where men are rarely allowed to originate paternity suits. Most statutes only allow the mother and/or the state to originate such proceedings. It is assumed that lawmakers did not foresee men wanting to claim paternity. This probably would not have occurred in previous generations where, due to social pressure and economic dependence, few women would have denied that a man was the father of their child. In today's society though there seem to be a growing number of people who are willing to raise a child by themselves and to be free from interacting with their sexual partner after the child is born. Further, until recently, few men would have taken the interest to claim paternity in situations where it was denied by the mother.

In the case of Roe v. Roe (316, NYS 2d, 94 1970) a putative father (unwed father) had no standing to originate proceedings for a declaration of paternity. This was just months after a judge in the same district had allowed a man to originate a paternity suit (which he won) (Crane v. Battle 307 NYS 2d, 355 1970). The judge in the Roe case said that the previous ruling had been based on too liberal an interpretation of the appropriate statute. It is interesting to note that only in one state (Michigan) can a putative father originate a paternity proceeding. This situation seems to be in direct violation of the 14th amendment's Due Process and Equal Protection clauses.

Other Issues

In a related issue a man is assumed by law to be the father of any child conceived by his wife while they were married. In some states the wife can claim that a man other than her husband is the father. However a man who is not the husband cannot claim paternity for himself. In Cunningham v. Golden the Supreme Court is currently deciding the constitutionality of a case based on this type of law in the state of Tennessee.

The final issue related to paternity is concerned with the statute of limitations for paternity cases. In the case of Mills v. Habluetzel (50 USLW 4372 1982) the U.S. Supreme Court struck down Texas' one year statute of limitations on paternity actions as unduly short. This one year limit denied a protection to illegitimate children that would have been available for legitimate children. The court did not go so far, however, as to say all such laws were illegal, only that one year was too short a period for the statute of limitations.

RIGHTS OF UNWED FATHERS

Historically, in common law, fathers of illegitimate children were a legal non-entity. It was obvious that someone had fathered the child but legally the mother was the only parent of an illegitimate child (Katz & Inker, 1979; Redden, 1982). These children suffered greatly for being born out of wedlock as they lacked almost any legal rights. Since no one was legally their father no one was required to provide support for the child. There were of course cases where support was quietly paid by men wealthy enough to afford it. But such support was rare.

In the twentieth century, two changes have affected this situation. First is that laws have been written to require unwed fathers to provide support for their offspring. This probably required a finding of paternity in courts before such support could be ordered. Secondly, unwed parents living together has created a new situation that the laws were not designed for, the unwed but participating father.

What has occurred in this century is a legal contradiction. While laws have required unwed fathers to support their offspring, the laws in almost every state remained consistent with common law and stated that the mother was the only legal parent of an illegitimate child. If the father was not legally the child's parent, why was he required to support the child? This question has never been addressed and as we will see it probably will not be.

In 1972, the most significant of cases involving unwed fathers was decided by the Supreme Court in Stanley v. Illinois (405 US 645 1972). Stanley was an unwed father who had sired and lived with his three children and their mother intermittently for 18 years. After she died the state of Illinois took possession of the children and set up an adoption hearing. Under Illinois law, Mr. Stanley was not a parent and was not entitled to due process of law. Eventually, the U.S. Supreme Court ruled that Stanley as an unwed father was being denied Equal Protection of the law and due process. The court stated that he should be given the same opportunity as unwed mothers and married mothers and fathers to notice of an adoption hearing and a hearing on their fitness before terminating their parental rights. They also added, in a note in the opinion, that notice must be given to putative fathers in all adoption cases. Following Stanley were similar decisions in Rothstein v. Lutheran Social Services and Vanderlaan v. Vanderlaan.

The court later qualified the rights of unwed fathers stating that an unmarried father does not have a "veto power" over the adoption of his children (Quillon v. Walcott 434 US 246 1978). In Quillon the court allowed a woman's second husband to adopt over the biological father's objections. This case differed from Stanley in that the children had always lived with the mother. Further the biological father had not regularly supported the children.

In Caban v. Mohammed the court did allow an unmarried biological father to block the attempted adoption of his children by the mother's new husband (Caban v. Mohammed 441 US 380 1979). In this case the biological father had lived with the mother for five years and had still contributed support and visited the children after the mother's marriage.

Although the rights of the biological father were upheld in this case the court did not say that unwed fathers have a "fundamental right" to their children, a right which *is held* by unwed mothers and married parents. The court did not use the same strict scrutiny standard of review that would be used for parents with a fundamental right. Instead an intermediate level of scrutiny was used (Weinhaus, 1981).

The court added that there might be a possible distinction between unwed fathers' rights when dealing with newborns v. older children (past infancy). In his dissent Justice Stevens suggested that mothers have the sole right to consent to adoption of newborns. This would further the state's interest in an expeditious adoption process. He claimed that mothers inherently have a closer relationship to the child due to her right to decide to bear or not and from the physical and psychological bond established between mother and child immediately following birth.

A final qualification in Caban was the statement that "where the father has never come forward to participate in the rearing of his child, nothing in the Equal Protection clause precludes the state from withholding the privilege of vetoing the adoption of the child.'' This certainly seems to give the father very little rights in those cases where the mother does not want the child but the father had not yet had time to establish his participation. This would be true in all cases where the child is a newborn.[2]

The issue of whether indigent non-custodial fathers have a right to counsel in termination of parental rights cases has varied from state to state. In 1981 North Carolina's Supreme Court ruled that they do not have a right to counsel (Lassifer v. North Carolina 101 Supreme Court 2153 1981). In the past year, however, nine states have ruled that indigent non-custodial fathers did have a right to counsel in such cases (i.e., *in re* Jay, California Court of Appeals 3rd District 12/28/83).

To bring unwed fathers' rights into perspective there are eight states that still do not require illegitimate fathers to consent to the adoption of their illegitimate children.[3]

CUSTODY

The topic in family law which affects the greatest number of men is the dispute over child custody. Of the more than one million divorces per year in the United States, more than sixty percent involve children (Orthner & Lewis, 1979). Estimates show that men receive custody in just ten to twelve percent of custody disputes. Statistics show that contrary to public opinion the rate of fathers getting custody has *not* risen substantially. News of fathers who win custody is widespread but most fathers are dissuaded from trying for custody even before the case goes to court. To better understand this important topic, a brief historical perspective will be offered.

History

Under ancient Roman law fathers possessed absolute power over their children. This power allowed the father to sell them into slavery and even order them put to death. The fathers' virtually unlimited control continued into the middle ages and into the industrialized 19th century (Orthner & Lewis, 1979).

In the 1800's laws in both the U.S. and Britain began to question the father's unlimited authority. By the 1840's British courts started awarding custody of young children to the mother. In the United

States in 1888 a Pennsylvania court gave custody of a four year old boy to his mother. In his opinion the judge stated that "the claim of a mother during the early years of an infant's life to the care of her child is to be preferred to that of the father" (Commonwealth ex. rel. Hart v. Hart, 14 Phil Rep. 352, 357 1880). This case was the first to establish what came to be known in American law as the tender years doctrine.

Tender Years Doctrine

The tender years doctrine essentially says that except under unusual circumstances young children should be awarded to the mother. This doctrine became standard practice in the U.S. by the 1940's. Mothers received custody of not only their young children, but, in practice, their older children as well. Fathers received custody in less than 10% of the cases.

The tender years doctrine was never a legal mandate to the courts. Rather it became a recommended practice that evolved into a legal standard. In 1970 the National Conference of Commissioners on Uniform State Laws demonstrated the power of the mother to gain custody when it stated "a uniform divorce act should contain a presumption that the mother is the appropriate custodian—at least for young children, and probably for children of any age."

Coupled with the tender years doctrine many judges used a rule which came to be known as the fitness test. In the late 1960's the Supreme Court of Minnesota said in Meinhardt v. Meinhardt that only when the mother was "unfit" as a parent was the father to receive custody (261 Minnesota 272, 276,111 NW 2d 782,784). A finding of unfitness however has been a rare occurrence.

Best Interest of the Child Doctrine

As men and women began to question traditional family roles in the late 1960's some courts and lawmakers began to question the practice of favoring the mother in custody cases. In Fish v. Fish in 1968 a Minnesota court said that "the principle that custody of young children is ordinarily best vested in the mother, vital and established as it may be, is "distinctly subordinate" to the "controlling principle" that the overriding consideration in custody proceedings is the child's welfare" (280 Minnesota 316, 159 NW 2d 271).

The principle discussed in Fish has been established as the "best interest of the child" doctrine.[4] This was established, not as a protection of the father's rights, but to allow more options to judges to do what was best for the child. It is also interesting to note that the tender years doctrine and best interest of the child doctrine have co-existed for the past two decades. "Best interest," however, has not resulted in fathers getting custody more frequently. Some states have passed laws against the tender years doctrine[5] and some have passed laws prohibiting preference for either parent.[6] But there are still cases where the tender years doctrine is being applied (eg. Albright v. Albright, Mississippi Supreme Court 9/21/83).

As noted before, the ultimate factor in custody disputes is the discretion of the judge to find for whoever the judge feels is in the child's best interest. This means that judges of today, most having been raised and educated in a more traditional era, still show a preference for the mother in eight out of nine cases. Knowing this, lawyers frequently dissuade male clients from spending thousands of dollars unless they have a very strong case. Added to this is the pressure in society against fathers who want to fight for their children's custody. This pressure is also put on lawyers not to waste the courts' time. Consider the lawyers who have read the following quote from the Family Law Committee of the Minnesota Bar Association (1971):

> Except in very rare cases, the father should not have the custody of the minor children of the parties. He is usually unqualified psychologically and emotionally; nor does he have time and care to supervise the children. A lawyer not only does an injustice to himself, but he is unfair to his client, to the state, and to society if he gives any encouragement to the father that he should have custody of his children.

Two points are important to consider here. First, the "unfitness test" is not the correct legal rule to determine custody. The fitness rule was designed to be used in custody disputes between a parent and a third party, not between two parents (Foster & Freed, 1967). Secondly, any predetermined preference for a parent is inherently not in the best interest of the child. The child's best interest is served when custody goes to the parent with whom the child has the best parent-child relationship.[7] As the court said in state ex. rel. Watts v. Watts, "sound application of the 'best interests of the child' criteria requires that the court not place a greater burden on the father in proving suitability for the custody than on the mother'' (Family Court NYC 350, NYS 2d 285 1973).

There has been progress for fathers on this issue. In Heyer v. Peterson, an Iowa court gave custody of a child to his father saying that he had demonstrated greater concern for the child's welfare and was the more mature and stable parent. The court added that the critical issue is not which parent has a greater right to the child but which parent fulfills the best interests of the child (307 NW 2d Iowa, 1981). This is an important case for fathers. It overrules a concept that mothers have a greater right to the child than fathers do. In the popular film "Kramer v. Kramer," Mrs. Kramer says in court "nobody can say that anyone has a greater right to this child than I do, I'm his mother." The Heyer case points out that "greater right" is not to be an issue in determining custody. No one has a greater right to the child before the law.

A final case that is important for fathers was the case *in re* Byrd. The court ruled that an unwed father who has participated in the nurturing process of the child has equality of standing with the mother with respect to the custody of the child (421 NE 2d 1284 1981). This ruling was made so as not to discriminate against the rights of illegitimate children. Legitimate children would have their case decided on their own best interest, but in previous cases involving illegitimate children the mothers' interests were considered as paramount. The court also reiterated that the unfitness argument is not valid in cases between two parents.

Joint Custody

A final change in recent years involving fathers' rights has been the increase in joint custody awards. This is not the place to discuss the pros and cons of joint custody. There are many arguments for and against joint custody. It is important though to briefly look at its effect on fathers' rights.

Joint custody refers to both parents retaining their parental rights. Major and even some minor decisions are to be made by both parents. It does not refer to the living arrangement of the children. The significance of this is that in sole custody awards the non-custodial parent has their parental rights terminated. They still have visitation rights but all decisions are legally given to the custodial parent. Since mothers are awarded *sole* custody most of the time, fathers lose their influence over their children's decisions. In joint custody cases, however, fathers still maintain their parental rights. The move to joint custody as a major option for the courts is gaining rapid strength across the states. It is not, however, appropriate for all individual cases.

Summary

To summarize the topic of custody, fathers have made some minor gains in the past fifteen years. Legally they should be guaranteed legal protection of the law under the 14th amendment. However in individual cases where judicial discretion is powerful, the burden of proof rests in all practicality on the father. Also, fathers are often pressured not to fight for custody and to pay expensive costs if they choose to fight. To close on a somewhat optimistic note almost fifty percent of those fathers who do fight for custody (only the very healthiest of cases) receive sole custody according to informal polls of judges in North Carolina and California (Orthner & Lewis, 1979).

SUPPORT

Child support is an issue which draws a great deal of emotional response from ex-spouses. Fathers often feel that support decisions are inequitable, especially because support is combined with termination of the non-custodial parent's parental rights. Mothers, often frustrated by the father's late or non-payment of support, react with anger when the courts seem powerless to guarantee payment. One would logically think the increase of women working outside the home would ease the situation. Unfortunately this is not yet the final solution as women still make less than 60 percent of that which men earn. This is even more pronounced for working mothers who cannot totally devote themselves to their careers.

According to a legislator's guide to support (Royce, 1979) only one-fourth of the families deserving and in need of support from the absent parent receive it. Further, in half of support cases the money received is less than ten percent of the receiver's family income. This guide states that it is a myth that men are unable to pay.

On the other side of the story, well known family law expert Harry Krause says that men suffer from unreasonable support obligations (Krause, 1982). Krause says that, since a high number of fathers remarry (five out of six), they essentially become responsible for helping support two families in the majority of cases. The second family's children are rarely considered when deciding support allocations to the first. Studies also show that non-custodial fathers usually take on more work in the first year after divorce to pay for the cost of maintaining two households. Finally, alleged fathers have been denied due process in paternity suits which will then be used to require support for the child. This is certainly a no win situation for all sides. Rather than blame one side or the other a brief mention of what has been done to provide support for children will be given. A few suggestions for improving the situation will also be offered.

In 1974 the Child Support Enforcement Program was founded by Congress to get support for children from their fathers. Created under this program, the OCSE operates a federal Parent Locator Service (PLS) to track down missing parents. This service works to reduce public expenditures for AFDC payments which are necessary when the father's support is not provided. Although this is a lengthy process it has been shortened by using computer records and IRS records to discover where the fathers are.

A second problem has been the difficulty in forcing fathers to make support payments. The process is expensive for the courts and time consuming. Also, men who refused to pay were rarely punished, since jail terms made payment even less likely. Lately, courts have gotten around this problem by using the IRS to deduct wages from the father's employment pay to guarantee payment. This is not, however, a standard practice.

Seeing this issue from a broader perspective, a Wisconsin bill has been proposed where the government would guarantee a minimum level of support to all eligible children. Fathers would make payments into a government fund based on the amount they are judged to afford without harming the child. Those who can pay more will still do so, and the child will receive an amount commensurate with what s/he had been used to. This system is similar to the one currently being used in Sweden. Both programs realize the economic hardship on all and refuse to punish the fathers for the dissolution of the marriage.

An astute reader has probably noted that this section has discussed fathers always paying support and mothers always receiving. The 14th amendment, however, makes it illegal to require only fathers to make payments and not to make mothers do so. This should make most state laws unconstitutional. Practice still shows, though, that only in rare cases do mothers pay child support. This is because mothers usually receive custody. When mothers do not receive custody they usually earn less than their ex-husband does. Rarely do the courts require both parents to share in the support payments.

CONCLUSIONS

Although fathers' legal rights are improving, there are many steps to go before they are equal with mothers' rights. The author makes the following suggestions that would be helpful in guaranteeing equality before the law.

In the issue of paternity suits, it is urged that state legislators update when and where necessary to provide for blood grouping tests in all paternity cases. This is not quite 100 percent effective but with recent advances in the medical field is far superior to any other method for excluding paternity.

Due Process also needs to be accorded to alleged fathers in paternity suits. These rights would include equal treatment with the plaintiff to originate proceedings and to provide evidence of the mother's sexual experiences with other men around the time of conception. It is time these men were treated like all other defendants, that is, that they are innocent until proven guilty.

The rights of unwed fathers are also in need of change. Ultimately it can be summed in one statement, give unwed fathers the same rights as unwed mothers. All states should require the father's okay for an adoption, if he can be located. It is recommended that states adopt a system similar to the one in Michigan where unwed fathers register their interest with the government. If the mother does not want to keep the child but the father does want the child, there should be no reason why his wishes should not be fulfilled. As in the case of *in re* Byrd, unwed fathers should be given equality in custody matters as well. If the father proves later to be unfit, then the law would, of course, step in. No other parents are required to prove fitness *before* getting custody. Unwed fathers deserve the same rights.

In custody suits between two parents the law requires equal protection for both. Judges need to be informed of the necessity of equal treatment if the child's best interests are to be served. Also, the "unfitness test" for mothers is incorrect for use in these cases and should be used only in those cases between a parent and a third party.

It has been suggested that social science research is important in influencing judicial decision making (Orthner & Lewis, 1979). Unfortunately for fathers, many early psychologists and sociologists (i.e., Freud, Bowlby) wrote of the unique mother-child relationship and of the relative unimportance of fathers. Numerous recent studies, however (i.e., Lamb, 1981; Parke, 1981), have shown that fathers are not only capable as parents but can be very important in the child's development. It is suggested that researchers of the father's role will work to make this research more available to lawmakers, lawyers and judges. It is hoped that judges will start to change some of their preconceptions about fathers and eliminate concepts like the tender years doctrine. Only then will fathers truly have a fair chance of getting custody of their children.

Finally, on the issue of support, it is urged that children be guaranteed a minimum payment by the government and that fathers *and* mothers be required to make fair contributions according to their abilities to pay for these payments. It must be remembered that approximately four out of five parents will remarry creating economic hardships which are difficult for all.

In summary, it seems that fathers have been discriminated against in American law because it is assumed they are irresponsible and uncaring. This is an unfair and incorrect assumption. Research shows fathers can be significant contributors to the child's development. It is time the law stopped discriminating against fathers.

NOTES

1. Although this case was not a family law case (it involved the buying of 3.2% beer in Oklahoma) the opinion has been cited in a number of family law cases since.

2. This could be helped by having states adopt laws similar to a Michigan law where putative fathers register their interest in the child with the local government.

3. Georgia, Kansas, Massachusetts, Mississippi, Missouri, Oklahoma, Pennsylvania and Vermont. Source: Washington University Law Quarterly Vol 1979, 1029 (1979), p. 1062.

4. See also Painter v. Bannister, 140 NW 2d, 152 (Iowa, 1966).

5. North Carolina law, 1977.

6. Section of Domestic Relations Law in NY "in all cases there shall be no prima facie right to the custody of the child in either parent."

7. See *Beyond the Best Interests of the Child*. Goldstein, J., Freud, A., Solnit, A. NY: Free Press, 1979.

BIBLIOGRAPHY

Cox, M., Cease, L. "Joint Custody," Family Advocate, Summer 1979 1 (1), 10.

Foster & Freed. *Law and the Family.* Vol. 2, NY, 1967.

Gasser, R., Taylor, C. "Role Adjustment of Single Fathers with Dependent Children," *Family Coordinator*, 25 (4), Oct. 1976.

Goldstein, J., Freud, A., Solnit, A. *Beyond the Best Interests of the Child.* NY: The Free Press, 1979.

Hetherington, E.M., Cox, M., Cox, R. "Divorced Fathers," *Family Coordinator*, 25 (4), Oct. 1976.

Katz, S., Inker, M. *Fathers, Husbands and Lovers: Legal Rights and Responsibilities.* Washington, ABA, 1979.

Krause, H. Child Support Enforcement: Legislative Tasks for the Early 1980's, *Family Law Quarterly.* Winter 1980, Vol. 15, 349.

Krause, H. *Child Support in America: The Legal Perspective.* Charlottesville, VA: Michie, 1981.

Krause, H. "Forcing Fathers to be Financially Responsible," *Family Advocate.* Summer 1982, 5 (1), 13–18.

Lamb, M. *The Role of the Father in Child Development.* 2d. NY: Wiley, 1981.

Melli, M. "The Changing View of Child Support," *Family Advocate.* Summer 1982, 5 (1), 16–17.

Orthner, D., Lewis, K. "Evidence of Single Father Competence in Childrearing," *Family Law Quarterly.* 13 (1), Spring 1979, 27–47.

Parke, R. *Fathers.* Cambridge: Harvard University Press, 1981.

Paulsen, M., Wadlington, W., Goebal, J. Jr. *Domestic Relations Cases and Materials.* 2d, NY: Foundation Press, 1974.

Redden, K. *Federal Regulation of Family Law.* Charlottesville, VA: Michie, 1982.

Royce, C. *A Legislator's Guide to Support Enforcement.* Washington: National Conference of State Legislatures, April, 1980.

Chapter 9

A Black Perspective
on the Father's Role
in Child Development

John Lewis McAdoo

The purpose of this paper is to examine the origins of some of the commonly held stereotypes of the Black father's role in the family, to review some of the empirical evidence related to these stereotypes and to present some empirical studies that evaluate the Black father's role performance and socialization practices from a more realistic perspective. A goal of this presentation is to present empirical evidence that evaluates the absent father as a by-product of slavery syndrome myth that has been perpetuated by social science literature. Another goal is to help the participants to understand that Black fathers in their socialization practices utilize the same range of parenting practices found in men of all ethnic groups. Further, that these behaviors, attitudes and beliefs vary in the same way given political, economic and social realities of their situation.

Our task has been made difficult by the fact that much of the social science empirical literature related to the family in general and the role of the father in the family has been a historical one. Further, the sociological, psychological and developmental empirical literature has focused upon the role of the mothers in the family process to the exclusion of the father's role. This research has been described as matricentric in character (Lamb, 1976; McAdoo, 1979, 1981). One could almost conclude that those aspects of the different professional disciplines studying the family might more accurately

John L. McAdoo, PhD, is Associate Professor, School of Social Work and Community Planning, University of Maryland at Baltimore, Baltimore, MD 21201.

117

be called matricentric sociology, matricentric psychology and matricentric developmental psychology for their almost pathological reliance on studies related to the role of the mother in the family process and her reports of the father's role in the family.

More recent efforts have focused on this imbalance in the empirical literature and this conference on fathering is a healthy indication that social scientists are beginning to understand that we cannot discuss the socialization of children without examining the father's role in that process. We are only beginning to develop methodologies that will help us in expliciting normative patterns of fathering, of their attitudes, behaviors and beliefs related to the socialization of their children and their roles in the family interactional processes.

If this conference on fathering is a signal of a new empirical beginning in terms of adding the father to our understanding of family interaction and socialization processes and patterns, then we need to find ways of evaluating Black fathers and their families in a less ethnocentrically biased way. We need to encourage mainstream social scientists to move beyond the studies that focused on the most problematic, economically devastated Black families, sometimes inappropriately comparing them to families who are most advantaged, i.e., families of college professors (McAdoo, 1981) and to develop new theoretical models of Black family functioning that are more scientifically and less politically motivated. We must give up the matricentric scientific notions that describe Black fathers as invisible men, who are not active in, have no power, control or interest in the socialization of their children (McAdoo, 1979). We must be willing to move away from what Jackson describes as the culture of investigative poverty, a research state of affairs where most of the contributors have been unduly possessed by a homogenous view of Blacks; an overconcentration upon abnormality; an apathetic lack of interest in interdisciplinary research; a short attention span; an exaggerated masculinity in defense of their adolescent knowledge; and an inability to defer gratification as evidenced by their relatively frequent utilization of inappropriate racial comparisons and insufficient empirical data, which, of course, usually produces invalid conclusions (Jackson, 1974). In celebrating fatherhood, we must be able, finally, to put to rest the stereotypes and myths that inhibit our understanding of the diversity of roles played by the Black father in his family.

MYTHS

Wilkerson (1977) uses the Random House dictionary definition of myths as an unproven collective belief that is accepted uncritically and used to justify a social institution as in the belief of biological inferiority of slaves used in support of slave societies. As Staples (1971) stereotypes of Black males as psychologically impotent and castrated has been perpetuated by both social scientists and the mass media and these stereotypes have been accepted by both Blacks and whites in this country. We submit that this has important implications related to the Black male's ability to function as a father in the family.

Along with the myth of the castrated marginal male, white social sciences have created the myth of the Black matriarchy, a hypothesis which suggests that the Black family and community are dominated by its female members and this is the direct result of the emasculation of the Black male by the historical vicissitudes of slavery and economic sources. The matriarchy is seen by some as perpetuating the impotent Black male syndrome in families while others see it as a subterfuge to hide the triple jeopardy that Black women must face being Black, female and their location in the working class strata of the country (Staples, 1970, 1971; Taylor, 1977).

What most of the authors (Staples, 1970, 1971; Wilkerson, 1977; Taylor, 1977) have attempted to convey is that the discrediting of the Black father is a political, economic and emotional one not based upon logic or scientific reason. We find that the literature related to myths on the Black father have overwhelmingly referred to the era of slavery as being the point in time where Black families were destroyed and the Black fathers emasculated. Many authors imply that female-headed households in Black families were the norm. However, until recently no empirical data was presented to support those conclusions. Several authors have presented empirical evidence that the predominate structure of the Black family shortly before the end of slavery and shortly afterwards was headed by two parents (Gutman, 1976; Furstenburg, 1975).

Gutman (1976) in a rather thorough examination of the persistent myths about Black families, reviewed U.S. Census and Freedman Bureau's data for the years 1850 through 1880 in thirteen American cities. He found in all of these areas the proportion of Black fathers present in families ranged from 70 to 90 percent. In 1880 the number of female-headed households with children present in seven southern cities and counties ranged from 9 to 21 percent. This data notes that the father was present in the home.

Furstenburg (1975) reviewed the census data for the city of Philadelphia and came to the same conclusions. Further, he compared Black, Irish, German and white American households in 1850 and 1880 and found that the Black family structural pattern was not significantly different from other ethnic groups living in Philadelphia at that time. He found that Black families in 1850 (23%) and in 1880 (25%) had more female-headed households than the white Americans (1850: 13%; 1880: 14%), the Irish (1850, 1880: 13%) and the Germans (1850: 3%; 1880: 8%). The great majority of the families lived in two parent families. When property holdings among different ethnic groups was held constant, variation among ethnic groups disappeared. Finally, the higher proportion of female-headed households appeared to be due to death of the males and not some of the stereotypic interpretations presented by others. He suggests that the harshness of the urban environment and impact on the Black family has not been greatly appreciated by researchers.

Both Gutman and Furstenberg have noted the economic difficulties that Black families faced in adapting to post-slavery society. Gutman was clear about the impact of racial discrimination in the decline of skilless workers in the labor force between 1865 and 1905, its impact on the political leadership structure of the Black community as well as the Black man's ability to support his family. Furstenberg's data indicates that matrafocal Black families are a product of economic discrimination, poverty and disease and not the result of some moral, intellectual or cultural deficit.

Even Moynihan's (1965) study noted that 75% of the Black families lived in nuclear or two-parent homes and this finding was remarkably similar to the historical and sociological studies of Gutman and Furstenberg and others. Since the degree of Black fathers' presence in the home has been found to be similar to the father presence of other ethnic groups, we can assume that he also played some role in the family process and the remainder of this paper will be devoted to examining empirical studies that will shed light on this assumption.

We will limit our discussion of the empirical literature related to fathering styles in Black families. Some of the literature relating to the role of the father as a provider, his influence in the decision-making process related to child rearing, his expectations for his children, his nurturing and controlling of his child's emotional growth and behavior and the interaction patterns that take place between the Black father and his child will be discussed.

PROVIDER ROLE

Most of the sociological literature relating to the provider role of the father follows Parson's (1955) description of the instrumental and expressive modes of family process. The father was described as playing only an instrumental role. That is, the father's role was seen as being primarily that of a provider who protected the family from the outside world and was the conduit of information and resources between the family and the outside world. The mother-child relationship was the key expressive relationship until the child had passed the preschool stage. While Parson's theories have served as a theoretical model in early family socialization literature, the empirical literature does not provide clear-cut support for his thesis. At least one researcher has provided evidence that suggests that fathers are engaged in expressive socialization functions (Cazenave, 1979).

Price-Bonham (1979) in her review noted that the effectiveness of the Black father in his role as a provider is viewed as being dependent upon his ability to aid in supporting his family and to share the provider role with his wife thus legitimizing his authority within the family and allowing him to serve as a model of responsible behavior to his children. Tausch (1952) noted that Black fathers and fathers of other racial and ethnic groups saw themselves as more than just economic providers to their families and they valued companionship with their children more than the provider role. The role of provider for these fathers may have presented a dilemma for them since the amount of time fathers spent with their children was partially controlled by employment pressures.

In analyzing the research of Maxwell (1976) and others (Cafritz, 1974; Fasteneau, 1976), Cazenave (1979) found that they overemphasized the provider role as parenting style in focusing exclusively on the lack of paternal participation involvement and expressiveness in white middle and upper-middle income classes. In his research with middle-income Black fathers, Cazenave notes that the greater the economic security, the more active the father becomes in the child-rearing function. His findings on 54 mailmen seem to support this conclusion, as these fathers were found to be more active in child-rearing activities than their fathers had been.

In summary, while many researchers appear to use Parson's theory as a guide, it now appears evident from Cazenave's and others' data relating to paternal nurturance (McAdoo, 1979; Radin, 1972, 1975), that Parson may have overemphasized the instrumental or provider role of the father. It is safe to assume that the American father has many roles that he plays in the family, that of provider, decision-maker, nurturer, husband and father. Research that isolates or focuses on any of these roles may provide misinformation about his role in the nurturing of his children. While this evaluation analyzes each of the roles of fathers separately, it is important to recognize the interrelationship of the roles the father plays and the reciprocity of father/mother, sibling/child roles in the socialization process.

DECISION-MAKING

Several authors have described the Black family as equalitarian in their decision-making patterns (Dietrich, 1975; Hill, 1971; Lewis 1975; Reuben, 1978; Staples, 1976; Tenhouten, 1970; Willie, 1978). Much of this literature was in reaction to social scientists' assertions that the Black family was matriarchical in structure (Moynihan, 1965). Willie (1978), in reviewing power relationship literature, found that Black families appear to be more equalitarian than white families, with the middle class Black family being more equalitarian than any other type. McDonald (1980), in an extensive review of the family power literature, suggests that because of theoretical and methodological problems inherent in family power research, we have not moved much beyond the original finding of Blood (1960) on this issue.

Blood (1960) and others have demonstrated that American fathers are moving toward an egalitarian relationship in the decision-making and power relationship in the home. Jackson (1978) reported that lower-class Black fathers tended to be more patriarchal in their decision-making patterns than lower-class white fathers and Black and white middle income fathers. Her review of selected literature on Black and white families noted that wife-dominant families (matriarchal) were more characteristic of white professional families with unemployed wives. Mack (1978) found that regardless of race or class, fathers perceived themselves as the dominant decision-makers.

The studies related to child-rearing decision-making in Black and white families indicate that the predominant pattern is egalitarian. That is, fathers share equally in the decisions about the child's needs (McAdoo, 1980). McAdoo (1979) had previously found that middle-income Black fathers shared equally with their wives in decisions on child-rearing activities. However, Cromwell's (1978) analysis of husbands' and wives' reports of dominance on child-rearing decision-making revealed conflicts in Black and Chicano homes on this issue.

Our conclusions, given the previous assertions, are that both Black and white middle-income fathers' involvement in decision-making around child-rearing practices appears to be changing in the same general pattern found by Bronfenbrenner's (1958) analysis of the literature twenty-three years ago. He found the predominant child-rearing decision-making pattern to be equalitarian and attributed the change to the influence of professional child development practitioners. These changes perhaps were also due to the addition of mothers to the work force and the use of television in getting child development practitioners' message to more people.

The question that troubles us in the review of both the Black and white empirical literature on this issue, is related to the degree of similarity found in all ethnic groups in the United States of this pattern of egalitarian in child-rearing decision-making in families. If this is so, from a Black researcher's perspective, then how can we scientifically justify the negative conclusions drawn only about Black families (Blood, 1967; Moynihan, 1965) and not white families with a similar pattern? What is needed to share the myth or destroy it as politically motivated and derisive?

PARENTING STYLE

Very few studies related to the Black father's expectations and parenting style were found. In a review of the literature Bartz (1978), in a study of 455 parents of different ethnic groups, noted that fathers of all socioeconomic classes shared similar expectations of their children's behavior. Ethnic differences in fathers' expectations of their children's behavior were a matter of degree and not kind. Working class fathers of all ethnic groups and races felt that children should help formulate rules and have the right to express their own ideas within the family. Black fathers and fathers belonging to other ethnic groups felt that parents earn the respect of their children by being fair, not by imposing parental will or authority.

While Bartz's data seems to suggest that lower socioeconomic Black fathers may be changing their traditional values to meet the new demands for socialization in society, it is clear from other literature (Staples, 1978; Taylor, 1978; Coles, 1978; Schulz, 1978) that many of them retain and support the values of their socioeconomic status. These men see themselves as the head of the family and they believe they are expected to provide punishment to their children for transgressing externally imposed rules and regulations. They describe themselves as strict, using physical as opposed to verbal punishment liberally. The child's punishment is related to the transgression's consequence rather than the intent of the child's actions.

Cazenave (1979), reviewing the changes in child-rearing activities in two generations of Black fathers, found that middle-income fathers reported being more actively involved than their fathers in child caring activities. This sample was more actively involved in changing their children's diapers, in babysitting and in playing with their children than their fathers had been. They reported spending more time with their children and claimed to punish their children physically less often than their fathers had punished them.

Black middle-income fathers in McAdoo's (1979) study resembled those in Cazenave's study in that they reported being equally involved in making child-rearing decisions. Most of these fathers could be described as traditional (Duvall, 1946) in their values toward child-rearing. They expected their child to respond immediately to their commands, would almost never allow angry temper tantrums from their child, and perceived themselves and their attitudes toward child-rearing as moderate to very strict. These fathers expected good behavior from their children as opposed to assertive and independent behavior. They were more likely to tell the child that they approved of his good behavior as opposed to hugging and kissing him. Their attitudes appeared to be like Baumrind's (1968) authoritative fathers.

In a comparative exploratory study observing Black and white fathers and their preschool children, Baumrind (1973) found sex differences in the fathers' expectations and the behavior of the children. There were few significant differences in black and white fathers' expectations of their sons' behavior. Black sons were expected to behave in a more mature fashion and the fathers were likely to encourage independent behavior. While no significant differences were observed in the behavior of the children, Black boys appeared to be less achievement oriented and more aggressive than white boys. Fathers of Black girls appeared to be significantly different from fathers of white girls in their parenting styles and child-rearing practices. The Black fathers did not encourage individuality and independence or provide enrichment of the daughter's environment. Black fathers did not promote nonconformity and were authoritarian in their practices.

The conclusion drawn by Baumrind was that socialization practices which would characterize Black families as authoritarian by white social science standards and therefore in need of change, actually benefit Black daughters. In comparing Black and white girls Baumrind found that Black daughters of authoritarian parents were exceptionally independent and at ease in the nursery school setting where the observations took place. The study provides us with an interesting observation which needs to be verified and clarified in future research. Black authoritarian fathers and families differ significantly from white authoritarian families in the degree to which they adhere to rigid standards. White fathers who were found to be authoritarian in Baumrind's studies were more likely to be seen as having an authoritarian personality syndrome (Adorno, 1950), i.e., dogmatic and intolerant attitudes being motivated by repressed anger, emotional coldness and a sense of impotence.

In summary to this section on parenting styles, it would appear that Black fathers socialize their children differently to some degree than white fathers and the impact of that process may lead to the development of high competence in girls. There appears to be a need for more research related to the Black father's attitude toward child-rearing, some observational validation of his behavior in relationship to his expressed values and some validation through data gathering from significant others in the family. However, it is important to note that they are more actively involved in child care, babysitting, changing diapers, playing with and controlling their children than popular literature would have us believe.

We need to determine the normative patterns of child care by Black fathers across both social class and ethnic group variables. As Pleck (1979) reminds us, the patterns of acculturation and family structure in Black families differed for northern and southern Blacks and for southern migrants to urban areas as well. Once these normative patterns are determined, then there is a need to follow fathers longitudinally over time to determine the impact of these patterns on the socialization of the children, the quality of the marital relationship and lifestyle of the family and the interactions of all of these variables. It is sad to note that little evidence of the existent empirical studies of normative patterns of parenting styles of fathers across ethnic groups has been found.

PARENT-CHILD RELATIONSHIPS

Walters and his associates (Walters and Stinnett, 1971; Walters and Walters, 1980) have done the most consistent reviews of the research related to parent-child relationships issues. Their latest work focused on the emerging research trends of physiological influences, parent-infant relationships, divorce, fathering, step parenting, child abuse and neglect, values of the child, methodological issues and intervention strategies.

Some of their conclusions were that patterns of parent-child relationships are influenced by parenting models which fathers and mothers provide to each other. To understand the concurrent contributions of parents to each other and to their children, research studies should focus on the mother-father-child relationship and on the mother-father-sibling-child relationship rather than on the father-child, mother-child relationship.

Walters' feelings are that a clearer picture or conceptualization is emerging from the research literature on the reciprocal effects of relationships between parents and children. Family researchers are moving away from a unidirectional model which sees the relationship going from parent to child toward one which emphasizes a reciprocal model of relationships between parent and child. Children not only influence their parents' behavior but are also important determiners of their own behavior patterns (Walters, 1980).

While Walters' review emphasizes the need for research on parent-child interactions and reciprocal relationships, it is also clear from his review and that of others (Lamb, 1977; Price-Bonham, 1979) that the role of the father in the parent-child relationship studies is not clearly understood. Studies of father-child relationships tend to emphasize the relationship between fathers and sons and leave the impact on daughters virtually unexplored (Walters, 1971). Further, as Staples (1970) notes, the role of the Black father in these studies is also not explored very well. He concludes that the Black male may be more difficult to reach. The implication being that social science researchers select other sources for their information on Black fathers.

Price-Bonham (1979), in her review of the literature, agrees with Staples' assessment and suggests that studies of Black father-child relationships suffer from the same deficiencies as studies of other ethnic groups. Most researchers doing family relationship studies generally collect data on fathers from mothers and/or wives (Walters, 1971; McAdoo, 1979), neglect to control for social class (Busse, 1972) and focus on the impact of absent fathers.

In summary to this section on father-child relationships, what seems lacking from the various literature reviews is a theory which describes how these relationships differ over the life span of the child's development within the family. This theory should address racial, ethnic and social class differences within the father-child relationship. There needs to be more descriptive research methodologies developed using both questionnaire and observational techniques to generate data bases related to the general concept of parent-child relationships and to particular aspects of that relationship. For Black father-child relationships, given socioeconomic class and other variables, there is a need to develop the boundaries, the quality and quantity of the parent-child relationship over time.

Once the relationships between fathers and children are identified, more sophisticated research designs can be used to determine the impact of mothers, siblings and the kin network system on the development and changes in the parent-child relationship process. This would suggest the use of multitraits and multimethod approaches with more complex research designs (Walters, 1980). Using such approaches, researchers could begin to measure the impact of the child upon the relationship and move away from linear models to curvilinear or other models that are appropriate.

FATHER-CHILD INTERACTION

The observations of father-child interaction patterns and their effect on the preschool child's social and cognitive growth is a relatively new phenomenon for social science researchers. The two most studied interaction patterns are nurturance and control. Nurturance may be defined as the expression of warmth and positive feelings of the father toward the attitudes and behaviors of his child.

Several researchers (Radin, 1972, 1975; Baumrind, 1971) have suggested that maternal warmth (nurturance) facilitates the child's identification with the mother, particularly the female child. Radin (1972) has suggested that paternal nurturance facilitates the male child's identification with the father. Identification with either parent should lead to an incorporation by the child of the parent's ideas, attitudes, beliefs and feelings about the child. The parent communicates to the child a positive acceptance of the child as a person. Nurturance is one of the patterns of interaction that is important in the development of social competence in preschool children.

Nurturance (warmth) is used most by parents who recognize and respond to their child's needs, who communicate acceptance, and who are available for interaction, than do parents who are inaccessible and insensitive. Warmth is seen as a characteristic of both parent roles (Newman, 1978). Newman notes that warmth is usually expressed in praise or approval in nonverbal interactions including patting, touching, stroking, hugging, kissing and in playful activities. Rodman (1978) suggests that there is evidence that warmth and rejection can be observed across a variety of cultural groups.

Parental control is another dimension of father-child interaction patterns. Control refers to the parent's insistence that the child carry out important directions and adhere to rules that the parent feels important. Control and nurturance are seen as necessary ingredients in authoritative parents' socialization patterns (Baumrind, 1973). Authoritarian fathers usually use restrictive control interaction patterns in socializing their children. These fathers' verbal interaction patterns with their preschool children are described in the literature as being restrictive, rather cold, unfeeling and aloof, and therefore, represent an expression of the authoritarian father's negative feelings towards his child's attitudes and behavior within the family (Radin, 1972).

Parental restrictiveness does not facilitate positive communication and identification (Radin, 1972) between the child and his parent. Restrictive behaviors are those behaviors that are not warm, loving, and supportive of the child. Nonsupporting behaviors are usually in criticism or expressed disapproval and may also include grabbing, pushing, restraining the child from some event or activity without explanation. It may be viewed as a negative reaction by the parent to the child's attitude, behavior and beliefs. Nonsupport may also lead the parent to handle the symptoms of the problem and not the needs of the child, or to controlling behavior on their part and the cutting off of the usual patterns of identification and communication of the child. Restrictiveness in the parents could lead the child to develop a negative image of himself and his worth as a human being, as well as having negative feelings about those around him.

Radin and her associates (Radin, 1972, 1975; Radin and Epstein, 1975; Jordan, Radin and Epstein, 1975) observed white lower and middle income fathers interacting with their preschool children. She found the predominant pattern of interaction to be nurturance. The fathers were warm and loving toward their children. She hypothesized that children of nurturant fathers would do well on cognitive tasks in kindergarten. They were able to support the hypothesis for boys of middle income fathers but not for boys of lower class fathers. Her studies also found that the relationship between paternal nurturance and the child's intellectual functioning was higher for boys than for girls. It was suggested that the fathers of girls may be sending mixed messages to their daughters and this may lead to a reduction in intellectual performance (Radin and Epstein, 1975).

McAdoo (1979) partially replicated Radin's work with Black middle-income fathers. He hypothesized that the predominant pattern of verbal interaction between Black fathers and their sons and daughters would be nurturance. He was able to support the hypothesis as 75 percent of the Black middle-income fathers were found to be nurturant toward their children. Fathers were equally nurturant toward their sons and daughters. One unanticipated finding was that children of restrictive parents initiated the interaction between them and their fathers significantly more often than children of nurturant parents. This finding supports Walters' (1980) suggestion that there needs to be an examination of the impact of the reciprocal nature of the pattern of interaction between the parent and child.

McAdoo was not able to find any relationship between a father's interaction patterns and his sons' and daughters' self-esteem. The children's positive self-esteem lead McAdoo to suggest that the relationship between father-child interaction and self-esteem may be an indirect one. Walters and Stinnett (1971), in their decade review of parent-child relationships, noted that the research results converge suggesting that parental acceptance, warmth and support are positively related to favorable emotional, social and intellectual development of children. They further found that extreme restrictiveness, authoritarianism and punitiveness without acceptance, warmth and love tend to be negatively related to a child's positive self-concept, emotional and social development. The studies they reviewed also indicate that parental attitudes and behaviors vary according to sex and behavior of the child.

Mackey (1979), in one of the most comprehensive cross-cultural observational studies involving father figures in the United States, Ireland, Spain, Japan and Mexico, found that American father figures did not interact much differently than father figures of other nations. They noted that father figures interacted more nonverbally with younger children and were closer to them. American men were as nurturant to their children as American women. No differences in intensity of interaction level between men and women were observed in American families.

SUMMARY

Selected literature related to the roles Black fathers play in the socialization of their children were reviewed. It was noted that when economic sufficiency rises within Black families, an increase in the active participation of the Black father in the socialization of his children was observed. Black fathers, like fathers of all ethnic groups take an equal part in the child-rearing decisions in the family. Their expectations for their child's behavior in the home also appears to be similar given socioeconomic status patterns. Unlike other fathers who are authoritarian, the Black fathers appear to be socializing their daughters to be more competent and independent at an early age. His predominant relationship and interaction pattern appears to be nurturant, warm and loving toward his children. Finally, as Lamb (1976) has suggested, the father's socialization role is defined by his position within the family system.

From a Black social science perspective, there is a need for more Black social scientists to be funded in doing empirical research related to the patterns of interaction and socialization of a Black father's children. Further, there is a need to evaluate the Black father's contribution to the total family experience and its effects on the competence of his children, the marital experience and other outcomes. Also, there is a need to evaluate the impact of the economic circumstances and climate of the family and the Black father's experience in employment as they influence his ability to carry out his role in the family. We need to develop normative patterns of the Black father's attitudes, behavior and beliefs related to the role of fathering and the socialization of his children. Only in this way can we begin to dispel the negative myths and stereotypes surrounding the role of Black fathers.

REFERENCES

Adorno, T.W., Fenkel-Brunswick, D.J., Levinson and Sanford, R.N. *The Authoritarian Personality.* New York: Harper, 1950.

Bartz, K.W. and Levine, B.S. "Child rearing by Black parents: A description and comparison to Anglo and Chicano, parents." *Journal of Marriage and the Family*, 40, 4 (November): 709- 720, 1978.

Baumrind, D. "Authoritarian vs authoritative parental control." In Scarr-Salapatek, S. and Salapatek, P. (Eds.) *Socialization.* Columbus: Merrill Publishing Company, 1973.

———. "Current patterns of paternal authority." *Developmental Psychology Monographs*, 4, 1, Part 2, 1971.

———. "An exploratory study of socialization effects on Black children: Some Black-white comparisons." *Child Development* 43: 261–267, 1968.

———. "Child care practices anteceding three patterns of preschool behavior." *Genetic Psychology Monographs*, 75, 43–88, 1967.

———. "Effects of authoritative parental control on child behavior." *Child Development*, 37(4): 887–907, 1966.

———. and Block, A.E. "Socialization practices associated with dimensions of competence in preschool boys and girls." *Child Development*, 38, (2), 291–, 1967.

Biller, H.B. *Parental Deprivation.* Lexington, Massachusetts: Heath Company, 1974.

Blood, R. and Wolfe, D. *Husbands and Wives.* New York: Free Press, 1960.

Bronfenbrenner, U. "Socialization through time and space." In Maccoby, E.E., Newcomb, T.M. and Hartley, E.L. (Eds.) *Readings in Social Psychology.* New York: Holt and Co., 1958.

Busse, T. and Busse, P. "Negro parental behavior and social class variables." *Journal of Genetic Psychology*, 120, 289–291, 1972.

Cafritz, J.S. *Masculine/Feminine or Human?* Itasco, Illinois: F.E. Peacock Co., 1974.

Cazenave, N. "Middle income Black fathers: An analysis of the provider's role." *Family Coordinator* 28 (November), 1979.

Coles, R. "Black fathers." In Wilkerson, D. and Taylor, R. (Eds.) *The Black Male in America.* Chicago: Nelson Hall, 1978.

Cromwell, V.L. and Cromwell, R.E. "Perceived dominance and conflict resolution among Anglo, Black and Chicano couples." *Journal of Marriage and the Family*, 42, 4, (November), 749–759, 1978.

Dietrich, K.T. "A reexamination of the myth of Black matriarchy." *Journal of Marriage and the Family*, 37 (May), 367–374, 1975.

Duvall, E. "Conceptions of parenthood," *Journal of Sociology*, 52, (November), 193–203, 1946.

Fasteneau, M. *The Male Machine.* New York: Macmillan, 1976.

Frazier, E.F. *The Negro Family in the United States.* Chicago: The University of Chicago Press, 1939.

Furstenburg, F.F., Hershberg, T. and Modell, J. "The origins of the female headed family: The impact of urban experience," *Journal of Interdisciplinary History,* 6, 211–233, 1975.

Gutman, H.G. *The Black Family in Slavery and Freedom: 1750–1925.* New York, Pantheon Books, 1976.

Hill, R. *The Strengths of Black Families.* New York: Emerson-Hall, 1971.

Jackson, J. "Ordinary Black husbands: The truly hidden men." In Staples, (Ed.) *The Role of the Father in Child Development.* New York: John Wiley and Co., 1978.

_____"Ordinary black husbands: The truly hidden men." *Journal of Social and Behavioral Science,* 20 (Spring), 19–27, 1974.

Jordan, B.E., Radin, N., and Epstein, A. "Paternal behavior and intellectual functioning in preschool boys and girls," *Developmental Psychology,* 11, 407–408, 1975.

Lamb, M.E. "The role of the father: An overview." In Lamb, M.E. (Ed.) *The Role of the Father in Child Development.* New York: John Wiley and Sons, 1977.

_____"Interactions between eight-month old children and their fathers and mothers." In Lamb, M.E. (Ed.) *The Role of the Father in Child Development.* New York: John Wiley and Sons, 1977.

Lewis, D.K. "The Black family: Socialization and sex roles," *Phylon,* 36, (Fall), 221–327, 1975.

Mack, D.E. "Power relationships in Black families," *Journal of Personality and Social Psychology,* 30, (September), 409–413, 1978.

Mackey, C.W. and Day, R.O. "Some indicators of fathering behaviors in the United States: A cross-cultural examination of the adult male interactions," *Journal of Marriage and the Family,* 41, 2, 287–298, 1979.

Maxwell, J. "The keeping of fathers in America," *The Family Coordinator,* 25, 387–392, 1976.

McAdoo, J. "Socializing the preschool child," Government grant funded by the National Institutes of Mental Health under contract No. 1 R01 MH25838-01, 1980.

_____"A study of father-child interaction patterns and self-esteem in Black preschool children," *Young Children,* 34, 1, 46–53, 1979.

McDonald, G.W. "Family power: The assessment of a decade of theory and research 1970–1979," *Journal of Marriage and the Family,* 42, 4, (November), 881–884, 1980.

Moynihan, D. *The Negro Family: The Case for National Action.* Washington, D.C.: Dept. of Labor, Office of Planning and Research, 1965.

Newman, B.M. and Newman, P.R. *Infancy and Childhood Development and its Contents.* New York: John Wiley and Sons, 1978.

Parsons, T. and Bales, R.F. *Family Socialization and Interaction Process.* Illinois: The Free Press, 1955.

Pleck, E.H. *Black Migration and Poverty: Boston 1865–1900.* New York: Academic Press, 1979.

Price-Bonham, S. and Skeen, P. "A comparison of Black and white fathers with implications for parents' education," *The Family Coordinator,* 28, 1, (January), 53–59, 1979.

Radin, N. "Observed paternal behaviors as antecedents of intellectual functioning in young boys," *Developmental Psychology,* 6, 353–361, 1973.

_____"Father-child interaction and the intellectual functioning of four-year old boys," *Developmental Psychology,* 8, 369–376, 1972.

_____and Epstein, A. "Observed paternal behavior and intellectual functioning of preschool boys and girls," paper presented at the Society for Research in Child Development, Denver, 1975.

Rapaport, R., Rapaport, R.N. and Strelitz, Z. *Fathers, Mothers and Society.* New York: Basic Books, 1977.

Reuben, R.H. "Matriarchal themes in black literature: Implications for family life education," *Family Coordinator*, 27, (January), 33–41, 1978.

Rodman, H. Cited in Newman and Newman (Eds.) *Infancy and Childhood Development and Its Contents*. New York: John Wiley and Sons, 1978.

Schulz, D.A. "Coming up as a boy in the ghetto," in Wilkerson, D. and Taylor, R. (Eds.) *The Black Male in America*. Chicago: Nelson-Hall, 1978.

Staples, R. "The myth of the Black matriarchy," in Wilkerson, D. and Taylor, R. (Eds.) *The Black Male in America*. Chicago: Nelson-Hall, 1978.

_____"The Black American family," in Mindell, C. and Haberstein, R. (Eds.) *Ethnic Families in America*. New York, Elsevier Press, 1976.

_____"The myth of the impotent Black male," *The Black Scholar*, 10, 1971.

_____"The myth of the Black matriarchy," *The Black Scholar*, 1, 1970.

_____"Educating the Black male at various class levels for marital roles," *The Family Coordinator*, 20, 164–167, 1970.

Taylor, R.L. "Socialization to the Black male role," in Wilkerson, D. and Taylor, R. (Eds.) *The Black Male in America*. Chicago: Nelson-Hall, 1977.

Tausch, R.J. "The role of the father in the family," *Journal of Experimental Education*, 20, 319–361, 1952.

Tenhouten, W. "The Black family: Myth or reality," *Psychiatry*, 2, (May), 145–173, 1970.

Walters, J. and Stinnett, N. "Parent-child relationships: A decade of research," in Broderick, C.B. (Ed.) *A Decade of Family Research and Action*. Minneapolis: National Council on Family Relations, 1971.

_____and Walters, L. "Parent-child relationships: A review 1970–1979," *Journal of Marriage and the Family*, 42, 4 (November), 807–824, 1980.

Wilkerson, D.Y. "The stigmatization process: The politicization of the Black male's identity," in Wilkerson, D. and Taylor, R. (Eds.) *The Black Male In America*. Chicago: Nelson-Hall, 1977.

Willie, C.V. and Greenblatt, S. "Four classic studies of power relationships in Black families: A review and look to the future," *Journal of Marriage and the Family*, 40, 4, (November), 691–696, 1978.

Chapter 10

Father/Child Relationships:
Beyond *Kramer vs. Kramer*

Shirley M. H. Hanson

Kramer vs. Kramer, a popular movie of the 1980's, was a story of a father raising his son alone. This story depicts a man struggling to parent a young boy after the mother walked out without warning. Dustin Hoffman, portraying Ted Kramer, learned how to cook and do housework, take care of a child's physical and emotional needs, and changed jobs to be more compatible with his new family structure. This warm-hearted but serious comedy exposed a lot of the general public with a version of life without a mother in the home. Although it is one impression, it is not the only way that single custodial fathers live and relate to their children. The purpose of this paper is to discuss what is known about the father-child relationship in single custodial father families. Material for this presentation was gleaned from the research literature as well as from the author's own research on single parent families.

Single custodial fathers are defined as male parents who have physical custody of their minor children. They assume primary responsibility for child care without the assistance of a co-parent or a co-habitating adult living in the family home. They may or may not have legal or sole custody but their children reside with them the majority of the time. Although many of the same issues to be discussed in this paper may pertain to single fathers who adopt or are widowed, the major focus of this discussion is on separated or divorced fathers.

It is important to review the statistics relating to single fathers. The Census Bureau reports about two million marriages a year and

Shirley M. H. Hanson, RN, PhD, FAAN, is Professor, Department of Family Nursing, The Oregon Health Sciences University, Portland, OR 97201.

135

one million divorces. About 60 percent of these divorces, or 600,000 families have children under the age of 18 years. One-parent families now account for 21 percent of the 31.6 million families in America, an increase of 111 percent since 1970. Correspondingly, nearly 12 out of 61 million children (one out of five) live with their single parents. Approximately 90 percent (10.5 million) live with their mothers, while 10 percent (1.5 million) live with their fathers (U.S. Bureau of the Census, 1980, 1982, 1984, 1985).

Lewis (1978) speculates that the number of children living with single fathers is closer to 3.5 million. The discrepancy between the official and unofficial statistics is due to the inaccurate way that data is collected on families. The numbers of children living with single custodial fathers increased 101 percent between 1970 and 1981. Fathers who live only with their children account for 35 percent of all male householders in the United States (U.S. Census Bureau, 1984). Thompson and Gongla (1983) believe that in the future, proportionally fewer single parent families will be maintained by the father, but that the absolute number of single-father families will continue to rise. In other words, the actual number of single parent families will continue to increase but the ratio between single mother and single father homes will continue as is. However, other predictions speculate that by 1990 single parent families will increase to 50 percent of all families in America and single father families will increase to 16 percent of this total (Masnick and Bane, 1980).

PROFILE OF SINGLE FATHERS

Since the primary thrust of this paper is the father/child relationship, only a brief composite description of single custodial fathers as described in the literature will be provided. Most single fathers have been separated or divorced. They assume custody through agreement with their former spouses. They usually enjoy a high level of education, income, and occupation. They are white, protestant, and middle-aged (35–45). They continue in the same job they had before the divorce and remain living in the same house and community. Housekeeping tasks are met with little difficulty and are shared with the children. They tend to join at least one singles group, usually immediately following the divorce. Single fathers do not appear to seek companionship or support from other single fathers, although they know at least one other man in similar circumstances. Fathers either seek custody or obtain it by default. They generally obtain legal sole custody while their former wives have the visitation privileges only. Few single fathers get child support monies from noncustodial working mothers.

CHILD IN SINGLE FATHER HOUSEHOLDS

Most of the work reported on single-father families is on men themselves and what they report about their children. A few studies collected data directly from children (Hanson, 1980, 1981, 1985a, 1985b, 1985c; Santrock and Warshak, 1979; Ambert, 1982). What does this material tell us about children in single father homes?

Sex of Children

The U.S. Census Bureau in 1980 reported that 57 percent of father-only households had custody of boys, whereas 43 percent had girls. In contrast, single mothers had an equal split between male and female children (U.S. Bureau of the Census, 1980). This higher incidence of male children living with single fathers is borne out in research studies and a child's sex may be a factor in men's decisions to seek custody and in the court's decision to grant custody. About one-third of single fathers have custody of females of all ages (Orthner and Lewis, 1978), with a few men reporting that girls are actually harder to raise than boys (Grief, 1982). Generally, there is still an overall belief in society that girls belong with their mothers whenever possible, primarily for sex role socialization. With the increasing incidence of child sexual abuse, the father-daughter incest issue is starting to become a question that is raised in some contested custody cases where fathers actively fight for legal custody of their daughters. The accusation of incest whether real or imagined has become a weapon in the arsenal of unhappy mothers even though the occurrence of this type of court dispute is not documented.

Age of Children

Although no exact figures are available, fathers have custody of all aged children, from infancy through teens. However, the "tender years doctrine" is still prevalent since the younger the child, the more likely they are to remain with their mother. Fathers more often get custody of preadolescent and adolescent aged children and, as mentioned above, these are usually boys. It appears that the average age of children living with fathers is getting younger as younger couples get divorced. Also, society is becoming more accepting of men who want to perform nurturing roles with smaller children.

Child Care Arrangements

Single fathers of younger children rely on the child care resources available in the community such as group day care centers. Contrary to myth, they do not coerce their families and/or neighbors in carrying out this responsibility for them. When the children begin school, neighbors are sometimes hired to tend them between the time that school is out and before the fathers get home from work. By age 10 or so, when the children are through the primary grades, they are often left responsible for themselves after school but accountable to dad vis-à-vis the telephone. Single fathers do not seem to exchange babysitting services with one another as single mothers frequently do. This "I can do it by myself" attitude appears to come from the fathers' need to demonstrate to the world that he can do it alone.

Linkages with Non-Custodial Mothers

When men have custody of children, it is likely to be sole custody either through legal or nonlegal means. A common example of nonlegal circumstances is where mothers have sole legal custody but the growing child decides to go live with the father sometime during the adolescent years. Mothers have and do exercise their right to visitation. It appears that children in father custody homes have more contact with their mothers than children in mother custody homes have with their noncustodial fathers (Santrock and Warshak, 1979). Single fathers report some of the same complaints that single mothers report about the noncustodial parent. That is, she spends too much time with the children, she doesn't spend enough time, she doesn't show up when she is supposed to, the children return upset after visitation, I don't like her boyfriend (lifestyle) and so forth.

A common problem in single parent families is where the custodial parent berates the non-custodial parent and vice versa. Although few researchers have studied this issue, one study reported that fathers were more likely than mothers to encourage children to take sides against the noncustodial parent (Defrain and Eirick, 1981).

Only 10 percent of noncustodial working mothers actually pay child support and the actual monetary amount is also very small (Hanson, 1981). As women began to obtain more education and higher paying jobs, the child support enforcement program may also pursue them as it now does fugitive fathers.

Linkages with Grandparents and Extended Families

One of the more interesting issues that has risen out of men's activist groups in the last couple of years, is that of the grandparents' right to spend time with their grandchildren after the parents' divorce. This is particularly a difficult problem when the grandparents' adult child is the noncustodial parent. If the custodial parent has sole legal custody, they can effectively keep the grandparents or extended family of any kind on the other side from seeing the grandchildren. Several states have introduced legislation making it illegal to withhold visitation from the ex-spouse's extended family, particularly biological grandparents; also many groups have sprung up around the country promoting grandparents' rights to visitation following divorce.

Single fathers who do obtain custody of their children, on the other hand, tend to keep very close contact with their own side of the family, particularly their parents and siblings. Most men report receiving a lot of moral support from their parents although they do not turn to them for financial or babysitting assistance. Men often name their parents as the most important people in their social support network.

FATHER/CHILD RELATIONSHIPS

The relationship between the single custodial fathers and children appears to be generally good. The present relationship is highly influenced by the quality and quantity of the earlier interactions when the mother was still in the home. Single fathers who interacted frequently and effectively with children from very early infancy, adjusted more readily to single parent roles (Orthner and Lewis, 1979; Gasser and Taylor, 1976), felt warmer and more comfortable with their custodial children (Lynn, 1979), were more likely to have actively sought custody (Hanson, 1980, 1985a, 1985b, 1985c) and they felt that they were doing a good job of parenting (Mendes 1976a, 1976b; Chang & Deinard, 1982). Additionally, fathers who have a quality relationship with their children actively sought the experience and education they needed for parenting, worked on nurturing interactions with their children, and had involved themselves in discipline prior to the divorce (Bartz, 1978).

Children who live in single father homes share in the household tasks that need to be done (Defrain & Eirick, 1982) and become more self-reliant than children from two-parent households (Katz, 1979). This finding is consistent with the hypothesis which states that the absence of hierarchy in the single parent household results in earlier maturation of children. Robert Weiss (1979) states,

> The single-parent family, insofar as it requires that the children within it behave responsibly, may be a better setting for growing up than the two-parent family . . . they must participate in their households as full members with the rights and responsibilities of full members. And this can be a useful experience which leads to self-esteem, independence, and a genuine sense of competence.

Discipline of children does not seem to be a big issue in single father homes as it is in single mother homes. Defrain and Eirick (1981) reported that dads did not change their disciplinary approach to the children after the divorce, whereas moms did. Smith and Smith (1981), however, found that fathers changed from a strict authoritarian approach to a more relaxed democratic approach following divorce and upon assuming the primary parenting role. Actually, it only makes sense that parents do change their disciplinary style when they no longer have a partner to mediate between themselves and the children. In one comparative study between single mothers and single fathers, Ambert (1982) found that fathers reported better child behavior toward them and that children of fathers also verbalized more appreciation than did children of single mothers. Too, fathers reported more satisfaction with their lone parenting role than did mothers.

Some scholars have been concerned about the influence of parental presence or absence on the sexual and social development of children. Santrok and Warshak (1979, 1982) studied the effects of father custody on children's social development comparing single mother, single father, and two-parent families. The obtained findings suggest that children living with the opposite sex parent are less well adjusted than children living with the same sex parent. That is, boys do better with fathers and girls do better with mothers. However, if both the father and mother custody families practiced "authoritative parenting" (extensive verbal give and take, warmth and use of enforcement of rules in a non-punitive manner), the results were increased competent social behavior in the children.

A common concern expressed about and by men serving as primary custodians to young children is their ability to provide emotional support and understanding as well as physical and psychological nurturance. The research that addressed this issue yields supportive evidence that men can and do fulfill this need in children (Hanson, 1981, 1985a, 1985b, 1985c; Smith and Smith, 1981; Ambert, 1982). Fathers not only view themselves as affectionate nurturing caretakers but children perceive them as loving and concerned parents. Children rate their single fathers as more nurturing than children rate either parent in two parent families. Fathers feel they best express their love to their children by how well they take care of them whereas children express love by how well they cooperate and show deference to their father. In several studies comparing children's behavior toward male and female custodial parents, single fathers reported more satisfaction with their roles than single mothers, and children appear to be happier with fathers (Ambert, 1982). Fricke (1982) found that fathers were more confident in their parenting ability and felt they had a better parent-child relationship.

Finally, a tenacity exists in the relationship between single fathers and their children. This seemingly tight relationship may be due to the mutual dependency, the uniqueness of the family structure, or the absence of the mother. In any event, strong and healthy parent-child relationships do exist in single custodial father families.

CONCLUSIONS

A number of conclusions can be made from this literature review. These will be summarized according to the problems and strengths commonly reported by single custodial fathers. Projections for the future of single father families will also be made.

Strengths of Single Custodial Father Families

Thus far in this essay, there has been a lot of discussion about the strengths of families where fathers are the primary custodian of dependent children. Rather than reiterate these strengths, one by one, they will be summarized. Single custodial fathers on the whole are doing quite well as primary caretakers of children. Those who are doing the best have actively sought additional parenting experiences or education prior to and following the divorce, have involved themselves in child discipline before the divorce, and have striven for more meaningful nurturing interaction between themselves and their children. They are able to fully use the resources that the community has to offer for themselves and for the children despite the fact that men are traditionally viewed as non-joiners of community related activities. Although most men reported little involvement in housework and child care prior to the divorce, they quickly learn the housekeeping tasks that are essential for running of a home. These fathers also learn if they had not used these skills before, to meet the emotional and psychological needs of their children. As more time passes following divorce, there is a decreasing need to find a surrogate mother for their children. For the most part, single custodial fathers are confident that they are doing a good job, and their children report them to be effective parents. There are fewer conflicts in this father/child relationship than there were in family interactions when the ex-spouse was still at home. A persevering relationship exists between these fathers and their daughters and these fathers and their sons. Most men report making special effort to get along with their children. Children of both sexes are reported to help with household duties and mature more quickly after living in a single parent home. Most dads are happy with their decision to have sought or agreed to custody and they feel that they were clearly the better choice of parent for the children under the given circumstances. Children also report satisfaction with this kind of arrangement and seldom yearn to live with their noncustodial mothers.

Problems of Single Custodial Father Families

Single custodial fathers are not without problems, and these problems involve a number of larger issues. First, divorcing fathers of today find themselves struggling with two competing paradigms in regard to child custody. Goldstein, Freud and Solnit (1973, 1979) proffer the notion that children need only one psychological parent following divorce; this parent (usually the mother) should make all the decisions on behalf of the best interest of the children. Contrariwise, joint custody and co-parenting is being promoted by a lot of other organizations, especially men's activist groups. So at a time when men in general and in specific are struggling for new identity and roles, they are not only experiencing difficulty in obtaining sole or joint custody, but also in deciding whether or not it is in their children's best interest.

Once fathers do receive custody, they report many problems, some of which are common to single parenthood and others which are specific to single fatherhood. For example, 33 percent of the men in Katz's study (1979) reported experiencing behavioral difficulties with custodial children and 69 percent of this group of fathers sought help for these or their own personal problems. In a study conducted by Chang and Deinard (1982) fathers reported their three major difficulties as: restricted chances to date, inability to pursue special employment opportunities, and a dearth of time and energy to spend with the children. Fifty percent of the men from this particular study also reported depression and loneliness; their health status diminished no doubt exacerbated by an increase in drinking and smoking. So there appears to be a decrease in the physical and mental health for both fathers and children alike, especially immediately following the divorce and when fathers first assume lone parenthood.

Other studies suggest that fathers who have custody of female children report difficulties with sex education (Grief, 1982; Bartz, 1978), and other issues related to femininity such as clothing and hairstyles. Men experience stress about leaving children at home alone between the time school is out and the time they themselves get home from work; this is an especially difficult issue when the children are too old to have "babysitters" but too young to stay alone for that length of time. Since most fathers still feel it is better for children to have two parents, they express concern about having to make decisions all by themselves in regard to the children. They would prefer to share decision making with someone else and commonly turn to their women friends for advice and council. Finally, single custodial fathers express the wish that they could spend more quality time with their children. Due to role overload from housekeeping, child care and job responsibilities, they find they do not have much time to be as involved in their children's world as they would like. They report having to make special attempts at keeping in touch with the emotional and psychological dimensions of childhood and sometimes have to force themselves to display physical affection toward the children—new behaviors in their repertoire since the divorce.

Future Directions

Times are changing and single fatherhood will change accordingly. More and more men are obtaining custody of children by choice or default. More courts are awarding either sole custody to men or designating joint custody arrangements. More attorneys are willing to support men who want to pursue a custody dispute in court. The incidence of contested custody is on the increase; in 1976, men won 10 percent of these cases but in 1982, they won 22 to 50 percent (Chang & Deinard, 1982; Burden, 1982). Too, courts have become more willing to award split custody. That is, as more couples divorce, and both parents are assessed as "fit" parents, several children go to live with one parent while the other children go to the remaining parent. Usually men are awarded the teenage sons and mothers receive the daughters, if not all the children of both sexes. Children are more frequently being asked with which parent they prefer to live. More mothers are choosing to leave the children in father's care as they seek options in the work world.

More people are thinking in terms of separation and divorce as a normal developmental stage in the lives of people rather than deviant behavior. Subsequently more support systems are evolving in communities and parents and children are taking advantage of them. Where single fathers used to come from higher socioeconomic classes, more and more men from the middle class are obtaining custody. Also, more men are receiving custody of younger children as well as female children.

It is not known whether or not these trends will continue but there seems to be little doubt that fathers of all kinds will increase their active involvement with children. With the progressive movement toward egalitarian roles in our society, with continued if not increasing rates of divorce, and with most women seeking opportunities outside the home, child care by all fathers as well as single custodial fathers is bound to change. In the future, the role of single custodial fathers will become more solidified, non-custodial fathers will find ways to remain potent in the lives of their children, and fathers in dual earner and traditional nuclear families will play a more active part in parenting children of all ages. The men who pioneered the role of single custodial fathers in this century have served as a prototype for the potential relationship that all fathers can enjoy with their children.

REFERENCES

Abarbanel, A. (1979). Shared parenting after separation and divorce. *American Journal of Orthopsychiatry, 49*, 320–329.

Albin, R. (1977). New looks at single parenting: Focus on fathers. *American Psychological Association Monitor, 8*, 7–8.

Aldous, J., & Dumond, W. (1980). *The politics and programs of family policy.* Notre Dame, IN: University of Notre Dame press.

Ambert, A. M. (1982). Differences in children's behavior toward custodial mothers and custodial fathers. *Journal of Marriage and the Family, 44*, 73–86.

Appleton, W. S. (1981). *Fathers and daughters.* Garden City, NY: Doubleday and Company, Inc.

Atkin, E., & Rubin, E. (1976). *Part-time father: A guide for the divorced father.* New York: The Vanguard Press, Inc.

Bain, C. (1973). Lone fathers: An unnoticed group. *Australian Social Welfare, 3*, 14–17.

Bane, M. J. (1976). Marital disruption and the lives of children. *Journal of Social Issues, 32*, 103–117.

Bartz, K. W., & Witcher, W. C. (1978). When father gets custody. *Children Today, 7*, 2–6.

Benson, L. (1968). *Fatherhood: A sociological perspective.* New York: Random House.

Biller, H. B. (1974). *Paternal deprivation: Family, school, sexuality and society.* Lexington, MA: D. C. Heath and Company.

Bird, R. (1975). Life with father. *Parents Without Partners, 18*, 18–20.

Bittman, S., & Rosenberg, S. (1978). *Expectant fathers.* New York: Ballantine Books.

Blechman, E. (1982). Are children with one parent at psychological risk? A methodological review. *Journal of Marriage and the Family, 44*, 179–195.

Boss, P. G. (Ed.). (1979, June). *The father's role in family systems: An annotated bibliography.* Madison, WI: University of Wisconsin.

Bozett, F. W., & Hanson, S. M. H. (1985). Perspectives of fatherhood. *American Behavioral Scientist, 28*(6).

Bradley, R. A. (1981). *Husband-coached childbirth.* New York: Harper and Row Publishers.

Brandwein, R. A., Brown, C. A., & Fox, E. M. (1974). Women and children last: The social situation of divorced mothers and their families. *Journal of Marriage and the Family, 36,* 498–514.

Burden, D. (1982). *Parental custody after divorce.* Unpublished manuscript, Brandeis University, The Florence Heller Graduate School for Advanced Studies in Social Welfare, Waltham.

Burden, D. (1979, August). *The single parent family: Social policy issues.* Paper presented at the annual meeting of the American Sociological Association, Boston.

Burgess-Kohn, J. (1976). *The fathers adjustment as a single parent.* Unpublished manuscript, University of Wisconsin, Department of Sociology, Waukesha, Wisconsin.

Cath, S. H., Gurwitt, A. R., & Ross, J. M. (Eds.). (1982). *Father and child: Developmental and clinical perspectives.* Boston: Little, Brown and Co.

Chang, P., & Deinard, A. (1982). Single father caretakers: Demographic characteristics and adjustment process. *American Journal of Orthopsychiatry, 52,* 236–243.

Colman, A., & Colman, L. (1981). *Earth father, sky father.* Englewood Cliffs, NJ: Prentice-Hall.

Cook, J. A. (1980). Joint custody, sole custody: A new statute reflects a new perspective. *Conciliation Courts Review, 18,* 1–14.

Daley, E. (1977). *Father feelings.* New York: Pocket Books.

Defrain, J., & Eirick, R. (1981). Coping as divorced parents: A comparative study of fathers and mothers. *Family Relations, 30,* 265–274.

Dempsey, J. J. (1981). *The family and public policy.* Baltimore, MD: Paul H. Brookes Publishing Co.

Dodson, F. (1975). *How to father.* New York: Signet Books.

Espenshade, T. J. (1979). The economic consequences of divorce. *The Journal of Marriage and the Family, 41,* 615–627.

Field, T. (1978). Interaction behaviors of primary versus secondary caretaker fathers. *Developmental Psychology, 14,* 183–184.

Fricke, J. M. (1982). *Coping as divorced fathers and mothers: A nationwide study of sole, joint, and split custody.* Unpublished master's thesis, University of Nebraska.

Gasser, R. D., & Taylor, C. M. (1976). Role adjustment of single fathers with dependent children. *The Family Coordinator, 25,* 397–401.

Gatley, R. H., & Koulack, D. (1979). *Single father's handbook: A guide for separated and divorced fathers.* Garden City, NY: Anchor Books.

George, V., & Wilding, P. (1972). *Motherless families.* London: Routledge and Kegan Paul.

Gersick, K. E. (1979). Fathers by choice: Divorced men who receive custody of their children. In G. Levinger & O. Noles (Eds.), *Separation and divorce.* New York: Basic Books, Inc.

Glick, P. (1975). A demographer looks at American families. *Journal of Marriage and the Family, 37,* 15–26.

Glick, P. (1979). Children of divorced parents in demographic perspective. *Journal of Social Issues, 35* 170–182.

Goldstein, J., Freud, A., & Solnit, A. J. (1973). *Beyond the best interests of the child.* New York: The Free Press.

Goldstein, J., Freud, A., & Solnit, A. J. (1979). *Before the best interests of the child.* New York: The Free Press.

Grad, R., & et al. (1981). *The father book: Pregnancy and beyond.* Washington, D.C.: Acropolis Books, Ltd.

Grady, K. E., Brannon, R., & Pleck, J. H. (1979). *The male sex role: A selected and annotated bibliography* (Superintendent of Documents, No. 79–790). Washington, D.C.: U.S. Department of Health, Education, and Welfare.

Green, M. (1977). *Fathering.* St. Louis: McGraw-Hill.

Greene, R. S. (1977). *Atypical parenting: Custodial single fathers.* Unpublished doctoral dissertation, University of Maryland.

Gresh, S. (1980). *Becoming a father*. New York: Butterick Publishing.

Grief, G. L. (1982). Dads raising kids. *Single Parent, 25*, 19–23.

Grief, J. B. (1979). Fathers, children and joint custody. *American Journal of Orthopsychiatry, 49*, 311–319.

Halverson, L. (1982). The joint custody alternative. *Washington State Bar News*, 12–17.

Hamilton, M. L. (1977). *Father's influence on children*. Chicago: Nelson-Hall.

Hanson, S. M. H. (1980). Characteristics of single custodial fathers and the parent-child relationship (Doctoral dissertation, University of Washington, 1979). *Dissertation Abstracts Index, 40*, 6438-A.

Hanson, S. M. H. (1981). Single custodial fathers and the parent-child relationship. *Nursing Research, 30*, 202–204.

Hanson, S. M. H. (1985). Single fathers with custody: A synthesis of the literature. In B. Schlesinger (Ed.), *The one-parent family*. Toronto, Canada: University of Toronto Press.

Hanson, S. M. H. (1985). Parent-child relationships in single father families. In R. Lewis & R. Salt (Eds.), *Men in families*. Beverly Hills: Sage.

Hanson, S. M. H. (1985). Fatherhood: Contextual variations. *American Behavioral Scientist, 28*(6).

Herzog, E., & Sudia, C. E. (1971). *Boys in fatherless families*. Washington, D.C.: U.S. Government Printing Office.

Hetherington, E. M., Cox, M., & Cox, R. (1977). The aftermath of divorce. In J. H. Stevens, Jr., & Marilyn, M. (Eds.), *Mother-child, father-child relations*. Washington, D.C.: NAEYC.

Hetherington, E. M., Cox, M., & Cox, R. (1976). Divorced fathers. *The Family Coordinator, 25*, 417–428.

Hetherington, E. M., Cox, M., & Cox, R. (1977, April). Divorced fathers. *Psychology Today, 42*, 45–46.

Hetherington, E. M. (1971). The effects of father absence on child development. *Young Children, 27*, 233–248.

Jenkins, S. (1978). Children of divorce. *Children Today*, 7(2), 16–21.

Kahan, S. (1978). *The expectant father's survival kit*. New York: Monarch.

Kamerman, S., & Kahn, A. (Eds.). (1981). *Child care, family benefits, and working parents*. New York: Columbia University Press.

Kamerman, S., & Kahn, A. (Eds.). (1978). *Family policy: Government and families in fourteen countries*. New York: Columbia University Press.

Katz, A. J. (1979). Lone fathers: Perspectives and implications for family policy. *The Family Coordinator, 28*, 521–527.

Kelly, J., & Wallerstein, J. (1976). The effects of parental divorce: Experiences of the child in early latency. *American Journal of Orthopsychiatry, 46*, 20–32.

Kelly, J. (1980). Myths and realities for children of divorce. *Educational Horizons, 59*, 34–39.

Keshet, H. F., & Rosenthal, K. M. (1978). Single-parent fathers: A new study. *Children Today*, 7, 13–17.

Keshet, H. F., & Rosenthal, K. M. (1978). Fathering after marital separation. *Social Work, 23*, 11–18.

Kohn, J. B., & Kohn, W. K. (1978). *The widower*. Boston: Beacon Press.

Lamb, M. E. (Ed.). (1981). *The role of the father in child development*. New York: John Wiley and Sons, Inc.

Lamb, M. E. (Ed.). (1982). *Nontraditional families: Parenting and child development*. Hillsdale, NJ: Lawrence Eribaum Associates, Publishers.

Lamb, M., & Bronson, S. K. (1980). Fathers in the context of family influences: Past, present and future. *School Psychology Review, 9*, 336–353.

Lamb, M. E., & Sagi, A. (Eds.). (1983). *Fatherhood and family policy*. Hillsdale, NJ: Lawrence Eribaum Associates, Publishers.

Levine, J. A. (1976). *Who will raise the children?* New York: Bantam Books.

Lewis, K. (1978). Single-father families: Who they are and how they fare. *Child Welfare*, *57*, 643–651.

Lewis, K. (1978). *Single father families*. Unpublished paper (Single Fathers Research Project, P.O. Box 3300), New Haven, CT.

Lewis, R. A. (1981). *Men in difficult times*. Englewood Cliffs, NJ: Prentice-Hall.

Lockerbie, D. B. (1981). *Fatherlove*. Garden City, NY: Doubleday and Co.

Loge, B. J. (1976). *Role adjustments to single parenthood: A study of divorced and widowed men and women*. Unpublished doctoral dissertation, University of Washington.

Lynn, D. B. (1979). *Daughters and parents: Past, present, and future*. Monterey, CA: Brooks/Cole Publishing Company.

McDonald, G., & Nye, F. I. (1979). *Family policy*. Minneapolis: National Council of Family Relations.

McFadden, M. (1974). *Bachelor fatherhood: How to raise and enjoy your children as a single parent*. New York: Charter Communications.

Marriage and Divorce Today Editorial. (1983). Majority of absent fathers don't pay support. *Marriage and Divorce Today*, *8*(47), 1.

Masnick, G., & Bane, M. J. (1980). *The nation's families: 1960–1990*. Boston: Auburn House.

Mendes, H. A. (1975). *Parental experiences of single fathers*. Unpublished doctoral dissertation, University of California, Los Angeles.

Mendes, H. A. (1976). Single fatherhood. *Social Work*, *21*, 308–312.

Mendes, H. A. (1976). Single fathers. *The Family Coordinator*, *25*, 439–444.

Metcalf, A. (1980). *Social networks in families headed by a single working mother*. Unpublished manuscript, University of Washington, School of Social Work, Seattle, Washington.

Mitchell, M., Redican, W. K., & Gomber, J. (1974). Males can raise babies. *Psychology Today*, *8*, 63–68.

National Association of Elementary School Principles (NAESP). (1980). One parent families and their children: The school's most significant minority. *Principal*, *60*, 31–42.

Nuta, V. R. (1981). Single parent children in school—What can you expect? *Single Parent*, *14*, 21–25.

Orthner, D., Brown, T., & Ferguson, D. (1976). Single-parent fatherhood: An emerging family life style. *The Family Coordinator*, *25*, 429–437.

Orthner, D., & Lewis, K. (1979). Evidence of single father competence in child rearing. *Family Law Quarterly*, *8*, 27–48.

Parke, R. D. (1981). *Fathers*. Cambridge, MA: Harvard University Press.

Pearson, J., Munson, P., & Thoennes, N. (1982). Legal change and child custody awards. *Journal of Family Issues*, *3*, 5–24.

Pedersen, F. A. (1980). *The father-infant relationship*. New York: Praeger Publishers.

Phillips, C. R., & Anzalone, J. T. (1982). *Fathering: Participation in labor and birth*. St. Louis: C. V. Mosby Company.

Ricci, I. (1980). *Mom's house, dad's house: Making shared custody work*. New York: MacMillan Publishing Company.

Richmond-Abbott, M. (1980). *Sex roles in single-parent families*. Unpublished manuscript, Eastern Michigan University, Ypsilanti, Michigan.

Roman, M., & Haddad, W. (1978). *The disposable parent: The case for joint custody*. New York: Holt, Rinehart and Winston.

Rosenthal, K. M., & Keshet, H. F. (1981). *Fathers without partners: A study of fathers and the family after marital separation*. Totowa, NJ: Rowman and Littlefield.

Rosenthal, K., & Keshet, H. (1978). The impact of childcare responsibilities on part-time or single fathers. *Alternative Lifestyles*, *1*, 465–491.

Rypma, C. (1976). Biological bases of the paternal response. *The Family Coordinator*, *25*, 335–339.

Santrock, J. W., & Warshak, R. (1979). Father custody and social development in boys and girls. *The Journal of Social Issues, 35*, 112–125.

Santrock, J. W., Warshak, R. A., & Elliot, G. L. (1982). Social development and parent-child interaction in father-custody and stepmother families. In M. E. Lamb (Ed.), *Nontraditional families: Parenting and child development*. Hillsdale, NJ: Lawrence Eribaum Associates, Publishers.

Schlesinger, B. (1974). *One-parent families in Canada*. Toronto: University of Toronto.

Schlesinger, B. (1977). One parent families in Great Britain. *The Family Coordinator, 26*, 139–141.

Schlesinger, B. (1985). *The one-parent family*. Toronto, Canada: University of Toronto Press.

Schlesinger, B. (1978). Single parent: A research review. *Children Today, 7*, 12–19, 37–39.

Schlesinger, B., & Todres, R. (1976). Motherless families: An increasing societal pattern. *Child Welfare, 55*, 553–558.

Schorr, A., & Moen, P. (1980). The single parent and public policy. In A. Skolnick & J. Skolnick (Eds.), *Family in transition*. Boston: Little, Brown and Company.

Schorr, A., & Moen, P. (1979). The single parent and public policy. *Social Policy, 9*, 15–21.

Seagull, A. A., & Seagull, E. A. W. (1977). The non-custodial father's relationship to his child: Conflicts and solutions. *Journal of Clinical Child Psychology, 1*, 11–15.

Shepard, M. A., & Goldman, G. (1979). *Divorced dads*. New York: Berkeley Books.

Sifford, D. (1982). *Father and son*. Philadelphia: Bridgebooks.

Silver, G. A., & Silver, M. (1981). *Weekend fathers*. Los Angeles: Stratford Press.

Smith, M. J. (1980). The social consequences of single parenthood: A longitudinal perspective. *Family Relations, 29*, 75–81.

Smith, R. M. (1978, October). *Single-parent fathers: An application of role transition theory*. Paper presented at the annual meeting of the National Council on Family Relations, Philadelphia.

Smith, R. M., & Smith, C. W. (1981). Child rearing and single-parent fathers. *Family Relations, 30*, 411–417.

Steinberg, D. (1977). *Father journal*. Albion, CA: Times Change Press.

Stevens, J. H., & Mathews, M. (Eds.). (1978). *Mother/child father/child relationships*. Washington, D.C.: The National Association for the Education of Young Children.

Sullivan, S. A. (1980). *The father's almanac*. Garden City, NY: Doubleday and Company.

Thompson, E. H., & Gongla, P. A. (1983). Single-parent families: In the mainstream of American society. In E. D. Macklin & R. H. Rubin (Eds.), *Contemporary families and alternative lifestyles*. Beverly Hills, CA: Sage Publications.

Todres, R. (1978). Runaway wives: An increasing North-American phenomenon. *The Family Coordinator, 27*, 17–21.

U.S. Bureau of the Census. (1980). *Marital status and living arrangements: March 1980* (Current Population Reports, Series P-20, No. 365). Washington, D.C.: U.S. Government Printing Office.

U.S. Bureau of the Census. (1980). *Child support and alimony: 1978* (Current Population Reports, Series P-23, No. 106). Washington, D.C.: U.S. Government Printing Office.

U.S. Bureau of the Census. (1984). *Statistical abstract of the United States*. Washington, D.C.: U.S. Government Printing Office.

U.S. Bureau of the Census. (1985). *Household and family characteristics: March, 1984* (Current Population Reports, Series P-20, No. 487). Washington, D.C.: U.S. Government Printing Office.

U.S. Bureau of the Census. (1982). *Marital status and living arrangements: March 1981* (Current Population Reports, Series P-20, No. 372). Washington, D.C.: U.S. Government Printing Office.

Victor, I., & Winkler, W. A. (1977). *Fathers and custody*. New York: Hawthorn Books, Inc.

Wallerstein, J., & Kelly, J. (1980). California's children of divorce. *Psychology Today, 13*(8), 57–65.

Wallerstein, J., & Kelly, J. (1979). Divorce and children. In J. D. Noshpitz (Ed.), *Basic handbook of child psychiatry*. New York: Basic Books.

Wallerstein, J., & Kelly, J. The effects of parental divorce: Experiences of the child in later latency. *American Journal of Orthopsychiatry, 46,* 256–269.

Wallerstein, J., & Kelly, J. (1975). The effects of parental divorce: Experiences of the preschool child. *Journal of American Academy of Child Psychiatry, 14,* 600-616.

Wallerstein, J., & Kelly, J. (1980). *Surviving the breakup.* New York: Basic Books.

Washington Chapter of U.S. Divorce Reform. (1978). *What you always wanted to know about divorce but were afraid to ask: A guide to divorce for the man (or woman) seeking child custody in a divorce or who wishes to have a joint custody arrangement* (P.O. Box 11). Auburn, Washington.

Weiss, R. S. (1979). Growing up a little faster: The experience of growing up in a single parent household. *Journal of Social Issues, 35*(4), 97–111.

Woody, R. H. (1978). Fathers with child custody. *Counseling Psychologists, 7,* 60–63.

Yablonsky, L. (1982). *Fathers and sons.* New York: Simon and Schuster.

Zimmerman, S. L. (1979). Policy, social policy, and family policy: Concepts, concerns, and analytic tools. *Journal of Marriage and the Family, 41,* 487–497.

Chapter 11

Men Caring for the Young: A Profile

Bryan E. Robinson

Deep in the heart of the Snow Bird Mountains of North Carolina, I was having lunch in a rustic mountaineer restaurant. On my placemat, surrounded by pictures of fish, fowl, and game, loomed a mountaineer "totin" a gun and draggin' his wife and child behind him—one in each hand!

Like the mountaineer on the placemat, men have often been pictured as the brute, the aggressor, and as being big, rugged, and independent. Traditionally, men were expected to be emotionally objective and to withhold feelings of tenderness, warmth, sensitivity, and nurturance. During the 1940s, for example, it was unheard of, even taboo, for men to work in nurturing situations with young children. As one educator put it: "One could hardly imagine a situation in which a man would be in his element teaching a class of kindergarteners. He would immediately become suspect" (Tubbs, 1946, p. 394). Another educator said: "Men should not be asked to play nursemaid to young children . . . No man should be assigned to teach children below the fifth grade level" (Kaplan, 1947, p. 368).

Decade by decade, views on the role and status of men in nurturing roles changed as society redefined its views on masculinity and femininity (Robinson, 1981a). As men and women crossed sex-role barriers and adopted nontraditional jobs and behaviors, both men and women were freed from previous sex-role constraints.

Bryan E. Robinson, PhD, is Associate Professor, Department of Human Services, College of Education and Allied Professions, The University of North Carolina at Charlotte, NC 28223.

SOME STATISTICS

Paralleling the loosening of gender-based sex roles, more male caregivers are on the scene, although the numbers remain quite low. In 1974, for example, male child care workers comprised only 4 percent of the total number of workers in this nation ("Drive to Open Up," 1974). And among the 1,170,000 elementary school teachers in the United States in 1979, only 15 percent were men (Phillips, 1979).

Nevertheless, male caregivers have become well organized. They have established the National Men's Child Care Caucus and founded a quarterly journal—*The Nurturant Male*—dedicated to increasing male involvement in the lives of young children on all levels in the home and on the job. More significantly, has been the founding of The Nurtury—a predominantly male-staffed child care center serving a population of single-parent children. Founded by Steve Brody in Sherman Oaks, California, The Nurtury's aim is to give consistent nurturing relationships with men for children from homes without fathers (Brody, 1978).

CONTRIBUTIONS OF MALE CAREGIVERS

Because of the low numbers of men in nurturing roles, the literature is full of impassioned pleas for their recruitment. Their presence is viewed as a panacea to provide a "masculine" balance in the child's so-called "feminized" world of predominantly women-staffed child care centers, increasing single-mother families, and greater numbers of families where both parents work. Educators claim that male caregivers prevent children from viewing school as a feminine environment (Kendall, 1972), improve school performance for boys (Smith, 1970), counteract urbanization and family disintegration problems (Johnston, 1970), provide masculine role models for boys (Sciarra, 1972), and prevent juvenile delinquency (Vairo, 1969). This rationale assumes, implicitly or explicitly, that men caregivers are like men in other roles, yet different enough from their female coworkers to make a significant difference. But research indicates that the very opposite is true. Men in nurturing roles are unique from men in other jobs and more similar to women in these same jobs. Ironically, it is these respective differences and similarities that make male caregivers valuable in the lives of young children.

Most of the claims that depict the male caregiver as the all-powerful miracle worker are based on subjective impressions of the writers and have little or no basis in fact (Gold & Reis, 1982; Robinson & Hobson, 1979). From reading these anecdotal reports, one surmises that male caregivers are valued solely for their macho presence and that any male figure would be satisfactory (Robinson, 1979b). Despite attempts on behalf of men in many quarters to minimize their masculine influence, this advantage continues to be the most cited benefit for employing men as child nurturers (Robinson, 1982).

This belief has also been perpetuated by early research during the 1970s that suffered from methodological shortcomings (Robinson, 1984). When researchers first addressed this question, they used inexperienced male students (Etaugh, Collins, & Gerson, 1975; McCandless & Bush, 1976), businessmen volunteers (Sciarra, 1970), and summer camp counselors (Alfgren, Aries, & Olver, 1979) as subjects in their studies due to difficulty in locating male child care workers. Generally, these studies concluded that the presence of men in child care has a masculinizing influence on children's sex-role development. These studies were criticized because the subjects were not full-time teachers and were not representative of men employed as preschool teachers (Robinson, 1979b). In most instances, the subjects had no intention of ever assuming a job in a female-dominated work world. They were part-time, were given less responsibility than the full-time female teachers, and did not have a voice in daily or long-term decision and policy making. In fact, investigators of one study admitted that children recognized the difference in status between the male and female teachers and perceived the females as their "real" teachers (McCandless & Bush, 1976).

In contrast, men who choose to become full-time caregivers have full responsibility for the children and actively participate in decisions concerning children's welfare and policies affecting the classroom. In addition, the fact that these men self-select their roles for their livelihood or perhaps for other reasons makes them different from students or volunteers participating solely for research purposes and from the macho male who prefers loading trucks or driving forklifts. At least two major differences have been identified from the research on men gainfully employed in nurturing roles: their motivations for entering their jobs and their personality traits.

First, when asked why they entered the child care ranks, full-time employed male caregivers do not give the same reasons as men in traditionally masculine jobs. Instead of money, prestige, or power, male caregivers said they selected their jobs because of altruistic concerns. They cited such reasons as love and enjoyment of working with children, appeal to the content of the day care program and curriculum, and desire to make a valuable contribution to this age group (Robinson & Canaday, 1977).

Second, Robinson and Canaday (1978) studied the personality traits of men actively employed as child care workers and found some interesting results. Twenty men (with an average of 2.7 years experience) were randomly selected from certified child care centers in one state. A group of 20 female caregivers was matched with the men by child care center, age, and education. And a third group of 20 men from the engineering field (99% of which is male-dominated) was matched with male caregivers on age and education. The overall personality traits of the male caregivers were similar to those of the women. The engineers had the most "masculine" personalities. The women had the most "feminine" personalities. And the male caregivers fell in between these two groups, but came closer to the profiles of the women. Moreover, both men and women rewarded children more for "feminine" behaviors than "masculine" behaviors and punished "masculine" behaviors more often than "feminine" behaviors.

Fagot (1977) also studied the sex-role behaviors of 20 male and 20 female caregivers. Ten teachers of each sex had formal training in a teaching program for young children and had three years teaching experience. Ten teachers of each sex also had no college training to work with children and had less than three years teaching experience. Inexperienced teachers of both sexes reinforced sex-stereotyped behaviors in both sexes of children. But experienced teachers of both sexes rewarded feminine behaviors more often than masculine behaviors in boys and girls. Fagot concluded that level of experience accounted more for sex-stereotyped treatment of children than did sex of teacher. This conclusion might also explain the sex-stereotyping of inexperienced male subjects in earlier studies.

Why did experienced men in these two studies encourage more feminine than masculine behaviors for children? One explanation for these findings is that many male caregivers do not view their role as strictly providing a male image for children. In the Robinson and Canaday study, male caregivers reported that it is equally important to break down stereotypes and to offer children another way of looking at men. They felt it necessary for children to see men in nurturant, warm, and intimate roles—roles traditionally assigned to women in our society. In Seifert's (1973) words, "The male's special contribution would consist not in 'acting like a man' for the children, but in disproving the idea that men need act in some special manly way" (p. 167).

Another explanation might be that males attracted to the care of children tend to be more nurturant, less aggressive, and noncompetitive types. So they allow these same behaviors to be expressed in children, while discouraging behaviors which counter these. Indeed, a conscious awareness of sexism led to deliberate attempts to combat sex-role stereotypes by some men. For example, one man said he sometimes deliberately guided girls into the block and truck play areas and boys into the housekeeping corner. So one might expect that male caregivers are making valuable contributions by modeling and rewarding traditionally feminine qualities as well as masculine ones.

A reasonable conclusion from these results is that male caregivers possess some "feminine" traits—perhaps more so than men in other job types. That's because work with young children requires both a male and female (or androgynous) orientation. Male caregivers are expected to be sensitive to young children's needs, but also to be assertive and show initiative where situations demand such a stance. Some children need help in learning to become toilet trained, while others just need to be held. Children need caregivers—men and women—who can be nurturant and warm, which historically carry "feminine" labels. According to the research of Sandra Bem and her associates, these are tasks which a highly masculine male would either feel uncomfortable about performing or be incapable of carrying out (Bem, 1975; Bem & Lenney, 1976). So, by definition, the successful male caregiver must possess some feminine traits which enable him to more comfortably perform the task of caring for young ones.

Several reviews of the literature examining the effects of male and female caregivers conclude that there are few differences that are significant and important (Brophy & Good, 1974; Gold & Reis, 1982; Robinson, Skeen, & Flake-Hobson, 1980a; Robinson, 1983). Compared to women, for example, men touch boys more often

(Perdue & Connor, 1978; Robinson, 1981b); give children more physical affection, make more favorable comments towards children, join in their play more often (Fagot, 1981; Perdue & Connor, 1978; Robinson, 1981b); and have a higher rate of job turnover (Robinson, 1979a). In general though, research on male caregivers shows that they are more similar than different from their female counterparts on a number of other significant factors: attitudes toward their work (Wright, 1977); attitudes toward children (Etaugh & Hughes, 1975; Good & Grouws, 1972; Robinson, Skeen, & Flake-Hobson, 1980b); personality traits (Biedenkapp & Goering, 1971; Robinson & Canaday, 1978); and sex-role behaviors toward children (Fagot, 1978; Robinson & Canaday, 1978; Whitney, 1981).

PROBLEMS OF ACCEPTANCE

Although similarities between men and women caregivers outweigh the differences, some factions continue to view the male caregiver as savior of children from their plight of skyrocketing family disintegration and father absence. In some instances, a halo effect for men preschool teachers has been reported by their colleagues. When a man nursery school teacher was on a teaching team, both teachers were more apt to rate boys and girls more favorably than when children were taught strictly by female teachers (Gold, Reis & Berger, 1979). But another faction suspiciously holds men at bay and views them as aliens invading foreign turf. Such contradictory messages have placed these men in a double bind and raised a major question for researchers and practitioners: " How far have men actually progressed in being accepted in nurturing roles?" One would expect that as gender roles loosened over the years, outmoded attitudes fell by the wayside. But James Levine (1977) contends that stereotyped notions and suspicions about male preschool teachers have lingered, partly because we are not socialized toward thinking of child care as a man's activity. And Seifert (1974) argues that the most important fact about men in nurturing roles with young children is the extent to which their work contradicts sex role conventions.

Generally, research has shown that when men or women cross sex-role lines and enter jobs of the opposite sex, they receive less acceptance (Simpson, 1974; Suchner and More, 1975). For example, studies surveying attitudes toward such nurturing roles as male nurse indicate sex bias towards men in these roles (Hesselbart, 1977; Lynn, Vaden and Vaden, 1975). Similar attitudes have been reported toward men in preschool settings. According to self-reports by men in these environments, stereotyped attitudes are shared by many of their colleagues and administrators. In a commentary on his thoughts on being a male caregiver, Sherman (1979) wrote that his most difficult problems were training to be a teacher, working mostly with women, and working in a profession shaped by women. A group of male adolescents placed in child care centers for research purposes, reported feeling awkward and less "masculine" when taking directions from female caregivers and said they had no intention of pursuing a profession in a female-dominated field (McCandless & Bush, 1976).

Other studies have reported some type of on-the-job difficulty based on sex-role conflict between the male minority and the female majority. In a two-year follow-up study of a group of male and female caregivers, 60 percent of the men reported experiencing conflict on their jobs because of their "maleness" (Robinson, 1979a). One man said he got all the "dirty work" at first because the women did not like men working with young children. He felt he posed a threat to the women because of possibilities of upward mobility. Another male respondent said he sometimes felt in the minority because there were things women would share among themselves that they would not share with him.

Three men reported that their women peers thought they, as women, were better equipped by nature to handle young children. Other men claimed that because they had never been mothers, their female coworkers felt they could not make accurate judgements concerning discipline, the health of children, approaches to teaching, supervising children and other traditionally "feminine" roles. Two other male respondents related conflicts between them and their female administrators because of what they believed to be a sense of threat on the part of the women because of their maleness. Although 100 percent of the men interviewed said they would encourage men to pursue jobs in childhood education, some of the women (11 percent) admitted they felt it was not the place for men—that men are out of their element.

These attitudes were based on the self-reports of a nonrepresentative sample of men and women or on the personal impressions of the writers. Other interviews of women preschool teachers revealed that women could not accept their male coworkers because they were engaged in a woman's job (Milgram & Sciarra, 1974). But these interviews were casual and nonscientific and neither the number of women interviewed nor the design and procedures of the interview process were reported. Do these isolated instances of suspicion and prejudice represent the extent of the problem? Or have generalizations been made on the basis of hearsay and a handful of experiences?

Until recently, no scientific attempt had been made to examine these allegations. But a recent poll of 141 college math students revealed that men child care nurturers were viewed as less competent than women and a day care program run by a woman was consistently rated better by males and females even though it did not differ from the one run by a man (Gordon and Draper, 1982).

Contrasting evidence indicates that men and women in the profession of childhood education hold similar views about the capability and role of men preschool teachers (Robinson, 1982). A national survey of 475 professionals, mostly classroom teachers and administrators disagreed with the popular notion that women are better suited by nature to work with preschool children or that women have greater sensitivity and ability to nurture children.

These data suggest that the extent of sex bias towards men caring for the young depends upon the age, years of experience, and amount of formal training of the respondent. High school and college students outside the field of child care are more likely to hold negative views (Gordon & Draper, 1982; McCandless & Bush, 1976). But more experienced practitioners in the field (average work experience 9.2 years) are less biased in their attitudes (Robinson, 1982). Statistically, in fact, the older the professionals and the more formal training they receive, the less likely they are to hold stereotyped views toward men in nurturing roles (Robinson, 1982). Additional research by Fagot (1977, 1978) also suggests that years of experience and amount of college training are also factors in the degree to which preschool teachers employed sex stereotypes with preschool children.

CONCLUSION

Despite earlier prohibitions of men in jobs with young children, campaigns for their recruitment have spiraled over the years. The man of the 80's is quite different from the man of the 40's. Over the past four decades, our society has redefined what is meant by masculinity and femininity. Both men and women have crossed sex-role barriers and adopted nontraditional jobs and behaviors. This has liberated women and freed men as well. Increased awareness of the importance of fathers in the rearing of children is an encouraging sign (Robinson & Barret, 1985). "Kramer versus Kramer," the critically acclaimed film, clearly demonstrated that when contemporary man is placed into a traditional female role, he can competently cope.

Although recent research indicates that male caregivers are unique and make very special and essential contributions in the lives of the children they touch, stereotyped notions and suspicions have lingered, partly because we are not socialized toward thinking of childrearing as a man's activity. As more men enter the child care field, researchers and practitioners have made awkward and conflicting attempts to explain and justify the presence of men whose lives take meaning from the nurturance of young children. As Levine (1979) suggests, this is perhaps a necessary step before our society can progress in its views of men in these roles:

> It's probably inevitable that we go through this phase of explanation—and a long one it no doubt will be. But at bottom, I suspect, we are simply trying clumsily—with our labels and reasons and scientific concepts and tests and measures—to say straight out something that sounds too simple, too unimportant, perhaps even too obvious: *For men as for women it is part of being human to care for our young.* (p. 15)

REFERENCES

Alfgren, S.H.; Aries, E.J.; and Oliver, R.R. (1979). Sex differences in the interaction of adults and preschool children. *Psychological Reports*, *44*, 115–118.

Bem, S.L. (1975). Sex-role adaptability: One consequence of psychological androgyny. *Journal of Personality and Social Psychology*, *31*, 634–643.

Bem, S.L., and Lenney, E. (1976). Sex typing and the avoidance of cross-sex behavior. *Journal of personality and social psychology*, *33*, 48–54.

Biedenkapp, M.S., and Goering, J.D. (1971). How "masculine" are male elementary teachers? *Phi Delta Kappan*, *53*, 115–117.

Brody, S. (1978). Daddy's gone to Colorado: Male-staffed child care for father-absent boys. *The Counseling Psychologist*, *7*, 33–36.

Brophy, J.E., and Good, T.L. (1974). *Teacher-student relationships: Causes and consequences.* New York: Holt, Rinehart, & Winston.

Drive to open up more careers for women. (1971). *U. S. News and World Report*, January 14, *76*, 69–70.

Etaugh, C.; Collins, G.; and Gerson, A. (1975). Reinforcement of sex-typed behaviors of two-year-old children in a nursery school setting. *Developmental Psychology, 11*, 255.

Etaugh, C. and Hughes, V. (1975). Teachers' evaluations of sex-typed behaviors in children: The role of teacher sex and school setting. *Developmental Psychology, 11*, 394.

Fagot, B.I. (1977). Preschool sex stereotyping: Effect of sex of teacher vs. training of teacher. Paper presented at the Society for Research in Child Development, New Orleans, Louisiana, March.

Fagot, B.I. (1978). Reinforcing contingencies for sex-role behaviors: Effect of experience with children. *Child Development, 49*, 30–36.

Fagot, B.I. (1981). Male and female teachers: Do they treat boys and girls differently? *Sex Roles, 7*, 263–271.

Gold, D., and Reis, M. (1982). Male teacher effects on young children: A theoretical and empirical consideration. *Sex Roles, 8*, 493–513.

Gold, D.; Reis, M.; and Berger, C. (1979). Male teachers and development of nursery-school children. *Psychological Reports, 44*, 457–458.

Good, T., and Grouws, D. (1972). Reaction of male and female teacher trainees to descriptions of elementary school pupils. (Technical Report No. 62). Center for Research in Social Behavior. Columbia, Missouri.

Gordon, T. and Draper, T.W. (1982). Sex bias against male workers in day care. *Child Care Quarterly, 11*, 215–217.

Hesselbart, S. (1977). Women doctors win and male nurses lose. *Sociology of Work and Occupations, 4*, 49–62.

Johnston, J.M. (1970). A symposium: Men in young children's lives. Part II. *Childhood Education, 47*, 144–147.

Kaplan, L. (1947). The status and function of men teachers in urban elementary schools. Unpublished doctoral dissertation, University of Southern California, Los Angeles.

Kendall, E. (1972). We have men on the staff. *Young Children, 27*, 358–362.

Levine, J.A. (1977). Redefining the child care "problem"—men as child nurturers. *Childhood Education, 54*, 55–61.

Levine, J.A. (1978). "Explaining" about men in early education. *Young Children, 33*, 14–15.

Lynn, N.B., Vaden, A.G., and Vaden, R.E. (1975). The challenges of men in a woman's world. *Public Personnel Management, 4*, 4–17.

McCandless, B.R.; Bush, C.; and Carden, A.I. (1976). Reinforcing contingencies for sex-role behaviors in preschool children. *Contemporary Educational Psychology, 1*, 241–246.

Milgram, J. I., and Sciarra, D.J. (1974). Male preschool teacher: The realities of acceptance. *The Educational Forum, 38*, 245–247.

Perdue, V.P., and Connor, J.M. (1978). Patterns of touching between preschool children and male and female teachers. *Child Development, 49*, 1258–1262.

Phillips, R. (1979). Searching for role models in the classroom. *The Chicago Tribune*, December 16.

Robinson, B.E. (1979a). A two-year followup study of male and female day care teachers. *Child Care Quarterly, 8*, 279–293.

Robinson, B.E. (1979b). Men caring for the young: An androgynous perspective. *The Family Coordinator, 28*, 553–560.

Robinson, B.E. (1981a). Changing views on male early education teachers. *Young Children, 36*, 27–32.

Robinson, B.E. (1981b). Verbal and nonverbal responsiveness of male and female preschool teachers to sex of child and sex-typed child behaviors. *Psychological Reports, 48*, 285–286.

Robinson, B.E. (1982). Professionals' attitudes towards men in early childhood education: A national study. Paper presented at the National Association for the Education of Young Children, Washington, D.C., November.

Robinson, B.E. (1984). Sex-role treatment of children by male preschool and primary teachers: A Decade review, *Child Study Journal*, *14*, 137–156.

Robinson, B.E. and Barret, R.L. (1985). *Fatherhood*. New York: Guilford Press.

Robinson, B.E. and Canaday, H. (1977). The male caregiver: Hero, humanist, and handyman. *Dimensions*, *5*, 113–116.

Robinson, B.E. and Canaday, H. (1978). Sex-role behaviors and personality traits of male day care teachers. *Sex Roles*, *4*, 853–865.

Robinson, B.E. and Hobson, C. (1979). ANDROGYNY: The essential ingredient for male teachers of young children. *Dimensions*, *7*, 49–51.

Robinson, B.E.; Skeen, P.; and Flake-Hobson, C. (1980a). Sex role contributions of male teachers in early childhood settings. *Childhood Education*, *56*, 33–40.

Robinson, B.E.; Skeen, P.; and Flake-Hobson, C. (1980b). Sex-stereotyped attitudes of male and female child care workers: Support for androgynous child care. *Child Care Quarterly*, *9*, 233–242.

Sciarra, D.J. (1970). A study of the effects of male role models on children's behavior in a day care center. Unpublished doctoral dissertation, University of Cincinnati.

Sciarra, D.J. (1972). What to do till the male man comes. *Childhood Education*, *49* 190–191.

Seifert, K. (1973). Some problems of men in child care center work. *Child Welfare*, *52*, 167–171.

Seifert, K. (1974). Getting men to teach preschool. *Contemporary Education*, *45*, 299–304.

Sherman, J.L. (1979). Thoughts on being a male teacher of young children. *The Nurturant Male*, *1*, 2–4.

Simpson, R.L. (1974). Sex stereotypes of secondary school teaching subjects: Male and female status gains and losses. *Sociology of Education*, *47*, 338–398.

Smith, D. (1970). A study of the relationship of teacher sex to fifth grade boys' sex preference, general self-concept, and scholastic achievement in science and mathematics. Unpublished doctoral dissertation, The University of Miami.

Suchner, R.W., and More, D.M. (1975). Stereotypes of males and females in two occupations. *Journal of Vocational Behavior*, *6*, 1–8.

Tubbs, E.V. (1946). More men teachers in our schools. *School and Society*, *63*, 394.

Vairo, P.D. (1969). Wanted: 20,000 male first-grade school teachers. *Education*, *89*, 222–224.

Whitney, M.F. (1981). Behavioral characteristics of male teachers in early childhood education. Unpublished masters thesis. University of California, Davis.

Wright, D. (1977). Attitudes of preschool caregivers toward their work. University of North Dakota: Unpublished doctoral dissertation.

Chapter 12

Friendship Between Men

Michael P. Farrell

INTRODUCTION

Although male friendship has been a central theme in American literature since the beginning of the 19th Century (Fiedler, 1982), it has become a subject of serious research only in the last decade. Prior to that point there were several well-known case studies and much research had been done on the role of friendship in the development of delinquent behavior and responsiveness to innovative ideas. There were points when reviewers reported the "rediscovery" of the primary group in modern society (Verba, 1961), but the systematic attempts to describe and explain the determinants of the properties of male friendship and its impact on personality and behavior have only recently begun.

The research is not yet cumulative, but it has been growing rapidly over the last decade and promises to continue over the 1980's. Several general interest books on friendship have appeared (e.g., Reisman, 1979; Bell, 1980; Duck, 1983). In the United States, Great Britain, Canada, England, and Russia there are several long term research projects in progress. Much of this work has been compiled in a series of four volumes on personal relationships edited by Duck and Gilmour (1981, 1981, 1982, 1982). In addition to research centering on the development and structure of friendships, there has also been an avalanche of studies centering around social support and networks, two subjects directly related to friendship. Until now the research on friendship has been published in a wide variety of journals, making integration and synthesis difficult, but

Michael P. Farrell, PhD, is Associate Professor, Department of Sociology, State University of New York at Buffalo, New York 14261.

the new Journal of Personal Relationships promises to be a central outlet for research in this area in the future.

Male Friendship as a Social Problem

Too often research or theoretical discussions of men's friendship are characterized by an evaluative tone, raising questions about which are better, men's or women's friendships. Perhaps Tiger's (1969) work started the argument with his theory that men are genetically programmed to bond into loyal, altruistic friendships, while women are not. Over the 1970's this position went into retreat, to the point that now men's difficulties with friendships are often viewed as a social problem (e.g., Bell, 1981, p. 92; Lewis, 1978; Pleck, 1975). For the most part male friendships are seen as less intimate than female friendships, and this is seen as detrimental to men's physical and psychological health (Hess, 1981), especially in old age.

This evaluative approach coincides with a tendency to draw stark categorical images of male and female relationships, ignoring the frequent findings of variation of friendship properties within sexes. To advance our theories of friendship it would seem wise to move away from the evaluative, social problems approach and move towards an approach based on propositions about the relationships between variables.

A full-fledged theory of friendship does not yet exist. Instead we are confronted with a wide array of descriptive studies, sometimes guided by an hypothesis or an empirical generalization, but more often interpreted with post-hoc theoretical analysis. The descriptive studies often compare male and female friendships, and the post-hoc analysis usually consists of speculations about how the observed differences can be accounted for by differences in sex role social-ization and development.

In this review we will follow the usual procedure of comparing male and female friendships, simply because comparative analysis of descriptive findings is an effective method for building theory. But throughout the paper we will attempt to stretch beyond description and point towards important determinants of friendship properties.

The objective of this paper is to selectively review the development of the field and the current state of knowledge about male friendship. We will first examine the portrayal of male friendship in literature, briefly highlighting some recurrent themes and archetypes. Then we will look at the current wave of research that has been growing exponentially over the 1970's and 1980's. This latter body of research will be grouped into four sections: (1) the impact of socialization and development on friendship; (2) the impact of social structure on friendship; (3) the developmental processes within friendships, and (4) the consequences of involvement in friendship relationships. In each section we will examine theoretical issues, research findings and methodological issues, briefly pointing to unanswered questions in each domain.

MALE FRIENDSHIPS IN AMERICAN LITERATURE

Beginning with Irving's Rip Van Winkle, and continuing through Cooper's Natty Bumpo and Chinkgachook, Melville's Ishmael and Quequeq, Mark Twain's Huck Finn and Jim, Steinbeck's Lenny and George to Kesey's McMurphy and Chief Broom, the romanticized image of friendship between males has been a central image in American literature. As Fiedler (1982) points out, the themes that recur include male friends, often of different races, moving away from women, the family, and the community into the wilderness (whether that be the forest, the ocean, outer space, or the inner city). The resourcefulness of the men and their loyalty or love for each other is tested and deepened by a series of challenges, often culminating in an act of violence.

This fantasy of male brothers finding fulfillment outside relationships with women and the family pervades American culture.* The theme appears in novels, movies, television serials and comedy, and in the Sunday comics. The sources of its appeal have not yet been uncovered. A systematic analysis of the structure of this fantasy and how it has varied over time may provide some important clues as to the meaning of male friendship in American culture. (See Swidler, 1983, for a recent analysis.)

---

*Recently this theme of rejecting the family and the opposite sex and pursuing adventure and fulfillment with a same-sex partner has become more salient in feminist literature. Brain (1976) claims it is also characteristic of Australian literature in stories about men and their mates.

Properties of Friendship

Although the field has not yet reached consensus about which properties of friendship should ultimately be included in a theory or how they should be measured, we are approaching that point rapidly. By 1970 some generalizations about friendship formation were well established. First, people who are physically near each other are likely to interact more often (Festinger, 1950; Newcomb, 1966; Nahemow and Lawton, 1975). Second, given that they are near each other, people with similar values are likely to be attracted to each other (Newcomb, 1961; Byrne and Nelson, 1965). The similar values finding have usually been explained by balance theory or cognitive consistency theory. Although the values-attraction hypothesis has been verified in field studies as well as experimental studies, sociologists are often critical of its limitations within a general theory of friendship. They point out that most studies testing this hypothesis have been done with undergraduate experimental subjects who are strangers to each other. Such studies may tell us something about initial attraction of people in similar roles, but it is questionable what they tell us about on-going friendship. In addition, although it may be true that similar values lead to attraction, it is also true that interaction alone leads to attraction (Homans, 1950) and to similar values (Newcomb, 1961). Furthermore, a subject often perceives more value similarity than actually exists in a relationship (Werner and Parmelee, 1979). To make things more complicated, while crude Likert scale measures of values and personality traits may be related to friendship in the early stages of acquaintance, at least one researcher has found that these kinds of indicators do not predict established friendships (Duck, 1972). To get around these limitations researchers have turned to field research or laboratory research using on-going friendships.

The properties of friendships chosen for study are usually divided into two types: network properties and relationship properties. The former consists of properties of the web of relationships between a man and two or more of his friends; the latter refers to properties of his relationships to each one of his friends. The relationship properties most often examined include (1) frequency of contact, (2) intimacy, (3) multiplexity or number of roles involved in the relationship, (4) duration, (5) proximity, (6) context of contact. The network properties usually examined include (1) size, (2) density or connectedness, (3) homogeneity of social characteristics.

There is still a lack of consistency in measuring these properties. Even the concept "friend" is notoriously vague. Unlike the concept spouse, there is no institutionalized means for acquiring the status of friend (although there are in some cultures, see Brain, 1975). Some people may claim as friends people a researcher might see as acquaintances, while others might say they have no friends when the researcher finds they have many relationships with properties we associate with friendship (Cohen and Rajkowski, 1982). Most researchers define friendship as a relationship characterized by voluntary interdependence with the parties oriented towards each other as persons rather than as occupants of roles (for elaboration and measurement of these concepts, see Wright, 1974). Reisman (1981) distinguishes between Associative, Reciprocal and Receptive friendships. Associative ties are casual, friendly relations that develop between people who find themselves in the same neighborhood, office, etc. They lack the commitment that would enable them to endure beyond the situation where they form, lasting only so long as the persons are in the situation. Reciprocal friendships involve commitment between parties who relate as equals, and who relate to each other's personalities. This kind of relationship usually begins as an associative relation, then continues beyond the initial context of formation. Receptive friendships are those in which one member is primarily a giver (usually higher status) and the other is a receiver. The receiver idealizes the giver, and the giver identifies with and vicariously participates in the experiences of the receiver. Reisman advises that researchers, depending on their objectives, provide definitions to subjects to ensure that "friend" means the same thing to subject and researcher. This seems like a good idea.

In measuring network properties researchers have asked subjects to list anywhere from three (Laumann, 1972) to twenty names (Hirsch, 1981) who meet some criteria of associative, reciprocal, or receptive friendship. (See Mitchell and Trickett, 1980 and Gottlieb, 1981, for reviews of network literature.) It may be that a sample of three to five names from a network of friends is a valid indicator of the properties of a whole network, but this possibility needs to be examined.

After obtaining a list of friends, a variety of methods have been used to measure properties of networks (density, overlap of kin and friends, etc.). Although there is still not consistency in measuring these variables, there is movement in that direction, particularly with the key variable of density (Mitchell and Trickett, 1980).

In measuring properties of relationships, researchers have focused on a wide variety of variables, ranging from intimacy, closeness, and trust, to ego-support value, maintenance difficulty, ease of communication, spontaneity, and multiplexity or number of roles in which the friend is contacted. Each of these concepts needs to be clarified, and redundancies need to be weeded out, but for our purposes the most important and problematic concept is intimacy. This concept has been operationalized with (1) a single question about how intimate or close a relationship is, (2) a question about how often personal problems are discussed, and (3) multiple dimensional measures of aspects of intimacy (Wright, 1974). There are some serious questions about validity using these different measures, especially when comparing male and female responses. Cozby's review of the self-disclosure literature (1972) shows as many studies finding no difference between men and women in self-disclosure, as find women disclose more. It may well be that discrepancies in findings occur because intimacy means different things to men and women. For example, Davidson and Duberman (1982) find that although men perceive themselves to be more trusting and spontaneous in same-sex friendships than women perceive themselves to be, men are likely to limit their disclosures to topics such as politics, current events and the movies, while women are much more likely to discuss personal issues or the friendship relationship itself. Laumann's (1972) findings are similar: less than two-thirds of his subjects would even discuss what kind of new car to buy and less than 10% would discuss troubles with their wives (Laumann, 1972, p. 125). In a study of college students Hacker (1982) finds only a weak relationship between self-reported closeness and self-disclosure.

Kahn and Antonucci (1979) have devised a technique for assessing the size of a person's network or "convoy" as well as differentiating reciprocal and associative relations. They present a subject with a drawing of three concentric circles. Assuming the center represents the subject, they ask the person to place in the surrounding rings the initials of those who provide them with support (Tangible *Aid*, *Affirmation* of their self concept, and *Affect* or emotional support). Those in the closest ring are the person's closest supporters (presumably reciprocal and receptive relations), those in the outer ring are associative relations. The usefulness of this procedure remains to be demonstrated, but it is a good start. It would be a great service to the field to develop consistent and valid measures of friends, network properties, and intimacy.

With these cautions in mind, let us examine findings on differences between male and female same-sex friendships.

DIFFERENCES BETWEEN MALE AND FEMALE FRIENDSHIPS

Children's understanding of friendship and behavior towards friends seems to unfold with their cognitive development (Bigelow and LaGaipa, 1975; Bigelow, 1977; Duck, 1975; Dweck, 1981). Younger children tend to have a concrete, egocentric orientation towards friendship, basing their choices on appearances, possessions, and external similarities to the self. In preadolescence there is a shift towards a more sociocentric perspective, taking into account the other's motives and emphasizing normative criteria such as loyalty and mutual aid. In early adolescence, girls, sooner than boys, shift to a more personal orientation, emphasizing psychological characteristics and intimacy (Douvan and Adelson, 1966; Kon and Losenkov, 1978). Vinacke and Gullickson (1964) find parallel shifts in behavior in their study of male and female differences in game playing in same-sex groups: at ages 7 and 8, both girls and boys display cooperative and accommodative behavior, being concerned that everyone experiences some gratification from the game; but by 14 to 16 years of age, boys change drastically, manifesting competitive and exploitive behavior in games, while girls remain accommodative.

Both qualitative and quantitative evidence indicates that boys tend to form larger friendship groups, while girls tend to pair off into dyads or, at the most, triads. For example, in a longitudinal study of classroom sociometric choices, Eder and Hallinan (1978) looked at the sex differences in the tendency of dyad members to accept third person into the group as a friend. They found that "dyadic friendships of girls are significantly more exclusive than those of males," (Hallinan, 1981). Studying 181 fifth graders Lever (1976) reports sex differences in game playing: boys more often play outdoors in large groups at competitive games that last longer and require more skill; while girls play indoors in private places with their best friend. Boys games tend to have extensive, explicit rules by which participants work towards a defined goal (Dweck, 1981). Boys' play is frequently interrupted by quarrelling about violations of rules, but boys seem to enjoy the disputes as much as the game. Such conflicts among girls often lead to ending the game in order to preserve the relationship.

Even outside of games boys' interaction is characterized by a competitive, combative orientation. As Schofield (1981) observes:

> A great deal of interaction within male peer groups seems directed toward proving and displaying athletic skill and physical strength. Informal arm wrestling tournaments are legion, as are a variety of behaviors such as playful shoving, tussling, mock boxing matches, wrestling and fun fights. (p. 64)

Such activity is more than just play. Boys often use these occasions to establish or maintain valued places in a dominance hierarchy.

Although in their review of research on sex differences, Maccoby and Jacklin (1974) report that girls and boys show no consistent differences in need for affiliation, most research has found that girls develop more intimate and exclusive relations with fewer friends (1 or 2) while boys develop more extensive ties with several friends (Dickens and Perlman, 1981; Kon, 1981; Eder and Hallinan, 1978). As Wright and Keple (1981) found in their study of adolescents, girls respond in a more intense and positive way to friends, while boys report their friendships with other boys as least rewarding in comparison to ties to mothers, fathers, or girlfriends. "Boys friendship . . . do not appear to be especially intense and do not constitute an important source of self-referent rewards."

This tendency for females to form more intimate ties than males persists into the college years (Wheeler and Nezlak, 1977) and into old age (Longino and Lipman, 1981; Powers and Bultana, 1976). There is some discrepancy in the findings about size of networks and amount of interaction with less close friends. While Fisher and Oliker (1980) note a trend towards men having larger networks than women early in the family life cycle, they report that women have more contacts later. However, several studies have found that men maintain an advantage in the number of "weak ties" (Granovetter, 1973) maintained into old age.

Most likely some of the discrepant findings are due to differences in measurement, as several reviewers have pointed out (e.g., Reisman, 1981; Chown, 1981). However, weighing all findings, it seems reasonable to conclude that men maintain larger networks with "weak ties" while women's networks, regardless of their size, are characterized by more intimacy and expressiveness.

How do we account for these differences? There are two basic paradigms for explaining the differences—a socialization-developmental paradigm and a structural paradigm. The former explains the difference on the basis of the experiences of males and females in their childhood and in their later socialization into sex roles. The latter explains the difference on the basis of the kinds of positions in social structures the different sexes occupy.

Socialization and Friendship

Although many researchers argue that the psychological basis for forming and maintaining friendship are laid down in childhood, there are virtually no tests of the hypotheses derived from this framework. Kahn and Antonnucci (1979), following Bowlby (1969) argue that the capacity for forming interpersonal relations are laid down in the infant's interactions with its mother. A mother who is consistent and nurturant provides her child with a sense of security. The child develops good object-relations, and this influences his orientations towards others. Vaillant (1978) argues that this foundation influences men's interpersonal relationships throughout adulthood.

Lynn (1976), Chodorow (1974), and Gilligan (1982) argue that there is a unique quality to male development that undermines their capacity for forming intimate ties and points them in the direction of greater individuation. They argue that all children begin life in a state of primary identification with their mothers—not differentiating themselves from their mother. Because mothers are females, they encourage this fusion more in their daughters than in their sons. With sons, mothers emphasize masculinity and encourage more differentiation. This process accelerates as sons approach school age, and they are urged to identify with males. Since fathers are not as continuously present as mothers, this identification must be with a position rather than a person. The elusiveness of masculinity leads males to define "masculine" as "not feminine." Therefore, to approach masculinity, sons move away from or repress the feminine identifications in themselves; they deny dependency needs that tie them to mothers, and degrade feminine activities. Thus for boys, to become masculine is to separate the self from mother and from the feminine. Females, on the other hand, experience a more continuous development within a strong, personal relationship based on identification. Later sex role socialization builds on this unconscious process, encouraging self-reliance and achievement in males and nurturance and responsibility in females. "Girls are thus pressured to be involved with and connected to others, boys to deny this involvement and connections" (p. 55). Because of these developmental differences, men are likely to experience difficulties in intimate relationships that call for identification, empathy and fusion, while females are likely to experience difficulties in situations that require individuation, differentiation and separation.

These are interesting hypotheses that need to be tested systematically. For example, one implication is that sons raised since infancy by fathers should resemble "typical" females in their interpersonal ties, while daughters in the same situation should resemble "typical" males. The theory may also lead us to conclude that androgynous males should have less difficulty with intimacy than masculine males. We will examine the evidence relevant to this hypothesis later.

Lewis (1978) is often cited as a source of a second line of thinking that accounts for men's difficulties with intimacy on the basis of socialization rather than development. (See Hess, 1981, for a comprehensive review.) This theory focuses on the ways that cultural expectations associated with masculinity conflict with the formation of intimate male friendships. As Lewis states ". . . a male's acceptance of traditional male role expectations strongly reinforces his efforts to be competitive, to fear homosexuality, and to avoid personal vulnerability and openness, all of which make emotional intimacy between men more difficult to attain."

Although socialization and development hypotheses sound plausible, the evidence to support them tends to be anecdotal or based on small samples. Many studies use these theories to interpret observed differences after the fact. Studies that purport to test the theories usually fail to measure the independent variables: developmental experience, competitiveness, fear of homosexuality and vulnerability, acceptance of male sex roles, etc. Instead they assume that simply being male makes it probable that these key variables will be at the appropriately high levels.

Among the studies that are this crudely designed, we can find as many that contradict the hypothesis as support it. If fear of homosexuality is a critical variable, we would expect homosexual men to have less difficulty with closeness and self-disclosure in male friendships than heterosexual men. I know of no direct tests of this hypothesis, but anecdotal evidence raises questions about it: homosexual relationships are reported to be non-committal and have difficulty with intimacy (Lee, 1981; Minnigerode and Adelman, 1981).

Lewis cites Jourard's studies of sex-differences in self-disclosure as evidence in support of the idea that men disclose less, but Cozby's (1973) review of that literature indicates conflicting evidence; half the studies show females self-disclose more than males, and the other half show no sex differences. In Hacker's (1981) study, she finds no differences between males and females in their likelihood of being high in self-disclosure in same sex friendships.

If socialization into the masculine role is a key determinant, then we would expect masculine men to disclose less than feminine or androgenous men (men high on both masculinity and femininity). Bem, Martyna and Watson (1976) did find that more masculine men were less responsive to the needs of a lonely, male stranger, but this tells us little about their behavior in friendship dyads. In a more direct test of the hypothesis, Narus and Fischer (1982) examine the relationship between scores on Bem's Sex Role Inventory and reports about "ease of communication" and "confidence sharing" with a male's closest friend, either male or female (128 subjects). Using analysis of variance to compare androgenous and masculine men, they find androgenous men more expressive (higher in ease of communication and confidence sharing). However, the differences between means are less than four points on scales that range from 7 to 42 (ease) and 6 to 36 (confidences). "The differences were in terms of degrees of expressiveness within a positive range, and not in terms of expressive versus inexpressive."

A high score on androgeny means that a subject is high on both masculinity and femininity. Since this is true, it becomes necessary to examine which component of androgeny is accounting for the differences between masculine and androgenous males. To unravel this question, the authors look within same sex and mixed sex friendships at the correlations between their measures of masculinity and femininity and their measures of expressiveness. Surprisingly, they find that masculinity is strongly correlated with expressivity (ease and confidences) in both same and mixed sex friendships, with the strongest associations occurring in same sex relationships. Femininity is unrelated to expressivity in mixed sex groups, unrelated to "ease" in same sex groups, and only weakly related to "confidences" in same sex groups.

Breaking the sex role scales into their component items, they then examine the correlation of each item with the expressiveness scales. Again they are surprised to find that the best predictors of expressiveness are items such as "defends own beliefs", "strong personality", and "willingness to take a stand". Ironically, several items from the femininity scale correlated negatively with expressiveness. In other words, it seems that the high scores on expressiveness for androgenous males were due to the masculine component of the androgeny scale. They conclude, "It is as though masculine qualities of strength and at times assertiveness enabled these men to share confidences and communicate easily with those to whom they felt close. Rather than assist expressivity, certain feminine qualities too often may have held back the men." Bem (1977) reports similar findings, and interprets them as indicating that men high on masculinity, because they conform more to the accepted male role, are less anxious about self-disclosure.

In a second study by Fischer and Narus (1981) comparing male and female same sex friendships they find male friendships less intimate than female friendships, but they report that androgyny is unrelated to intimacy for men.

The implications of these findings are that the assumptions behind the socialization-development theory of sex differences in friendships should not be taken for granted. Before we suggest socializing men into more androgynous sex roles as a solution for male reticence, we need more evidence that socialization is what is accounting for the reticence. It may be that the theory has some merit, but there is enough contradictory evidence to raise questions. We will never be sure as long as results are interpreted post hoc and key explanatory variables are not measured. Future research should be designed so as to measure the critical dimensions of socialization and development that are purported to account for the properties of male friendships.

STRUCTURAL INFLUENCES ON FRIENDSHIP

Much of the research on friendship has been done within a social psychological perspective, testing hypotheses about personality characteristics that lead to mutual attraction and the growth of relationships. (See Duck, et al., Vols. 1 through 4 for an overview of this field.) However, another tradition of research has pointed to the impact of social structure in creating conditions for friendship formation or disruption, and creating the motivation for "dyadic withdrawal." The structural influences we will examine are urbanization, social class, organizational position, and stages of the marital and adult life cycles.

Urbanization and Friendship

One of the oldest structural arguments is that industrialization and urbanization undermine the development or maintenance of friendship bonds (Wirth, 1938; Packard, 1972). A great deal of research has discredited this theory. In his well-known case study Whyte (1955) set out to study the "disorganization" of an Italian slum and found men bonded together with strong friendship ties. Gans (1962) findings support Whyte's. Liebow (1967) and Anderson (1978) found similar friendship groups among Black men in urban inner cities. Using survey techniques, Lowenthal et al. (1975) report that 74% of their male subjects have friends they see weekly or more often. Farrell and Rosenberg (1981) find 80% of the men in their Boston study reporting they have male friends they see regularly. Laumann (1972) finds that 69% of the men in his Detroit study report participating in closely knit networks. Using the same data base, Fisher, et al. (1977) report that men at all stages of life labeled more than half their best friends as "very close." Even frequent moving is not associated with isolation and loneliness. Fisher and Stueve (1977) attribute this finding to several factors: (1) most moves are short distances, (2) many ties are replaceable, (3) frequent movers are likely to have social skills, (4) people tend to choose compatible neighborhoods, (5) people are likely to move voluntarily to improve their circumstances.

Fisher, et al., argue that rather than urbanization mechanically leading to less dense and multiplex friendship networks, the structural constraints of modern systems set limits within which an individual constructs his friendship network based on rational social exchange principles. The myth of the anomic, isolated man in urban areas has been dispelled, and researchers have gone on to map out the variations in the properties of friendship ties. Those men who become friends through a shared work setting or neighborhood (associative friends) are likely to be seen frequently, ethnically heterogeneous, but not particularly intimate. Intimate childhood friends (reciprocal) are likely to be living further away, contacted less often, more ethnically similar to the respondent, and less multiplex in their exchanges.

Social Class and Friendship

Not surprisingly, men tend to choose friends who are in the same or adjacent socio-economic statuses (Laumann, 1972; Jackson, 1977). White collar men, having more resources and fewer constraints, tend to report more friends. Their friendships tend to be occupationally homogeneous and ethnically heterogeneous. The reverse is true for the working class men. Entry and exit into the occupational system influences the age of friends: while most men choose friends who are similar in age, those close to age 21 or age 65 are far more likely to choose friends from within the range of 21 to 65 than outside this range. Participation in the labor force creates a boundary "fault" (Jackson, 1977).

The Life Cycle and Friendship

There have been several recent studies that have described changes in the size and quality of men's friendship relations over the life cycle. Apart from the studies of the relationship between cognitive development and conceptions of friendship in childhood, there have been few attempts to relate theories of adult development to theories of friendship participation. If adult males develop more differentiated and integrated cognitive and emotional structures in adulthood (Farrell and Rosenberg, 1981), or if there are predictable transitions in their life-structures (Levinson, et al., 1978) or if they develop less defensive personalities (Vaillant, 1977), then it may be that their modes of relating to friends change in predictable ways. However, like theories of the impact of socialization and development, these theories have not yet been adequately tested.

Several recent studies have attempted to explain life-cycle variations in men's friendship behavior on the basis of variations in their role sets or positions in social structures (e.g., Farrell and Rosenberg, 1981; Stensrud, 1981; Stensrud and Feldman, 1982; Fisher and Oliker, 1980). They argue that changes in a man's role set or position generate changes in his focal concerns. Men with mutual concerns generated by similar structural positions are likely to form friendships. However, it may be that role obligations or structural constraints prevent the formation or maintenance of friendship. Finally, some theorists suggest that people have a limited need for friendship (a "fund of intimacy," Nelson, 1966; Farrell and Rosenberg, 1981). The more this need is gratified in one domain, for example, in the marital relationship, the less pressing is the desire to have intimate ties in other domains. Much of this theory and research centers around changes in friendship patterns over the family life cycle.

Marriage and Friendship

Lowenthal, et al. (1975) report daily contact between friends for three quarters of their adolescent sample. Steuve and Gerson (1977, p. 84) report 73% of their sample of young single men arranging more than weekly contact. As couples get more deeply involved emotionally—going from casual dating to engagement, the overlap of their friendship networks increases (Milardo, 1982; Johnson and Leslie, 1982), but the size of the network decreases and the involvement with friends declines.

Marriage brings an abrupt decline in frequency of contact, with the decline continuing until middle age (Stueve and Gerson, 1977, p. 89; Schulman, 1975; Farrell and Rosenberg, 1981; Tamir and Antonnucci, 1981). The arrival of children and the addition of the father role seems to speed the decline. However, both Lowenthal and Farrell and Rosenberg find an increase of involvement with friends as subjects approach retirement, Ross-Franklin (1983) finds an increase of involvement after retirement. In contrast, Fisher and Oliker (1980) find a decline in the number of friends reported by men over 65. What happens in this stage of the life cycle (post-retirement) is unclear. Fisher and Oliker also report that women in this stage maintain more friendships than men; they attribute the differences to the greater likelihood of men's friends dying and the greater disposition of women towards forming friendships. However, interviewing 235 noninstitutionalized men and women over 70, Powers and Bultena (1976) report that men have regular contact with more friends than women do. While they agree that men are less likely to replace lost friends, they claim that " . . . older men, as a group, regularly interacted with a greater number of persons and had more frequent contact with several categories of interactants. Intimate friends, however, seem to be a relatively small part of their world." This configuration of findings is consistent with Longino and Lipman's (1981) findings in their study of 488 elderly people in two life-care communities. When asked to list all the people who "mean a lot to you or who are important in your life," men and women both list an average of 10 people, however, men have a smaller network of primary relations and a larger network of secondary relations than women. And compared to women, men receive less emotional, social and instrumental support from their relationships.

Finally, the death of a man's wife leads to changes in association patterns. Longino and Lipman (1981) report that widowed men have the least number of primary relations and the largest network of secondary relations. However, both Power and Bultena (1976) and Petrowsky (1981) report that widowed men are more likely than married men to report frequent contact with close friends. Ward's (1981) analysis of NORC data from 1972 to 1977 supports these findings, with married men seeing friends and neighbors least frequently in comparison to men who are widowed, divorced, or never married.

Although there is disagreement on some fine points, there is a growing body of research that indicates that both frequency of contact and intimacy vary in a curvilinear fashion for men over the adult life cycle. Taking on familial role responsibility reduces friendship participation; discarding roles increases it.

Organization Structure and Friendship

Dunphy (1972) has suggested that position in an organizational hierarchy influences the quantity and quality of informal ties, as well as the culture and role-structure of the groups that do form. Kanter (1977) developed a similar theory in her case study analysis of a large corporate structure. She argues that three properties of positions are critical in influencing informal ties: Power, Opportunity for Advancement, and the degree to which one is in the minority at one's status level. Those low in opportunity and power develop a "horizontal reference group," turning to their peers to gripe, gossip and seek assurance and protection, but not mobilizing for action and change. The roles of Agressor and Seducer are likely to be salient in these groups (Dunphy, 1972). Those high in opportunity are more competitive, identifying with groups with power, and forming informal groups aimed at exerting power and bringing about change. Dunphy argues that such groups are likely to crystallize around a "wheeler-dealer" who has a record of successful accomplishment. At the top of the system are groups that are closed and exclusive that emphasize loyalty and conformity. "Tokens," persons who are few numerically at their status level, are likely to be excluded from informal peer networks.

It might be possible, as Kanter implies, that variation within and between men's and women's friendships occur because they occupy different points in status hierarchies. Since women are more likely to be found in positions lower in power and opportunity, it may be that the greater intimacy of female friendships is due to those conditions. What Kanter calls gossip, griping and seeking reassurance from a horizontal reference group might be considered intimate, self-disclosure by other researchers. The competitive, action-oriented relationships of those higher in power might be considered less intimate. Looking at men's friendship alone then, we would expect to find greater intimacy in lower status, low-opportunity positions. However, Jackson, et al. (1977, p. 29) report just the opposite—men in higher status positions tend to report "closer" relations than men of lower status. Having higher status is also associated with having more friends numerically (Farrell and Rosenberg, 1981) and fewer friends who are kin and neighbors (Komarovsky, 1967; Verbrugge, 1972; Laumann, 1972). Jackson, et al. conclude that " . . . high status seems to provide more opportunity and fewer constraints in network formation" (p. 49). Thus, at least for adults, position in status hierarchies does not seem to account for the differences between male and female friendship.

However, if we examine the effects of position in hierarchies on children's friendship we get a different picture. Hallinan has argued that the different properties of friendship among classmates may be related to properties of the classroom structure. For example, she finds (1976) that an open classroom structure, where several groups of children work on separate tasks with open interaction allowed, generates less hierarchical distributions of sociometric choices (fewer stars and isolates), fewer asymmetric dyads, and fewer intransitive triads. In a longitudinal follow-up she finds that asymmetric relationships last a shorter time when they do occur in open classrooms. In all cases she reports that girls have more mutual choices than boys. In a later article (1981) she speculates that some of the differences between girls and boys friendships may be due to the fact that girls are likely to have higher status in the classroom than boys. Because teachers are likely to be female, and because students may assign higher status to girls who often show greater maturity and higher academic achievement, there may be some qualitative differences between male and female groups. In a sense, boys may be the "alienated" workers in classrooms, and this condition may lend a different quality to their friendships.

Long ago Cohen (1955) argued that experience in the classroom hierarchy was a key determinant of delinquent subcultures that turn adult value structures upside down. The low self-esteem generated by experiences of failure is counteracted by a reaction-formation. Supported by the culture of his friendship group, a boy comes to value exactly what his teachers condemn: dirtiness, violence, invasions of property, etc. Liebow (1967) suggests similar defensive dynamics occur in groups of lower status adult men, who repair their damaged self concept through participation in a culture that redefines their failures at marriage and work as signs they are real "men," a success within the group's subculture. Farrell and Rosenberg (1981) provide evidence that contact with friends has a different impact on young lower class, as compared to middle class men. For the former, the more often they see their friends, the more alienated they are likely to be and the fewer chances for advancement they see at work. For middle class young men the reverse is true, frequent contact is associated with reduced alienation and perceptions of more opportunities. More research needs to be done to determine the conditions in which friendship contributes to adaptation to system demands or defensive withdrawal from the larger system into a self-enhancing deviant subculture.

Job Conditions and Friendship

Recently Kohn and Schooler (1983) have presented evidence that status alone is not as good a predictor of men's values and behavior as the actual conditions where he works. He and his colleagues have shown that the degree of job complexity, routinization, and freedom from supervision on the job are related to values in childrearing as well as intellectual flexibility. Recently it has been shown that properties of one's job are also related to properties of one's marriage (Spade, 1983). It may well be that a closer look at job characteristics other than status will find stronger relationships between work and friendship properties.

In support of this position Stensrud (1982) found that delivery men in a cookie company who held similar jobs, with low supervision and high security in a non-competitive environment developed intimate friendship ties and met frequently off the job. On the other hand, people working in a highly differentiated factory in a competitive environment developed only associative ties with infrequent outside contact.

In reviewing literature on informal relations in work settings, Shils (1951) reports that the quality of leadership in a structure influences interpersonal relations. Impersonal, arbitrary decision-making generates alienated primary groups, while more inclusive leadership generates less alienated primary groups (also see Mangham, 1982). Working within this perspective Smith (1978) argues that a clearly specified normative structure insulates workers from the effects of leadership. Looking at the degree to which state police officers form friendships within their units, he finds that when job clarity (specification) is low, the more alienating the supervisor, the more friendships formed in the environment. He refers to these relationships as "dyadic withdrawal," suggesting that they form defensive functions similar to Bion's (1959) concept of a "pairing group." However, since he examines only socio-metric choice, it is not possible to say anything about the properties of these relationships.

In his cross-cultural analysis of friendship, Brain (1976) points to the importance of variables similar to those isolated by Smith. For example, he argues that the "taboo on personal friendship" found in the Norwegian merchant marine is due to the competitive, individuated positions of men. Each person has a clearly specified work role with clear criteria for advancement and, each man is "in a unique position through pay, shift arrangements, and chances of advancement." On the other hand, deck hands on trawler ships who share a percentage of the profits and share equal ranks relative to the officers form strong friendship bonds.

Clearly more research needs to be done on how the properties of roles in work environments influence the properties of friendship. The finding of less intimacy in male friendship groups may well be due to the fact that they are more likely to occupy positions in organizations that are organized into hierarchies with competitive relations between members and varying degrees of external threat from supervisors as well as natural and man-made forces. Even among children's groups the differences observed may be due to these structural factors. That boys spend more time than girls in organized competitive sports is a consequence of concerted efforts made by decision-makers since the turn of the century. Boys clubs, YMCA's, Little League baseball and football and most high school sports are social structures created by adults for boys. They provide boys with experience in hierarchical structures governed by clear rules in which differentiated groups pursue clear goals. If these structures are responsible for some of the observed differences between male and female friendships, it may be that those differences will diminish as more and more females enter such structures both as children and as adults.

STAGES OF FRIENDSHIP DEVELOPMENT

There has been very little research on the stages of friendship development. Most research has focused on the stage of initial attraction or has simply assumed that existing friendships are all at the same stage of development. Brain (1976) has argued that friendships in America lack institutionalization and tend to be relatively underdeveloped as social systems: "Friends in our culture are left to find their own symbols and make up their own rituals— private jokes, special greetings, nicknames, regular meetings" (p. 106). Brain implies that a fully developed friendship would resemble what Naroll (1982) calls a "moralnet"—a primary group or social support network with a moral order or world view consisting of:

1. central values embodied in cultural themes
2. governing normative code justified by core values
3. dramatic tales or "legends" that embody central themes
4. rituals or ceremonies that emphasize central values or events in the tales.

In a recent analysis of the enduring friendship group formed by the Impressionist painters, Farrell (1982) finds many of these criteria. The members negotiate a shared subculture of values in art and a normative code about painting and members' behavior toward the market and each other. In later stages they ritualize their meeting time, and their interaction centers around old stories and new gossip that clarify their values, often by pointing out the deviance of those boundary-markers who violate group norms. Throughout its existence the group members exchange aid, emotional support, and validations of each others self-concepts as artists. Eventually the friends mobilize for collective action, drawing heavily on the resources of their socio-emotional leaders to resolve strains and their executive leader to evaluate courses of action and monitor progress towards the goals.

The development of this friendship group resembles that of other primary groups (Tuckman, 1977; Farrell, 1976). As Mills (1984) describes the fully developed primary group system, the Impressionists' group sustained commitment from its members, developed open communication, differentiated roles, and capacities to monitor internal processes, external threats and opportunities, as well as progress towards its goals. It had the capacities to nurture its members, resolve conflict, obtain and exchange resources, set priorities and achieve collective goals.

Such fully developed friendships proceed through stages. There have been several recent reviews of attempts to characterize at least the initial stages of friendship formation (Levinger, 1977; Morton and Douglas, 1981; Emerson, 1981). Much of the recent theory stems from a cognitive perspective, stressing the processes whereby persons sift through a field of eligibles and evaluate their possibilities for friendship. Levinger and Snoek (1972) argue that relationships begin with unilateral awareness, proceed to surface contact then to mutuality. During the unilateral awareness stage external characteristics are important: perceived similarity, appearance, etc. During the surface contact stage persons exchange information about roles and status, and finally they disclose information about themselves as unique individuals. Exchange theory has dominated attempts to conceptualize this process. It is argued that people first weigh rewards minus costs of a relationship as compared to alternatives (Kelly, 1979). Next they begin an exchange process, first on a surface level then at levels of greater personal concern. At each stage the participants weigh the rewards and costs, degree of equity, distributive justice, and reciprocity in the relationship. Beyond the initial stages of attractions, much of this literature remains speculative.

Critics of this perspective point out that it assumes a rational, calculating model of human behavior and ignores the extent to which social structure and non-rational emotions influences relationships. The focus on exchange and cognitions also ignores the emergent structural properties of relationships—role differentiation, creation of group norms, rituals and values, etc.

The theory and research on the development of primary groups is relevant to the phenomenon of friendship, but it has rarely been used to guide research. Male friendships often involve more than two members, or else the dyadic relationships crystallize out of a larger network of associative relations. Most likely these relationships manifest the same developmental stages observed in other groups.

Probably the most influential theory of primary group development is Bennis and Shephard's (1955). Tuckman's (1977) review of research shows their hypothesized stages supported by most research. They argue that as relationships develop they confront two obstacles to authentic communication: (1) conflicted orientations toward authority, and (2) conflicted orientation towards peers. Members orientations toward authority range from dependent to counterdependent or rebellious. Orientations toward peers range from over-personal (overexposing the self so that over-vulnerability will inhibit attack) to counter-personal (hiding personal information to avoid attack). Conflicts about these issues are confronted in phases: members first resolve conflicts about how to orient towards authority both in the group and outside the group; then they confront conflicts about how personal the relationships should be. A fully developed group negotiates a culture in which members are neither dependent upon authority nor counter-dependent or rebellious. Instead they value independence, allowing leadership and outside authority to dominate when appropriate. A fully developed group also negotiates a culture in which members are neither over-personal, nor counter-personal. Instead they regulate personal exchanges on the basis of their appropriateness to the group's activities. (For a more detailed picture of variables apparent at each stage of development see Farrell, 1976 and 1982.)

If the findings on the differences between male and female groups are accurate, it would seem that neither type becomes fully developed. While female groups remain overly dependent and overly personal, male groups remain counter-dependent and counter-personal.

Two recent studies show that male and female friendship relationships differ in their movement through the phases. In a cross-sectional study of male and female friendships of varying degrees of duration (one to twelve or more months), Wright (1982) reports that (1) both men's and women's friendships rapidly developed into relationships in which plans and activities were interdependent; but (2) while women also rapidly developed "personalized interest and concern for each other" that leveled off after six months, men showed only a slight increase in personal relations during the first six months, but then increased rapidly during the last six months so that they eventually were equal to the females (p. 18).

In a longitudinal study of male and female friendship in which college freshmen kept logs of their contacts with friends over 2 week periods in the fall and spring, Wheeler and Nezlak (1977) find that while female relationships are more intimate in the fall, males increase intimacy during the second semester and females decrease intimacy. Wright concludes his review of ten years of research by noting that ". . . the differences between women's and men's friendships diminish markedly as the strength and duration of the friendships increases" (p. 19) (also see Hacker, 1981).

This conclusion should be qualified to state that differences in self-reports of quality of the interpersonal relationships diminish, but one still wonders if the friendships retain differences that were not measured. If Bennis and Shephard are correct about the necessity of working through conflicts about authority and intimacy issues before a relationship can achieve authentic communication and effectively confront joint tasks, then it may be that female friendships tend to be "underdeveloped" in the area of authority relations. That is, since they so quickly move into an overpersonal modality and neglect working out of authority and leadership problems, it may be that they are characterized by an overly "nice" quality, suppressing conflicts and having difficulty working together towards joint goals that require conflict resolution, decision-making, and differential authority within the relationship or working with authority outside the relationship. Some empirical evidence for this conclusion of less authenticity in female dyads is Hacker's (1982) finding that males are more likely than females to reveal both strengths and weaknesses in their same-sex friendships while females were more likely to reveal weaknesses, but not strengths. Some qualitative evidence of women's difficulty in dealing with conflict and strain in a relationship comes from Wright's report on post-experimental interviews with subjects which, he states, "have suggested rather strongly that maintenance difficulty (conflict of goals, motives, wishes; time spent clarifying actions or comments, etc.) is a more inhibiting factor to the growth of friendship for women than for men . . ." (p. 13). He finds men report more of this type of activity. These are only small pieces of evidence, but they are consistent with the hypothesis that female friends spend less time developing capacities for decision-making and goal-seeking.

On the other hand, men's friendship may often get stuck in dealing with authority issues and have capacities for intimacy and nurturance undeveloped. Using General Inquirer content analysis to compare the formation of all male and all female groups, Aries (1977) finds that male groups develop a more stable dominance order, while female groups develop less stable hierarchies, with leaders reporting they feel uncomfortable in leadership positions. But male groups show less talk about their feelings and personal lives, and they show more of a tendency to size each other up for knowledge and competence. They made efforts to see where they stood with each other, swapping stories about sports, pranks, politics, etc.* As mentioned earlier, even in childhood boys spend much interaction testing and maintaining the dominance order, defining norms, confronting deviants, and resolving conflicts. These preoccupations in male groups may prepare them for situations that require decision-making and action, but may handicap them in situations that require nurturance.

It may be that density of a friendship network is an indication that a friendship relationship is likely to be more fully developed. Interlocking networks are likely to have been in existence longer than radial networks. They are likely to be composed of members who are similar in religion, ethnicity, occupation and political preference. They are also likely to interact more often and be more intimate. Intimate topics likely to be discussed include difficulties with the boss, medical problems, marital difficulties and changing jobs (Laumann, 1972, p. 124–126). They are more common among Catholics and Jews than Protestants, but their appearance is unrelated to education, occupation, or social mobility. They seem to be more effective in generating conformity in their members, amplifying the behavioral and attitudinal characteristics of men at the class level of their members (Laumann, 1972; Farrell and Rosenberg, 1981). Laumann finds 27% of the friendships he observed manifesting this kind of relationship.

The question of the differences between male and female friendship will remain unresolved as long as we do not take into

---

*It may be that these stories are used as projective vehicles through which members communicate to each other indirectly (Farrell, 1979; Bales, 1971).

account the stage of relationship development. The processes that go on between two strangers in a laboratory tell us little about the ultimate processes that occur in fully developed friendships. Selman and Selman (1979) have suggested that friendship development recapitulates the development of friendships from childhood to adulthood, beginning with an egocentric, concrete orientation and reaching maturity in a sociocentric, intimate tie that recognizes the autonomy of each member. Hypotheses like these should be tested, or at least we should develop a descriptive map of developmental processes.

It would be very useful to have a means to measure the stage of development of relationships. With such an instrument it would be possible to refine our theories about the effects of socialization, development and social structure on friendship—qualifying our hypotheses to take into account stage of development.

EFFECTS OF FRIENDSHIP

The effects of friendship can be divided into the social-emotional and the instrumental. Most of the recent research has been on the social-emotional effects, examining the impact of social support on various indicators of physical and psychological health. The variables examined are tangible aid and services, emotional support, and affirmation of one's opinions and self-concept. Instrumental effects include role socialization, access to information about innovations and opportunities, creativity and advances in science and art.

Social-Emotional Effects

In an ongoing friendship, stress or illness in one of the members may throw the relationship into a state of disequilibrium. Plath (1979) provides detailed illustrations of the ways in which "consociates" or "convoys" relationships respond to normal life events of their members. In the midst of such life events or other more tragic ones, the presence of a friend who monitors a person's stress, provides emotional support, validates his self-image, advises about decisions, and assists in achieving goals can have beneficial effects. (See Thoits [1982] for an excellent discussion of conceptualization and measurement of social support.)

French (1974) finds that supervisors have more stressful job roles than either scientists or engineers, often being confronted with urgent decisions, interruptions, work overload and ambiguous tasks. Such conditions are associated with high blood pressure, serum glucose, and serum cortisal levels. Under conditions of high social support from friends and others, this relationship between stress and strain is reduced. House and Wells (1977) find similar buffering effects of support in their study of 2,000 hourly workers. Some studies have found that support reduces psychological strain but not physical strain (Pinneau, 1975). Kasl and Cobb (1979) report that under conditions of high social support, unemployed men experience less depression and anomie and greater chances of being reemployed, but their physiological symptoms are not affected (also see Gore, 1978; and Liem and Liem, 1979). In one of the few longitudinal studies that examines the long-term effects of social support, Berkman and Syme (1979) in a nine year mortality study of over 6,000 subjects present evidence that contact with friends reduces the likelihood of death at all age levels from 30 to 69. The effects hold up after controlling for SES and a variety of self-destructive health habits. An important point for our purposes is that they find that the effects of social support are stronger for women than they are for men, though the effects are significant for both. Sarason et al. (1983) report similar findings. Tamir and Antonnucci (1981) report that men are less effective than women at mobilizing social supports. To the extent that the nurturant, over-personal qualities of female friendships are the critical factors in buffering the impact of stress, men's friendships may be less effective than women's.

Kadushin (1983) attempts to unravel some of the complexity around the question of the conditions in which men's friendships provide reduction in stress. In a study of Vietnam Veterans in cities, towns, and rural areas he finds that having a dense network of non-veteran friends or a circle of veteran friends has different effects in different environments. In urban areas, having a circle of veterans is associated with less stress. However, in rural areas and small cities, being in a circle of veterans is associated with more stress. Kadushin argues that the greater freedom to choose and create relationships in urban areas makes the culture of the circles more supportive of adaptive behavior; but in rural areas and small towns, where less choice is available, such circles serve defensive functions, retard adaptive responses and are associated with more post traumatic stress disorders. He states: "Network analysis . . . begins to allow us to specify what kinds of effects on individuals in what kinds of social systems" (p. 197).

Kadushin's findings suggest that the differential effectiveness of male and female groups in relieving stress may have as much to do with structural as socialization factors. This line of thinking should be explored in future research.

Instrumental Effects

Socialization, Identity Maintenance, and Change. Several studies have argued that friendship is a critical vehicle of socialization, particularly during childhood, adolescence, and during episodes of role change. Much of the early delinquency research came to this conclusion (e.g., Thrasher, 1926). Dunphy (1969) argues that adolescent friendships play a part in the socialization of men into sex roles. Fine (1981) argues that preadolescent friendships operate as staging areas for behavior, where boys learn interactional skills, obtain didactic training, and develop sophistication in a self-image appropriate to social situations. Dunphy's and Fine's post hoc analyses seem plausible, but they should be tested by comparing the behavior and degree of socialization of boys who do and do not participate in such friendship groups. One study, (Mannarino, 1975) testing Sullivan's theory of the constructive effects of chums in preadolescence, finds that boys with chums tend to be more altruistic than those without.

Much of the research on identity maintenance and change has been carried out with females. Blau (1973) finds that aging females who are enmeshed in friendship relationships do not think of themselves as being "old," whereas those of similar age without such friendship do. Hirsch (1981) finds that women going through or returning to college adjust more readily if they have little overlap of family relations and their friendship networks. Presumably a person in a disconnected network is less likely to be confronted with significant others with consensus about the person's identity. The lack of consensus allows for more freedom, experimentation and gravitation towards the friends who are most supportive of changes. The relevance of these findings to men's friendship needs to be explored in future research. Since many men are likely to maintain friendships that are separate from family relationships (particularly working class men), it may be that men with such disconnected networks adapt more readily to identity changes.

Opportunities and Productivity

Granovetter (1973) argues that the weak, associative ties characteristic of many men's friendship are more effective than strong, dense networks in dealing with more instrumental goal-oriented problem solving. Persons in dense networks tend to close out contacts and information from outside sources. For example, Laumann (1972) shows that they are less open to extremes in political attitudes. To the extent that access to innovative ideas requires a member of a friendship network to maintain a wide array of weak ties rather than a small array of dense ties (Mullins, 1975), men in large, associative networks should have more access than those in dense networks. This access enables them to make more original contributions to their fields. Granovetter (1973) provides evidence that job opportunities are more likely to be available to men in weak networks. (See Lin, 1982 for some qualifications.) He also suggests that a community with many disconnected, dense networks would be less effective in mobilizing for political action than one with more wide ranging weak ties. This whole line of thinking suggests that the kinds of networks men form as compared to women (larger, with weak ties), will be more effective in obtaining innovative information and mobilizing for collective action. Much of this reasoning remains speculative and needs to be tested with research.

CONCLUSIONS

Carrying out a review of current literature is like painting a group portrait. The reviewer wants to be sure that everyone gets into the picture, and that each person is positioned correctly with regards to his or her relationships to other people. But inevitably, as the painter imposes his own organization on the portrait, some people are going to feel misplaced; others may feel they have been bent into inappropriate postures. Nevertheless, the article reflects how this author views the field at this point. It is time to summarize that view.

Reisman (1981) has commented that the field of friendship

research is still in its infancy. After reviewing the current literature, it is difficult not to agree. There are hopeful signs in the explosion of interest recently, but there are many problems that must be resolved if we are to achieve a cumulative body of knowledge about men's friendship.

First, it is necessary to move beyond post hoc evaluative analyses towards theoretically guided research. The post hoc analyses have generated a number of hypotheses that need to be tested. If research is to be cumulative, it is necessary to gather the many hypotheses into a logically coherent set of propositions and design research to test hypotheses deducted from those propositions.

At the same time it is necessary to develop some consistency about measurement of friendship, network properties, and relationship properties. Wright has made progress in developing valid and reliable measures of dimensions of friendship. Researchers studying social support have made progress in measuring properties of relationships and networks. Future research should incorporate these advances.

Theorizing about properties of male friendship should take into account:

1. socialization and development
2. social structure
3. developmental processes within friendships.

The socialization and development theory has been particularly favored in post hoc analysis. However, like past research on attitudes and character structure (House, 1981), the effects of socialization are assumed rather than tested. When dimensions of socialization or development have been measured, their relationships to friendship properties have not supported common assumptions. One direction for future research is to sort out what aspects of socialization do make a difference in friendship properties.

Research making use of hypotheses derived from a structural perspective have usually been more carefully designed. Hypotheses are deducted, and independent as well as dependent variables are measured. Progress is being made, but thus far very few studies have been completed from this perspective. It would seem particularly useful to use this perspective in answering some of the perennial questions about the differences between male and female friendships. We need to sort out to what extent the differences are accounted for by sex roles, and to what extent differences are due to the different kinds of positions men and women occupy in social structures, and the different types of organizations to which they belong.

Finally, a great deal of research has shown that primary relationships develop through stages. It would seem appropriate for future research to take this developmental variable into account, at least using the crude indices of duration and density as indicators of development. As several researchers have shown (Farrell, 1982; Tuckman, 1977) different types of processes occur at different stages of relationships.

In testing socialization and structural hypotheses, this developmental factor generates "noise" or error variance. For example, if male college friendships are in a different stage of development during the fall than female friendships, then generalizations about the ultimate differences between male and female friendships based on one-shot observations in the fall will be wrong. We do not yet have a simple indicator of stage of relationship development. Until one is developed, the duration and density variables will have to suffice.

This review has shown once again what a "young" science sociology is. There is still much to be done.

REFERENCES

Anderson, E. (1978). A Place on the Corner. Chicago: University of Chicago Press.

Aries, E. (1977). "Male-female interpersonal styles in all-male, all-female, and mixed groups." Pps. 292–310 in A. Sargent (ed.), Beyond Sex Roles. New York: West Publishing Company.

Backman, C. W. (1981). "Attraction in interpersonal relationships." In M. Rosenberg and R. Turner (eds.), Social Psychology. Washington, D. C.: American Sociological Association.

Bales, R. F. and Cohen, S. P. (1979). "Images from Fantasy, the FAN Level." Pps. 229–230 in SYMLOG: A System for the Multiple Level Observation of Groups. New York: Free Press.

Bell, R. R. (1981). "Friendships of women and men." Psychology of Women Quarterly, Vol. 5(3):402.

———(1981). Worlds of Friendship. Beverly Hills: Sage Publications.

Bem, S. L., Martyna, W., and Watson, C. (1976). "Sex-typing and Androgyny: Further Explorations of the Expressive Domain." Journal of Personality and Social Psychology, 34:1016–1023.

Bem, S. L. (1977). "On the utility of alternative procedures for assessing psychological androgyny." Journal of Consulting and Clinical Psychology, 45:196–205.

Bennis, W. F. and H. A. Shepard. (1956). "A theory of group development." Human Relations, 9:415–437.

Berkman, L. F. and S. L. Syme. (1979). "Social networks, host resistance, and mortality: a nine-year follow up study." American Journal of Epidemiology, 109:186–204.

Bion, W. R. (1959). Experiences in Groups, and Other Papers. New York: Basic Books.

Blau, Zena Smith. (1973). Old Age in a Changing Society. New York: New Viewpoints.

Bowlby, J. (1969). Attachment and Loss, Vol 1. New York: Basic Books.

Brain, R. (1976). Friends and Lovers. New York: Basic Books.

Bunker, B. B. (in press). "Women in groups." In B. E. Wolman (ed.), International Encyclopedia of Neurology, Psychiatry and Psychoanalysis and Psychology.

Byrne, D. and Nelson, D. (1965). Attraction as a linear function of proportion of positive reinforcements." Journal of Personality and Social Psychology, 4:699–702.

Caldwell, M. A. and L. A. Peplau. (1982). "Sex differences in same-sex friendship." Sex Roles, Vol. 8, No. 7:723–732.

Chodorow, N. (1974). "Family structure and feminine personality." Pps. 41–66 in M. S. Rosaldo and L. Lamphere, Women, Culture and Society. Stanford: Stanford University Press.

Chown, S. M. (1981). "Friendship in old age." Personal Relationships, Vol. 2:231–245 op. cit.

Cohen, A. K. (1955). Delinquent Boys. Glencoe, Ill.: Free Press.

Cohen, C. I. and H. Rajkowski. (1982). "What's in a friend? substantive and theoretical issues." The Gerontologist, Vol. 22, No. 3:261–266.

Cozby, P. C. (1973). "Self-disclosure: a literature review." Psychological Bulletin, 73:73–91.

Davidson, L. R. and L. Duberman. (1982). "Friendship: communication and interactional patterns in same-sex dyads." Sex Roles, Vol. 8, No. 8.

_____(1982). "Friendship: a comparison of same-sex dyads." Sex Roles, Vol. 8, No. 8:809–821.

Dickens, W. J. and D. Perlman. (1981). "Friendship over the life-cycle." In S. Duck and R. Gilmour (eds.), Personal Relationships, Vol. II. New York: Academic Press.

Douvan, E. and J. Adelson. (1966). The Adolescent Experience. New York: Wiley.

Duck, S. W. (1973). "Personality similarity and friendship choice: similarity of what, when?" Journal of Personality, 41:543–558.

Duck, S. W. (1983). *Friends for Life*, New York: St. Martin's Press.

Duck, S. and R. Gilmour. (1981). Personal Relationships, Vol. I. New York: Academic Press.

Duck, S. W. and R. Gilmour. (1981). Personal Relationships, Vol. 3. New York: Academic Press.

Duck, S. and R. Gilmour. (1981). Personal Relationships, Vol. 2. New York: Academic Press.

Duck, S. and C. Spencer. (1972). "Personal constructs and friendship formation." Journal of Personality and Social Psychology, 23:40–45.

Dunphy, D. C. (1969). Cliques, Crowds, and Gangs. Melbourne, Australia: Cheshire Publishing Co.

_____(1972). The Primary Group. New York: Appleton-Century-Crofts.

Dweck, C. S. (1981). "Social-cognitive processes in children's friendship." Pps. 322–334 in S. R. Asher and J. M. Guttman, The Development of Children's Friendships. Cambridge: Cambridge University Press.

Eder, G. and M. Hallinan. (1978). "Sex differences in children's friendships." American Sociological Review, 43:237–250.

Emerson, R. M. (1981). "Social exchange theory." In M. Rosenberg and R. Turner (eds.), Social Psychology. Washington, American Sociological Association.

Farrell, M. P. (1976). "Patterns in the development of self-analytic groups." Journal of Applied Behavioral Science, Vol. 12, No. 4:523–542.

_____(1979). "Collective Projection and Group Structure," Small Group Behavior, 10, Feb., 81–100.

_____(1982). "Artists' circles and the development of artists." Small Group Behavior, Vol. 13, No. 4:451–474.

Farrell, M. P. and S. D. Rosenberg. (1981). "Friendship groups and male development." Pps. 189–204 in Men at Midlife. Boston: Auburn House Publishing Company.

Fennell, M. L., P. R. Barchas, E. G. Cohen, A. M. McMahon and P. Hildebrand. (1978). "Perspective on sex differences in organizational settings: the process or legitimation." Sex Roles, Vol. 4:589–603.

Festinger, L., Schacter, S., and Back, K. (1950). Social Pressures in Informal Groups: a Study of Human Factors in Housing. New York: Harper and Row.

Fiedler, L. (1982). What Was Literature? Class Culture and Mass Society, New York: Simon and Schuster.

Fine, G. A. (1981). "Friends, impression management, and preadolescent behavior." Pps. 29–52 in S. R. Asher and J. M. Gottman (eds.), The Development of Children's Friendships. Cambridge: Cambridge University Press.

Fischer, C. S., R. M. Jackson, C. A. Stueve, K. Gerson, L. M. Jones, and M. Baldassare. (1977). Networks and Places. New York: The Free Press.

Fischer, J. L. and L. A. Narus. (1981). "Sex roles and intimacy in same-sex and other sex relationships." Psychology of Women Quarterly, Vol. 5(3).

Fisher, C. S. and S. J. Oliker. (1980). "Friendship, sex and the life cycle." Berkeley: University of California, Institute of Urban and Regional Development, Working Paper, No. 318.

French, J. R. P. Jr. (1974). "Person-role fit," in Occupational Stress, edited by A. McLean, Springfield, Ill.: Charles C. Thomas.

Gans, H. (1962). The Urban Villagers. New York: Free Press.

Gilligan, Carol. (1982). In a Different Voice. Cambridge, Mass.: Harvard University Press.

Gore, Susan. (1978). "The effect of social support in moderating the health consequences of unemployment." Journal of Health and Social Behavior.

Gottlieb, B. H. (1981). Social Networks and Social Support. Beverly Hills: Sage Publications.

Granovetter, M. S. (1972). "The strength of weak ties." American Journal of Sociology, Vol. 78, No. 6:1360–1381.

Hacker, H. M. (1981). "Blabbermouths and clams: sex differences in self-disclosure in same-sex and cross-sex friendship dyads." Psychology of Women Quarterly, Vol. 5(3):385–402.

Hallinan, M. T. (1976). "Friendship patterns in open and traditional classrooms." Sociology of Education, Vol. 49:254–265.

Hallinan, M. T. (1981). "Recent advances in sociometry." Pps. 91–115 in The Development of Children's Friendship. op. cit.

Hess, Beth B. (1981). "Friendships and gender roles over the life course." Pps. 104–114 in P. J. Stein (ed.), Single Life. New York: St. Martin's Press.

Hirsch, B. J. (1981). "Social networks and the coping process." Pps. 149–170 in B. H. Gottlieb, (ed.), Social Network and Social Support. Beverly Hills, Sage Publications.

Homans, G. C. (1951). The Human Group. New York: Harcourt, Brace, and World.

House, J. S. (1981). "Social Structure and Personality," Pps. 525–561 in Social Psychology; Sociological Perspectives, edited by M. Rosenberg and R. H. Turner, New York: Basic Books.

House, J. and Wells, J. A. (1977). "Occupational Stress, Social Support, and Health." Paper presented at the Conference on Reducing Occupational Stress. White Plains, New York.

Johnson, M. P. and L. Leslie. (1982). "Couple involvement and network structure: a test of the dyadic withdrawal hypothesis." Social Psychology Quarterly, Vol. 45, No. 1:34–43.

Kadushin, C. (1983). "Mental Health and the Interpersonal Environment," American Sociological Review, Vol. 48, No. 2:199–210.

Kahn, R. L. (1979). "Aging and social support." In M. W. Riley (ed.), Aging From Birth to Death. Westview Press.

Kahn, R. L. and T. C. Antonnucci. (1979). "Convoys over the life course: attachments, roles and social support."

Kanter, R. M. (1977). Men and Women of the Corporation. New York: Basic Books.

Kasl, S. and S. Cobb. (1979). "Some mental health consequences of plant closing and job loss." Pps. 255–300 in L. A. Ferman and J. P. Gordon (eds.), Mental Health and the Economy. Kalamazoo, Michigan: Upjohn Institute.

Kelley, H. H. (1979). Personal Relationships. Hillsdale, N. J.: Erlbaum.

Komarovsky, M. (1967). Blue-Collar Marriage. New York: Vintage.

Kon, I. S. (1981). "Adolescent friendship: some unanswered questions for future research." Pps. 187–203 in Personal Relationships, Vol. 2, op. cit.

Kon, I. S. and V. A. Losenkov. (1978). "Friendship in adolescence: values and behavior." Journal of Marriage and the Family, 40:143–155.

LaGaipa, J. J. (1981). "Children's friendship." Pps. 162–186 in S. Duck and R. Gilmour, (eds.), Personal Relationships, Vol. 2. New York: Academic Press.

Laumann, E. D. (1973). Bonds of Pluralism. New York: John Wiley and Sons.

Lee, J. A. (1981). "Forbidden colors of love: patterns of gay love." Pps. 128–139 in P. Stein (ed.), Single Life. New York: St. Martin's Press.

Lever, J. (1976). "Sex differences in the games children play." Social Problems, 23:478–487.

Levinger, G. and Snoek, J. D. (1972). Attraction in Relationships: A New Look at Interpersonal Attraction. Morristown, N. J.: General Learning Press.

Levinger, G. (1977). "Reviewing the close relationship," in Close Relationships, edited by G. Levinger and H. L. Rausch, Amherst, Mass.: University of Massachusetts Press.

Lewis, R. A. (1978). "Emotional intimacy among men." Journal of Social Issues, Vol. 34, No. 1:108–121.

Liebow, E. (1967). Tally's Corner, A Study of Negro Streetcorner Men. Boston: Little, Brown.

Liem, G. Ramsey and J. Hauser Liem. (1979). "Social support and stress: some general issues and their application to the problem of unemployment." Pps. 347–377 in L. A. Ferman and J. P. Gordon, (eds.), Mental Health and the Economy. Kalamazoo, Michigan: Upjohn Institute.

Lin, N., Ensel, W. M., and Vaugn, J. C. "Social resources and strength of ties: structural factors in status attainment." American Sociological Review, 1981, Vol. 46: 393–405.

Lockhead, M. E. and K. P. Hall. (1976). "Conceptualizing sex as a status characteristic." Journal of Social Issues, 32:111–124.

Longino, C. F. and A. Lipman. (1981). "Married and spouseless men and women in planned retirement communities: support network differentials." Journal of Marriage and the Family, Vol. 43, No. 1:169–177.

Lowenthal, M. F., M. Thurnher and D. Chiriboga. (1975). Four Stages of Life. San Francisco: Jossey-Bass.

Lynn, D. B. (1976). "Father and Sex-role Development." Family Coordinator, 25:403–428.

Maccoby, E. and C. Jacklin. (1974). The Psychology of Sex Differences. Stanford: Stanford University Press.

Mangham, J. L. (1981). "Relationships at work." Pps. 197–214 in S. Duck and R. Gilmour (eds.), Personal Relationships, Vol. 1. New York: Academic Press.

Mannarino, A. P. (1975). Friendship Patterns and Altruistic Behavior in Pre-Adolescent Males. Unpublished PhD Thesis, Ohio State University.

Meeker, B. F. and P. A. Weitzel-O'Neill. (1977). "Sex roles and interpersonal behavior in task-oriented groups." American Sociological Review, 42:91–105.

Milardo, R. M. (1982). "Friendship networks in developing relationships." Social Psychology Quarterly, Vol. 45, No. 3:162–172.

Miller, P. M. and J. G. Ingham. (1976). "Friends, confidants and symptoms." Social Psychiatry, 11:51–58.

Mills, T. M. (1984). The Sociology of Small Groups. 2nd edition, Englewood Cliffs, N. J.: Prentice-Hall.

Minnigerode, F. A. and Adelman, M. R. (1981). "Elderly homosexual women and men." Pps. 334–341 in Peter Stein, (ed.), Single Life. New York: St. Martin's Press.

Mitchell, R. E. and E. J. Trickett. (1980). "Task force report: social networks as mediators of social support." Community Mental Health Journal, Vol. 16 (1):27–44.

Morton, T. L. and M. A. Douglas. (1981). "Growth of relationships." Pps. 3–26 in S. Duck and S. Gilmour, Personal Relationships, Vol. 2. New York: Academic Press.

Mullins, N. C. (1975). "A sociological theory of scientific revolution." Pps. 185–203 in Knorr, Strasser and Silian, Determinant and Controls of Scientific Development. Dordrecht-Holland: D. Reidel Publishing Company.

Mullins, N. C., et al. (1977). "The group structure of cocitation clusters: a comparative study." American Sociological Review, Vol. 42:552–562.

Nahemow, L. and M. P. Lawton. (1975). "Similarity and propinquity in friendship formation." Journal of Personality and Social Psychology, Vol. 32:205–213.

Naroll, R. (1983). The Moral Order. Beverly Hills, California: Sage Publications.

Narus, L. R. and J. L. Fischer. (1982). "Strong but not silent: a reexamination of expressivity in the relationships of men." Sex Roles, Vol. 8, No. 2:139.

Nelson, J. (1966). "Clique contacts and family orientations," American Sociological Review, Vol. 31:663–672.

Newcomb, T. (1961). The Acquaintance Process. New York: Holt, Rinehart and Winston.

_____(1966). "The General Nature of Peer Group Influence", pps. 2–16 in College Peer Groups, edited by T. M. Newcomb and E. K. Wilson, Chicago: Aldine Publishing Co.

Packard, V. (1972). A Nation of Strangers. New York: David McKay.

Petrowsky, M. "Marital status, sex and the social networks of the elderly."

Pinneau, S. R. (1975). "Effects of social support on psychological and physiological strains. Unpublished PhD Thesis, University of Michigan.

Plath, D. M. (1979). "Contours of consociation: lessons form a Japanese narrative."

Pleck, J. (1975). "Man to man: is brotherhood possible?" Pps. 229–244 in N. Glazer-Malbin, Old Family/New Family. New York: D. Van Nostrand Company.

Powers, E. and G. Bultena. (1976). "Sex differences in intimate friendships of old age." Journal of Marriage and the Family, 38:739–747.

Reisman, J. M. (1979). The Anatomy of Friendship. New York: Irvington.

_____(1981). "Adult friendships." Pps. 205–230 in S. Duck and R. Gilmour, Personal Relationships, Vol. 2. New York: Academic Press.

Ross-Franklin, J. (1983). The Impact of Retirement on Marital Dyad Members. Unpublished PhD Thesis, State University of New York at Buffalo.

Sarason, T. G., H. M. Levine, R. B. Basham and B. R. Sarason. (1983). "Assessing social support: the social support questionnaire." Journal of Personality and Social Psychology, Vol. 44, No. 1:127–139.

Schofield, J. W. (1981). "Complementary and conflicting identities: images and interaction in an interracial school." Pps. 53–90 in The Development of Children's Friendships, op. cit.

Selman, R. L. and Selman, A. P. (1979). "Children's ideas about friendship: a new theory," Psychology Today, 114:71–80.

Shils, E. A. (1951). "The Study of the Primary Group." Pps. 44–69 in The Policy Sciences, edited by D. Lerner and H. Lasswell. Stanford: Stanford University Press.

Shulman, N. (1975). "Life cycle Variations in patterns of social relationships." Journal of Marriage and the Family, pps. 813–821.

Smith, T. S. (1983). "Personal ties and institutionalized action: an aggregate analysis of reciprocated choice in friendship markets." University of Rochester, unpublished manuscript.

Spade, J. (1983). The Nature of Work Activity: Its Impact on the Family. Unpublished PhD Thesis, State University of New York at Buffalo.

Stensrud, J. R. and K. A. Feldman. (1982). "The structural effects of life course change in patterns of friendship." New York State Sociological Meetings.

Stueve, C. A. and K. Gerson. (1977). "Personal relations across the life-cycle." Pps. 79–100 in C. S. Fischer, Networks and Places. New York: The Free Press.

Swidler, Ann. (1983). "Love and Adulthood in American Culture." Pps. 286–317 in Family in Transition, Skolnick, A. S. and Skolnick, J. H., (eds.) Boston: Little, Brown.

Tamir, L. M. and T. C. Antonnucci. (1981). "Self-perception, innovation and social support through the family life course." Journal of Marriage and the Family, Vol. 43, No. 1.

Thoits, P. A. (1982). "Conceptual, methodological, and theoretical problems in the study of social support as a buffer agent against life stress." Journal of Health and Social Behavior, 23, 145–159.

Thrasher, F. M. (1926). The Gang. Chicago: University of Chicago Press.

Tiger, L. (1969). Men in Groups. New York: Random House.

Tuckman, B. W. and Jenson, M. A. (1977). "Stages in Small-Group Development, Revisited," Group Organizational Studies, 2, No. 4, Dec., 419–427.

Vaillant, George E. (1977). Adaptation to Life. Boston: Little Brown.

Verba, S. (1961). Small Groups and Political Behavior. Princeton, N. J.: Princeton University Press.

Verbrugge, L. (1973). "Adult friendship contact." Unpublished PhD Thesis, University of Michigan, Ann Arbor, Michigan.

Ward, Russell (1981). "The never-married in later life." Pps. 342–356 in P. Stein, (ed.), Single Life. New York: St. Martin's Press.

Werner, C. and P. Parmelee. (1979). "Similarity of activity preference among friends." Social Psychology Quarterly, Vol. 42, No. 1:62–66.

Wheeler, L. and J. Nezlak. (1977). "Sex differences in social participation." Journal of Personality and Social Psychology, Vol. 35:742–754.

Wheeler, L., H. Reiss and J. Nezlak. (1977). "Loneliness, social interaction and sex roles."

Whyte, William Foote. (1955). Street Corner Society. Chicago: The University of Chicago Press.

Wiggins, J. L. and A. Halzmuller. (1978). "Psychological androgyny and interpersonal behavior." Journal of Consulting and Clinical Psychology, Vol. 42, No. 1:40–52.

Wirth, L. (1938). "Urbanism as a way of life." American Journal of Sociology, 44:1–24.

Wright, P. H. (1974). "The delineation and measurement of some key variables in the study of friendships." Representative Research in Social Psychology, 5:93–96.

Wright, P. H. (1982). "Men's friendship, women's friendships and the alleged inferiority of the latter." Sex Roles, Vol. 8, No. 1:1-20.

Wright, P. H. and T. W. Keple. (1981). "Friends and parents of a sample of high school juniors: an exploratory study of relationship intensity and interpersonal rewards." Journal of Marriage and the Family, Vol. 43, No. 1.

Chapter 13

Family Versus Career Responsibilities

Harlan London
Katherine R. Allen

The socialization process of males generally instills the primary importance of work roles over family roles. Adult males today were reared in an era of the separation of men's and women's roles: fathers as breadwinners and mothers as caretakers. Signs of change are reflected in the behaviors and attitudes of both younger age groups and men of all ages who ascribe to a more egalitarian perspective. As women gain greater economic and social power, the male monopoly on power within the home and in intimate relationships is decreased.

Although there are signs of change, full transformation of gender roles has not occurred. Many professions still remain male dominated. Furthermore, husbands are not sharing equally in homemaking tasks, even if their wives are employed outside the home. Certainly, inroads have been made in terms of fathering, but true gender equality is far from secured (Lewis, 1982).

Religious institutions have long been conservative in outlook and patriarchal in composition. Recent exceptions do exist, such as the increasing enrollment of women in Protestant seminaries. Yet, the Church, like corporate America, maintains the image of traditional family and career structure, where the husband is the major breadwinner and thus the head of the household and his wife is in a supportive, expressive position.

The number one priority of the male clergy is his calling as a minister, just as the corporate executive's main function is to

Harlan London, PhD, is Associate Professor, Department of Child and Family Studies, College of Human Development, Syracuse University, Syracuse, NY 13210. Katherine R. Allen, PhD, is Assistant Professor of Child Development and Family Living, Texas Woman's University, Denton TX 76204.

subordinate all other roles to his career position. Both occupations require the investment of time and energy beyond the typical 40 hour work week. Family needs are auxiliary, and the head of this auxiliary is a "lady", who, in this case is the clergyman's or the executive's wife.

In the following discussion, we will consider the particular case of the male clergy. As noted above, this profession tends to reflect the traditional arrangement of males as having primary responsibility for the economic needs of the family and females as having primary responsibility for the emotional needs of the family. Following the research report, there will be a discussion of the changes that are altering this traditional structure and thus reflecting current trends in the lives of modern men.

THE HIERARCHICAL SYSTEM OF THE UNITED METHODIST CLERGY

This article will provide a descriptive account of data gathered on a national sample of United Methodist clergy families in the United States. The purpose of this study was to assess the levels of satisfaction among clergy and spouses regarding their family relationships, financial compensation and career progress within the itinerancy of the United Methodist Church. In keeping with the theme *Men in Families*, this discussion will focus primarily on men's roles in the United Methodist Church as clergy themselves and as spouses of female clergy.

The United Methodist Church is the only protestant denomination with a hierarchical system. Clergy in this denomination are appointed by bishops to serve as pastors of local parishes. In terms of the clergy career path, most begin their career in the ministry as a student supply. They may then be appointed as pastor of a small parish, or as an assistant or associate pastor of a large parish. Next, the clergy may be appointed as a senior pastor of a larger parish.

District superintendents are pastors selected by the Bishop to serve as an administrative supervisor or liaison between the Bishop and the local parishes in a given area. They serve as an advisor to the Bishop in parish management and may suggest to the Bishop the appointment of clergy from one location to another. The Bishop is an administrator of a given region within the Church's jurisdictional region or area. Appointment of clergy to their parish assignment is made by the Bishop.

The development of the clergy career path in the United Methodist Church has been described by Mills (1969) as a three level scheme. Mills describes new pastors in the early stages of their career as *neophytes*. *Veterans* represent established clergy in the middle of their career, and *leaders* are at the top of the career path. This scheme provides a way to group the clergy in this sample by age, as will be discussed later in this article.

DEMOGRAPHIC PROFILE OF THE SAMPLE

Data for this study were obtained from the national file of all (35,000) United Methodist pastors, district superintendents and clergy appointed beyond the local church. Every twentieth pastor and clergy appointed beyond the local church was included. The district superintendents represent a 50% sample of all district superintendents in the various conferences across the United States. A total of 1,803 questionnaires were mailed to clergy and spouses in the above three groups. A response rate of 60% was obtained, with 1,083 usable questionnaires returned by clergy. In addition, 993 spouse questionnaires were returned.

The demographic analysis shows that the clergy and their spouses are a very homogeneous group. The typical clergy is a middle-aged, white, married man with children. Professionally, he is likely to be a senior pastor who has earned a master's degree. The typical spouse is a somewhat younger, middle-aged, white married female. She is likely to be a homemaker, who has completed some college, but has not earned a degree. If she is employed, she is likely to be working in a professional or technical capacity.

Demographic data on the clergy and spouse groups show that 80% are 36 years of age or over. Nearly 95% of both groups are white. Only 6% of the clergy are female and the majority of these women are under age 36. The overwhelming majority of all of the clergy are married: 85.6% are still in their first marriages, and an additional 7% have remarried. Thus, only 7.4% of clergy in this study are unmarried at the present time. Considering the fact that at any point in time, at least one third of all adults are unmarried (Macklin, 1980), this sample is not representative of the population at large. The clergy families average between 2 and 3 children.

Professionally, the majority of clergy are highly educated, with 68% holding a master's degree. They are likely to be in a leadership position (65% are pastors; 16% district superintendents). Fifty-one percent of the clergy earn between $10,000 to $20,000 in addition to their housing allowance. Nearly half of the spouses (49%) are not employed outside the home, and 71% have no income or earn under $10,000 per year. While there are signs of change, especially among younger, unmarried clergy, the predominant pattern revealed in this investigation is that of a male-headed household, a supportive wife and 2 or 3 children.

The clergy role appears to be a demanding one in that it requires a commitment from all members of the clergy family. This observation is based on the fact that clergy spend about 54 hours per week fulfilling their professional duties, while only about 23 hours per week are spent with their families, and 15 hours per week are spent alone with their spouse. The clergy families in this sample are also quite mobile. A third of the families have moved between 6 and 10 times, during their career and on the average, they have moved about four times.

SOME REALITIES OF THE CLERGY ROLE

The results of the present study indicate that major differences among male clergy appear to be dependent on either the clergy's age or level of advancement within the appointive system.

In order to investigate the relationship of age to other variables, the clergy sample was grouped as followed: 23–35, 36–54, 55 and over. Several interesting trends appeared as a result of these age groupings. For instance, the oldest group (55 and over) tended to be the group which indicated the most satisfaction in terms of their income and career progress. This is not surprising due to the fact that the oldest group tended to hold the highest clergy positions and higher incomes associated with these advanced positions. This group, as well as the middle age group, tended to give priority to their careers over the career of their spouses.

In contrast, while the youngest group tended to be equally well educated, they also were most likely to hold lower positions within the clergy hierarchy and had the lowest income levels. As might be expected, the youngest group was far more likely to express dissatisfaction with income and career progress. In addition, this group was most likely to give equal priority to their spouse's career as well as their own. This finding may reflect the current economic trends in that dual careers are not only more acceptable to this group but also may be an economic necessity.

Position within the clergy hierarchy also tended to influence the clergy's perceptions of career and personal satisfaction. The relationships here are rather straightforward. The higher clergy positions are associated with higher salaries, and personal and career satisfaction. Education level also tended to be associated with higher clergy position, but this finding is misleading given that 82% of the clergy in the sample held advanced degrees.

The majority of the sample indicated that their career progress was about what they had expected or better than they had expected. While these findings may appear contrary to the findings concerning career satisfaction for the youngest group, this group represents only 17.6% of the sample. Therefore, while the *majority* of the sample expressed satisfaction in the careers, this majority does not include the youngest group.

By contrast to male clergy, the women were significantly different. Female clergy held the lowest positions, were represented most frequently in the youngest group and not surprisingly, received the smallest salaries. These women, in general, expressed dissatisfaction with their career progress. Their husbands represent a highly diverse group and few general statements can be made about them. However, male spouses of clergy did tend to earn more income than their wives, even though they held less advanced degrees than their wives. Again, these findings may tentatively suggest an increased acceptability and necessity for dual careers at least for young people entering the ministry.

CLERGY REACTIONS TO FAMILY VERSUS CAREER RESPONSIBILITIES

In addition to demographic variable and issues related to satisfaction the investigators in the study posed three hypothetical situations regarding family and career commitments. Clergy and spouses were asked to respond to what influence certain family problems and needs might have on the appointive system. The three open-ended questions are stated below:

Situation #1

Suppose you have a sick child and the community in which you live has excellent health, hospital and medical facilities to assist you and your family in providing care for this child. You are asked to move to another community and church where the medical services are very limited and you will have to travel great distances to find medical care for your child. What would you say or do when asked to move?

Situation #2

Suppose your spouse is just beginning a career and the children are away in college, the clergy-person is asked to move to a small community with limited opportunity for the spouse to continue to work and the additional income is needed to finance the college education of a child. What would you say or do?

Situation #3

Suppose you and your spouse have had difficulty adjusting to parish life and you have not been able to find a parish situation in which you felt comfortable and happy and this has caused some marital stress. In addition to these problems, you have a teenage youngster who has not done well academically, has many friends, was selected to serve on the high school yearbook committee and wants to stay and finish high school in the community where you are now living. Given the many ways of responding to a move, if you were in this situation and asked to move, what would you say or do?

A content analysis of twenty percent (n = 405) of the entire sample of clergy and spouse responses to the open-ended situations was conducted to examine their perceptions of the kind of experiences that influence their lives in the itinerancy system of the United Methodist Ministry. These situations, which include the care of a sick child, the need for a spouse's income, and a teenager's success in high school, indicate the potential conflicts between family and career commitments.

The results suggest that the response may be classified along a continuum of most to least committed to the appointive system. Seven categories were elicited from the data—move/compromise, undecided, indiscernible, stay/compromise, stay, conditional/leave the ministry if necessary—representing the full range of options subjects suggested in their responses. For the most part, clergy and spouses attempted to seek a compromise situation. This finding indicates that, yes, indeed, clergy and their spouses are willing to move if required. Elaborate solutions are often suggested so that a choice for or against their family or ministerial vows does not have to be made. In contrast, a large percentage of clergy and spouses indicate they would stay without hesitation, on the one hand, or, at the other extreme, would even leave the ministry altogether if they were not satisfied with the suggested appointment. Those people who would leave the ministry altogether are either very disappointed with the itinerancy or are simply not convinced that the ministry is their only option.

The content analysis also revealed that those who are the most satisfied with their career as clergy are likely to be the ones with the most options. This group includes well-paid male pastors, district superintendents, and their wives. They are likely to be at least middle aged and to have grown children.

The dissatisfied appear to be in one of two groups. Either they are highly educated, younger clergy, with few or no children, who are just beginning their careers, or they are the older, disillusioned group. Here, we find a lot of wives of clergymen, who have sacrificed for their husband's career, only to have him in later life married to the church. The divorced clergy, though a small proportion of the sample, also appear to be disillusioned in their personal lives and their careers.

IMPLICATIONS

The results of this study reveal that, on the whole, this sample of United Methodist clergy and their spouses are generally satisfied with their career progress and family circumstances. These conclusions appear obvious in that the clergy profession requires a high degree of commitment, not just from the pastor, but from the entire family, particularly the spouse (Hoge, Dyble & Polk, 1981; Mills, 1969). While our industrialized society is characterized by a relative separation of private and professional roles, the Protestant minister is unable to separate the two. All the aspects of the clergy's personal life—from the marital relationship to recreational preferences to childrearing practices—are visible and occupationally relevant (Mills, 1969). Family and vocational roles are, thus, enmeshed. However, due to the nature of the clergy career, as demonstrated in the results of our study of United Methodist clergy, the vocational realm is expected to take first priority.

These conclusions are more true of older clergy than of younger clergy. While the entire sample as a whole demonstrated that a great deal of creative problem solving is undertaken in the daily lives of clergy families, younger clergy appear to be less tolerant of the sacrificial nature of the itinerant system. There is an indication that younger clergy are less willing than older clergy to sacrifice their time, their financial compensation, and the quality of their marriages in the service of the church. A social-exchange perspective offers an explanation. The more time and energy one had invested in a career, the more one will be committed to that career. A similar analogy has been made regarding marriage. The longer one remains married, the greater the likelihood that one will continue in that marriage, as evidenced by the fact that most divorces (about two-thirds), occur during the first ten years of marriage, while only a third occur after the tenth year (Eshleman, 1984).

Yet another explanation exists in the gap between the satisfaction level of younger and older clergy. Dissatisfaction is seen primarily in the youngest group. They come into the system at a higher education level than the two older groups. They earn a very low salary which makes it difficult to support a family. Often, two incomes may be required "just to get by." This may account for the fact that this group holds a more equalitarian perspective concerning clergy/spouse career priorities in that two incomes may be required today for economic survival. As previously noted in the clergy responses to the three family versus career dilemmas, the youngest group was least willing to compromise and was most willing to leave the ministry if required to choose between family and career responsibilities.

While recognizing this apparent discontent is evident among only 17.6% of our sample, (i.e., the youngest group who are in the 23 to 35 age range) they are still the future veterans and leaders of the church. Given their dissatisfaction, it becomes obvious that some changes are required within the system if the United Methodist Church is to continue to attract and retain young, high quality candidates for the ministry. Our data suggest that these changes should focus on monetary incentives, more flexibility concerning family related issues, and fewer mobility demands.

One of the most outstanding differences between male clergy under age 35 and their older counterparts revolves around the issue of equality between spouses. The data clearly indicate that it is in the youngest group of clergy that equal priority is most likely to be given to the spouse's career (i.e., 46% of the 23 to 35 age group versus 15% of the 36 to 54 age group). It is unclear whether this more egalitarian perspective in the younger group is due to their more liberal view of the female role or results from the increasing necessity for a dual income. Whatever the reason, this is an interesting finding.

In reviewing the responses of the youngest group of clergy, the most significant change the church might make to enhance satisfaction among this group would be to increase entry level salaries. A change such as this may offer an additional incentive to compensate for the tremendous demands placed on clergy as they begin their careers in the ministry and family. Similarly, since it is the age group that is called upon most often to move, these moves might be made more appealing if additional financial rewards were offered as an incentive. Our data suggest that many of the younger clergy hold high anticipation of career and salary advancement as they move from one position to the next. Clearly, this is not the case for clergy at the lower end of the hierarchical system.

While these solutions may not be appropriate in all cases, there appears to be a need to re-evaluate entry level clergy positions, in this denomination, in order that their level of satisfaction may more closely coincide with the level of satisfaction found among clergy who have progressed to the more prestigious positions in the hierarchical system.

SUMMARY

As we examine the overall results of this study of United Methodist clergy, we see an initial profile of reasonably satisfied older clergy and spouses who have committed themselves to a type of career pattern which has been described as essentially a two-person career. They share this type of experience with many professional families in the same age cohort and seemingly have no desire to alter their situation. By contrast to this group, we then see a younger cohort of people who have entered their occupations with different expectations and ways of handling occupational and family responsibilities. This latter group is less likely to favor the two-person career option and reflects a much broader range of characteristics. Possibly, due to differences in age and a less advantaged position, many of these younger people are disenchanted with their prospects. If this continues, the outcome is likely to be a major shift from the traditional paths experienced by the older people or it may result in the younger people seeking other careers. In any event, traditional clergy paths may be altered, these people may change their own family pattern, or they will leave the ministry. Something will have to change. At this time, it is unclear whether the institution of the church or the families themselves will benefit or suffer.

REFERENCES

Eshleman, J.R. (1984). The family: An introduction. 4th edition, Boston: Allyn & Bacon.

Hoge, D.R., Dyble, J.E. & Polk, D.T. (1981). Organizational and situational influences on vocational commitment of Protestant ministers. *Review of Religious Research*, *23*, 133–149.

Lewis, R.A. (1982). *Men in Difficult Times*. Englewood Cliffs, New Jersey: Prentice Hall, Inc.

Macklin, E.D. (1980). Nontraditional family forms: A decade of research. *Journal of Marriage and the Family*, *42*, 175–192.

Mills, E.W. (1969). Career change in the protestant ministry. *Ministry Studies*, *3*, 5–32.

Chapter 14

The Honey Moon—Some Options

Kris Jeter

The Honey Moon, defined as the wedding night and approximately the first month after the marriage ceremony, has historically been recognized as a time of wonder and astonishment for the partners in connubial bliss. In the Orient, the bride groom would, during the course of the 28-day lunar month honey moon, have sexual relations with the bride during her menstrual period. This would be the man's first contact with "moon honey," the menstrual blood regarded as the source of life, an elixir. In Greece, the Goddess Hymen (veil) and the Hymenoptera (the veiled-winged bee) were sources of honey, a food stuff and burial preservative as well as symbol of regeneration of female potency. Hymen was called forth with the invocation of "O Hymen Hymenaie," to preside over the honey moon, the ritual penetration of the veil (Walker, pages 407–408).

The folklore and mythology expressed in varied art forms about the honey moon are rich, providing us with varied bride and bride groom characters and role models and prototype options for honey moon behavior. Immersed in the depths of the human psyche is the universal, primordial, collective unconscious inhabited by archetypes, internal forces of energy which seek to organize the psyche's varied interactions and sustain the endurance of the ego consciousness. These archetypes are spontaneously expressed cross culturally as vital life forces and archetypal images in art, fantasies, dreams, fairy tales, and myths. It is through the archetypal images that the human being reveals profound unconscious longings and yearnings (Jung).

Thus, it is to the ancient stories, "the depersonalized dream," that we search for the bride and bride groom archetypes, "the personalized myth" (Campbell). In this analytical essay, one

209

Arthurian legend, one Danish and one German fairy tale tell of climactic honey moons. These ancient stories are presented and investigated individually and as a group to determine significant longings and roles of the bride and bride groom in the honey moon as expressed in mythology. The unconscious pinings and yearnings of men, women, couples, kin, and communities rise in the sacred honey moon time when the veil is penetrated and the moon honey discovered.

> That for which you yearn
>   yearns as much for you.
> Listen to its call
>   of longing to come through.
> Stay with your desire;
>   feel the power grow.
> As two lovers come together,
>   yearning makes it so. (Taylor)

THE BOY WHO SET OUT TO LEARN FEAR

Carl-Heinz Mallet, a German school administrator, believes that fairy tales have meandered through centuries and cultures on the lips of storytellers and in the hearts of listeners. Each fairy tale is a fine crystal which concentrates the color and spectrum of human behavior, emotion, and knowledge of the life-death cycle. He relates and analyzes "The Boy Who Set Out to Learn Fear" in *Fairy Tales and Children: The Psychology of Children Revealed through Four of Grimm's Fairy Tales*.

The Fairy Tale

Once upon a time there lived a father and his two sons. The older son was considered much more intelligent and obedient than the younger. However, when the older son was ordered to go to scary places, he would say, "I'm afraid." The younger would nonchalantly go to these places. He began to wonder if fear was a skill that he should learn and so started to often say, "Ah, if only I could be scared."

The sexton of the local church parish offered to teach the younger son fear. One midnight, the sexton woke the boy and ordered him to climb the church steeple and ring the bell. *The sexton hurried ahead to the tower and crouched covered in white to appear as if a ghost. The boy saw the figure, called out three times, and then threw the ghost down the staircase. He pulled the bell rope as instructed and returned to his bed and deep sleep. Later in the evening the wife of the sexton woke the boy inquiring of her husband's whereabouts. He said that there was a figure who did not disclose her or his identity and so was dealt with as a thief. The sexton's wife found her wounded husband and complained loudly to the boy's father.*

The father gave 50 pieces of gold to the boy and ordered him to leave and tell no one of his father's or hometown's name. The boy left saying, "Ah, if only I could be scared."

Hearing him, a man showed him the gallows and told him to spend the night and he would be scared. In exchange for being afraid, the boy would pay the man fifty gold pieces. The boy sat in the gallows and built a fire to warm himself from the brisk wind. He looked above and saw seven hanged men. Still being chilled, he, with empathy for their cold bodies, brought them down and placed them by the fire. The bodies being dead, with tongues hanging out, sat upright by the fire and were unable to protect their clothing from fire scattered by the wind. The boy placed them up on the tree again, He slept by the fire without fear. The man did not earn the fifty gold pieces. The boy left the gallows saying, "Ah, if only I could be scared."

An innkeeper overheard him and said that the king would give his daughter's hand in marriage and treasures to the man who could successfully spend three nights in an "enchanted castle." The boy asked the king for the chance to sleep in this castle. The king granted the boy's wish and asked him if there were three inanimate items he would want for his visit. The boy requested that he have "a fire, a lathe, and a carving bench with a knife."

On the first midnight two large black cats leaped on his right and left side, looked at him with feral, blood thirsty eyes, and asked him to play a card game. The boy asked them to lay open their paws. The boy exclaimed at the sight of the lengthy claws, offered to clip them, instead slew them and pitched them into the castle moat. No sooner than he had accomplished this, a horde of black cats and dogs attached to fire-hot chain link leashes attacked the boy. The boy leaped at them, slaying some with his knife and throwing them into the moat and frightening others to escape.

Tired from the battle, he saw a bed in the corner of the room. As soon as he lay down, the bed stirred and moved throughout the whole enchanted castle. He exclaimed, "faster." The bed came to an abrupt halt, landing on top of the boy's body. He untangled himself and slept by the fire till dawn. The next day he told the king and the innkeeper, "Ah, if only I could be scared."

The second midnight the boy heard raves, screeches, and yowls. One half of a male figure fell down the chimney followed by the remaining half. The man was followed by other men carrying "two human skulls and nine human bones." The boy asked if he could join them in a game of ninepins. The boy filed and smoothed the skulls with his lathe. They played; he lost some money. As suddenly as the men had appeared, they disappeared. Accordingly, the boy slept soundly. He again reported to the king, "Ah, if only I could be scared."

On the third midnight, six large men marched into the castle bearing a coffin. The boy looked in calling out "Cousin," felt the cold dead man, and laid down beside the man to warm him. The thawed man said, "Now I'm going to strangle you!" The boy cast him into the bier, and the six men removed it from the enchanted castle.

Immediately, an even larger man of considerable age with snow-white hair flowing from his face confronted the boy, "Oh, you insect, you'll soon learn what it is to be scared, for you are going to die." Each said that he had most power and strength. The boy positioned the beard to his advantage and beat the man. The ancient man moaned and beseeched the boy to stop, promising gold. The boy stopped. They went to the basement and the ancient designated one chest of gold for the needy, the king, and the boy. At midnight the ancient left and the boy had fitful sleep. The next morning, he reported to the king, "Ah, if only I could be scared." The king replied, "You have broken the spell on the castle, and you shall marry my daughter."

The boy distributed gold to the king and to the poor and retained a portion. All of the royal subjects of the kingdom celebrated the marriage with great festivity. The boy continued saying, "Ah, if only I could be scared."

The wife, irritated at her husband's constant repeating of his wish spoke with her chambermaid who offered to satisfy his desire. The chambermaid obtained a bucket of gudgeons. While her husband slept, his wife removed the bedcovers and unloaded the bucket of squirming and wiggling small carp fish in cold water over

*him. The boy, now the young king awoke and exclaimed, "Oh, I'm
so scared, I'm so scared, dear wife! Yes, now I know what it's like
to be scared* (Mallet, pages 15–25). *"And if they haven't died, then
they're still alive today!"* (Mallet, page 208).

The Analysis

On one glance, a reader might predict that the message of a fairy
tale with such a title as related to the honey moon would be that fear
can enhance the nuptial bed. Carl-Heinz Mallet believes that "The
Boy Who Set Out to Learn Fear" is a story which outlines the
developmental stages from boyhood to adolescence to young
manhood.

The child feels safe in the family nest and is comfortable with her
or his unaffected, unsophisticated spontaneous behavior. With
adolescence, though, the freedom from cares disappears. The body
no longer looks or feels or acts the same as before. For boys, the
voice cracks and facial hair pops out. For girls, the breast and hips
increase in size and menstruation commences. Pimples burst out on
both. Having not yet attained sexual maturity, the adolescent is
haunted by it. The body movements followed by deportment
become clumsy and ungraceful. Raw energy slowly takes purpose
and form. Not understanding the personal changes, empathy for
others is at a low point. Careless and tactless comments are made in
either bristling boasts or enthralled dependency.

Hans comes from a family of origin in which the elder brother,
Matthes, is the favored son. Matthes obeys commands and does his
assigned tasks well. He is fearful of walking through cemeteries and
hearing ghost stories during the evening hours. Hans envies Matthes
his popularity and believes, that if he learns how to be afraid like his
brother, he can also win the approval of his family and community.
Thus, the goal Hans sets for himself is to learn the skill of fear. He
then does the unusual; he states his personal adage, "Ah if only I
could be scared," often with great yearning. Such truthfulness is not
appreciated by others. Hans is the hero in this fairy tale because he
acts without self consciousness to achieve his stated goal. He pays
no attention to the social norms of behavior and shows little respect
for institutional values. Rather, he acts in accordance to his
idiosyncratic value system.

As all boys, Hans enters into conflict with his father. This is the
only way for a boy to develop knowledge about personal latent

powers, limitations, skills, and tenacious traits which he can call
forth to surmount obstacles. Even in the conflict, Hans is mannerly
when his father does not understand his actions with the Sexton.
And so, the adolescent leaves his childhood home to achieve his
goal. Upon leaving his family and community, he is promptly
acknowledged as a young man by adults that he meets.

Hans fearlessly follows his path, facing and meeting head on all
obstacles. He meets the King, who is an exemplary father figure.
The King actively listens to Hans' yearning and provides him with
practical items and tasks to further his quest. Of course, in actuality,
such a father does not exist.

Hans accepts the challenge of liberating the castle of ghosts and
spirits and moves to bring with strong effort illumination to the
bewitched castle. This castle symbolizes Hans' internal self. He
confronts the trials offered him by the charmed and enchanted
castle.

Upon liberating the castle, he presents one chest of treasure to the
King, showing his respect for the father figure; one to the poor,
indicating his awareness of others' existence; and keeps one for
himself, rewarding his good deeds. Yet, everything that he has
earned—the princess, the treasure, and the castle—were not his
stated goals. He has not satisfied his yearnings to be scared.

Hans' unspoken yearning is for warmth. Throughout his journey
he meets cold cats, corpses, partial men, and skeletons. He attempts
to warm each, yearning for the warmth of his parental and familial
home life. He does, on his trek, learn how to be alone.

Marriage is a union of two adults. The wife is not a "surrogate
mother for bestowing warmth" (page 173); her gifts are in contrast
to the gifts of a mother. "Life is not a warm bed, it is bubbly, lively,
tingling—at least for those able to free themselves from the
attachments and entanglements of childhood" (page 173).

Thus, the princess disentangles Hans from his need to be afraid
so that he could be as his brother—afraid and liked. She follows the
advice of the chambermaid, well experienced in the affairs of the
honey moon. She provides him with the unexpected as he lies
immersed in sweet dreams. She throws a bucket of sharp, piercing,
cold water inhabited by a multitude of twisting, shimmering, lively,
tiny fish. Suddenly, Hans feels overrun with sensations unknown to
him in his past. The fish cannot be avoided. He cannot withdraw
into himself. In this honey moon, Hans' lonely, masculine castle
from which he has ousted the terrors is now striken with the

exquisite, feminine fish. In the best of times, their union can bring forth volts of intense energy that can enhance, nurture, and elevate vitality.

Hans embarked on his journey yearning to be contacted by a significant event which would alter his perception of life. During the honey moon, a time of novelty, wonder and astonishment, the feminine aspect, so foreign to his way of being, perforated his inner self so that he can engage in a lively, adult, marital union as an equal.

KING LINDWORM

Marie-Louise von Franz, Swiss psychologist and collaborator and friend of Jung, tells and discusses "King Lindworm," a Danish story, in the 1980 book, *The Psychological Meaning of Redemption Motifs in Fairytales* based on lectures she presented in 1956. The Celtic-Germanic word, "Lindworm," translates to mean dragon and snake.

The Fairy Tale

Once upon a time there were a king and a queen who awoke from the first eve of their honey moon to find a prediction of their barrenness engraved on their bed. Despairing, they looked high and low for a way to reverse this cruel curse.

One day, an old woman counseled the queen. "Leave a bowl bottom side up in the north-west corner of the garden. Upon waking, you will find two roses. Should you partake of the white rose, you will bear a girl child. Should you partake of the red rose, you will bear a boy child. Under no circumstances are you to eat both roses."

The queen projects into the future. She wonders what would happen to a girl child who would marry outside of the family and a boy child who would go to fight in the wars. Thus, she eats both roses wanting to conceive twins.

Nine months later, Lindworm, a male dragon is born. Without delay, Lindworm, in ominous voice, announces that he will demolish the castle and eat every living thing—human and animal. The king arrives home from war, quite unaware of the queen's pregnancy and of the birth of the male dragon. Lindworm orders the king to bestow upon him all of the rights due him as a son or he will demolish the castle and eat every living thing. Lindworm rules the castle and all obey his every bid and call.

When Lindworm becomes twenty years of age, he asks for a bride, threatening his wrath if he has no bride. There then begins a progression of marriages, each ending with the bride being eaten by Lindworm on the first eve of the honey moon. In time, Lindworm has eaten all but one of the maidens residing in the kingdom who are eligible to marry. The king asks an old shepherd to give his daughter in marriage to Lindworm and consent is given with much sorrow.

The shepherd's daughter knowing of her future, walks to the forest crying large tears. She receives advice from an old woman.

After the wedding ritual and feast, the princess enters the honey moon chamber, wearing nine shirts, one upon the other. When Lindworm asks her to remove her shirt, she, in turn, asks him to remove a skin. After she removes nine shirts and he nine skins, she finds a heap of blood, fat, and muscle. The princess soundly thrashes this heap with a hazel switch dipped into a vat of lye. When the heap is almost disintegrated, the princess gently swabs it with sweet milk, enclosing it with a wrap made of nine shirts. She lays down, falling asleep embracing the heap in her arms.

The next morning the honey moon couple awake. The princess lies in the arms of a handsome prince, redeemed by his new wife from the curse. They live happily every after, blessed with the bliss of marriage, in the grand circle of life (von Franz, pages 76–77).

The Analysis

Marie-Louise von Franz discusses this Danish story in *The Psychological Meaning of Redemption Motifs in Fairytales*. The bewitched or cursed archetype disrupts, disorganizes, and consumes people and objects. A portion of the bewitched one's psyche is maimed or paralyzed which, in turn, incapacitates the functioning of the entire psyche. It is the task of the female or male hero to liberate, recover, and restore the bewitched person to full redemption.

In "King Lindworm," the bewitched prince is a hermaphrodite, a regressive being formed internally of masculine blood, fat, and muscle contributed by the red rose and covered by nine layers of dragon scales contributed by the femininity of the white rose.

The bride is tutored by a wise woman, experienced in the honey moon ritual herself. The prince is recognized to be a man paralyzed under the encasement of nine skins. The bride dons nine layers of shirts in order to veil, to protect herself.

During the honey moon, the couple in a "simultaneous transformation" (page 87), slowly divest one layer at a time, both responding authentically to each unveiling, until the true character is revealed. The bride then whips her groom with hazel tree branches dipped in strong alkaline lye, symbols of unbiased truthfulness. She cleanses him of his curses with sweet milk, the feminine source of nurturance, reconstituting and amplifying him to completeness. And she re-covers him in nine shirts and restores him with her loving presence.

Throughout the ages, there have been and will continue to be folk who enter a marriage wounded and seeking wholeness in the partner. Likewise, there have and will be persons in search of a bewitched one to mend. Regardless of the degree of curse and quality of redemption, an orderly, "simultaneous transformation" to authenticity is one prototype option for the honey moon as well as courtship and marriage.

SIR GAWAIN'S MARRIAGE

During the middle 1800's, Harvard professor, Thomas Bulfinch, wrote classical mythology of the varied ages in a clarified, crystaline form for reading by the masses. One Arthurian legend he tells is "Sir Gawain's Marriage," which is abridged below.

This story has surfaced through the ages. In the fourteenth century it was told by English poets Geoffrey Chaucer as "The Tale of the Whf of Bathe" and John Gower as "Tale of Florent." In the middle fifteenth century it appeared as a poem, "The Weddynge of Sir Gawan and Dame Ragnell." This was followed in the seventeenth century by a ballad, "The Marriage of Sir Gawaine (Campbell, page 118). The message of the story is relevant in times past as it is now.

The Arthurian Legend

Once upon a time, King Arthur, in order to save the virtue of a fair damsel, took revenge against a fierce baron. The "grim baron" lived in a castle which "stood on magic ground." Thus, as King

Arthur approached the land, he lost his confidence and power. The baron agreed to allow King Arthur one year to determine the correct answer to the question, "What thing is it which women most desire?" or else the baron would be awarded all of King Arthur's lands and treasures.

The King rode up and down mountains and plains, and to the north, south, east, and west asking the question. He heard the answers of adulation, grandeur, knights, merriment, and wealth. On the day he was to give the answer to the baron, he happened to ride by an abominable looking woman, so ugly he turned away from her. She said, "What wight art thou that will not speak to me? It may chance that I may resolve thy doubts, though I be not fair of aspect." The woman told him the answer to the question in exchange for his arrangement of her marriage to a handsome and favored knight.

King Arthur arrived at the baron's castle and provided many answers to the question, "What thing is it which women most desire?" Adulation, grandeur, knights, merriment, and wealth were incorrect. He then repeated the ugly woman's answer, "all women would have their will." Thus, King Arthur redeemed his kingdom, however at the price of the married life of a knight.

He related his problem to his nephew, Sir Gawain, the Knight of the Splendid Golden Hair, who quickly agreed to marry the lady. King Arthur said: "The loathly lady's all too grim, And all too foule for thee." The lady was brought to the castle from the forest. The marriage ritual was performed, however, there was no celebration or feast.

When alone at nightfall, the bride asked her husband why he breathed with great heaviness. Sir Gawain admitted his true feelings. He was uncomfortable with her age, her low status, and her grotesqueness. Not insulted, she rebutted that these qualities were actually attributes. Age was simply a matter of taste, status depended on parents and character was much better, and there would be no competitors vying with the Knight for her ugly body.

Saying nothing, Gawain looked into his bride's eyes, seeing a woman more beautiful than he thought possible. She said that her true appearance was concealed by the power of her brother, the "grim baron." The baron had doomed her to a life of appearing abominable unless two conditions be met. She had satisfied one condition, marrying a handsome and favored knight. Thus, she was

free now to be either beautiful by day and ugly by night or beautiful
by night and ugly by day. She allowed Gawain to make the choice.
   Sir Gawain pondered the options—his pride in her public
appearance and his joy in her private attentions. He granted his
bride her will over her fate. This act satisfied the second condition;
she was beautiful by day and by night.

> *Sweet blushes stayned her rud-red cheek,*
>   *Her eyen were black as sloe,*
> *The ripening cherrye swelled her lippe,*
>   *And all her neck was snow.*
> *Sir Gawain kist that ladye faire*
>   *Lying upon the sheete,*
> *And swore, as he was a true knight,*
>   *The spice was never so swete.* (Bulfinch, pages 347– 349)

The Analysis

In 1982, Jungian therapist, Edward C. Whitmont, in his book,
Return of the Goddess, analyzed the King Arthur legend and
recognized Sir Gawain as Grail Hero. The story of Gawain's active
life, including his marriage, is hypothesized to be a disguise for
Parsifal's inner growth.

Gawain is historically called "bright hair," "the Fountain of
May," "he who is given eternal youth," and "the new year's god
who heals and renews the old god, who has guarded the cauldron
and now must die" (page 167). Gawain serves the Grail goddess,
represented in the entire Arthurian legends by Lady Ragnell,
Kundrie, Morgan le Fay and other women.

Lady Ragnell is the physically ugly wellspring who challenges
Sir Gawain to risk and trust in order that he may grow. Lady Ragnell
replaces Sir Gawain's departmentalized, divided view of good life
and bad life with a holistic view of living as a harmonious
movement of creation and destruction. Gawain, as a knight, is to be
prepared for combat, dressed in masculine armor of self discipline.
With a lady, the knight is to remove his armor and meet the
feminine. Gawain encounters his fear of the opposite, the feminine,
and vitality. Gawain acknowledges Lady Ragnell's sovereignty,
accepting the lovely and the grotesque, the brilliant and the obscure
while being true to his own integrity. He provides and accepts
empathy and love, cooperatively sharing responsibility. When Sir

Gawain accepted Lady Ragnell, she conferred the sovereignty of the land upon him.

The honey moon and marriage portrayed in this legend are a prototype of an opportunity to greet a world which is delightful and frightful, to consciously risk pain while attending to the self and the other. Each seeks and penetrates personal psyche and relationship archetypes. Each partner wishes ''sovereignty''— affective and behavioral response and respect.

CONCLUSION

These three myths (''depersonalized dreams'') about honey moons, provide us with varied bride and bride groom characters, role models, archetypes, and prototype options for honey moon behavior. The honey moon, in ''the personalized myth,'' symbolizes the unconscious yearning of the man to integrate his anima archetype and, the woman, her animus archetype. In the conclusion to this analytic essay, several strong yarns which have emerged— role theory, anima and animus archetypes, marriage, yearning, and honey moon—will be woven together to form a full bodied hawser. From these concepts are distilled yearnings and roles of the bride groom and bride in the honey moon of ''the depersonalized dream'' and ''the personalized myth.'' These are charted in Table One and are discussed.

Role Theory

Social psychologists have hypothesized that people do not behave in a random manner. Individuals in social situations occupy a position and fulfill a role dependent upon their perceptions with reference to expectations (Jeter).

Transpersonal psychologists believe that the role is an object of perception of unconscious archetypical images and dependent upon a person's actions, feelings, and thoughts. Carl Jung observed that the male fetus contained female genes and the female fetus contained male genes. He was curious to know of the path that these genes took in the growing male and female. Jung hypothesized that each man and woman is biologically and psychologically ambisexual, possessing both masculine and feminine traits. Male and female roles are molded by genetic sex differences amplified by

TABLE 1

YEARNINGS OF THE BRIDE GROOMS AND BRIDES IN THREE MYTHS

Title of the Myth	Names by Which The Bride Groom is Called before and after the Honey Moon	Names by Which The Bride is Called before and after the Honey Moon	Bride Groom's Yearning	Bride's Yearning	Bride's Means Derived from Inner Knowledge and Female Counsel
"The Boy Who Set Out to Learn Fear"	Boy to "Young King" (Hans)	King's daughter to "dear wife"	"Ah, if only I could be scared"	to scare him so that he would enter the marriage as an adult	threw bucket of gudgeons and cold water on Hans
"King Lindworm"	King Lindworm	Shepherd's daughter to princess	to receive his entitlement of a wife, even if it extinguishes all womankind and life	to redeem the bewitched bride groom and to live	during "simultaneous transformation" she divests 9 shirts and he 9 skins; she then whips him with hazel branches dipped in lye, cleanses him in milk, covers him in 9 shirts, and hugs him in sleep
"Sir Gawain's Marriage"	Sir Gawain	"loathly" "lady of such hideous aspect" to the "lovely" Lady Ragnell	as a Knight to fulfill King Arthur's pledge, to "find some fare and courtly knight to be her husband"; to give sovereignty while being sovereign	to return to her true form by fulfilling the 2 conditions: marriage to "some young & gallant knight" & her husband's giving "his will to her"	asks him "why he sighed so heavily" without offense answers that his objections of "age," "ugliness," & "low degree" are attributes (in some versions she requests a kiss)

the process of socialization. In the course of this formation process, the human often neglects attending to the opposite sex traits within.

Anima and Animus Archetypes

Jung believed that the opposite sex traits within the collective unconscious are in the form of archetypes. The archetypes, internal forces of energy, seek to organize the psyche's varied interactions and sustain the endurance of the ego consciousness. In men resides the anima, the soul, the God Eros, god of relatedness. In women lives the animus, the spirit, the God Logos, god of form.

The anima and animus are immutable inhabitants in the psyche. They involuntarily come forth in dreams and fantasies which we may project upon another person. If a person is captivating and enamoring, he or she is probably a projection of the anima or animus. A living human generally does not bewilder a person to obsession.

The anima and animus entice and lure. When perceived, regarded, and interrelated to the consciousness, the positive anima and animus emerge. In men, the positive anima could be exhibited in being, gathering, listening, nurturing, unifying behaviors. In women, the positive animus could be expressed in action, analysis, definiteness, discrimination, structure behaviors.

However, when the anima and animus are doubted, refused, or opposed, the negative archetype rises. In men, the negative anima could be represented in capricious, effeminate, gloomy, maudlin, and mawkish behaviors. In women, the negative animus could be revealed in argumentative, dogmatic, inflexible, prejudiced, unyielding behaviors.

A person through conscious work can distinguish the actuality of the anima and animus, a process Jung called a "master-piece" of individuation (page 29). This work involves recognition of ambisexuality and the authenticity of inner and outer worlds.

Marriage

Jung proposed that the human being chooses a marital partner who depicts a yet-to-be-learned inner knowing. An authentic marital relationship occurs when two distinct individuals attend to, share, and accept personal growth and developmental issues.

In a marriage, the unconscious of two humans collide. It is

important for a person to distinguish between projected anima and animus images and actual marital partners. The baffling, flaming, and inexplicable projection of the anima and animus is the affair of the gods. In comparison, love of a marital partner may seem common, unexceptional, and usual. Consciousness of the divine inner love and the human outer love can further authenticate personal and marital life.

Yearning

The English word, "yearning," is derived from and akin to a multitude of ancient Sanskrit, Greek, Latin, Gothic, and other Indo-european words. The meaning of the word is "to be filled with desire, to be uneasy with eager longing and anxiety . . . to feel compassion or tender love, to be moved with pity, grief, or sympathy" (Neilson, page 2968). The words in Amanda Mc-Broom's song, "The Rose," provide a summary meaning—"a hunger, an endless aching need."

Betsy Caprio, parish minister, describes the source and dynamics of yearning.

> We are surrounded by the interplay of the two opposite flows in the universe. These complements confront each other in our souls, in the natural world in which we move, in our encounters with others, in the cosmic dance. They may war . . . or be in occasional dialogue . . . or, best of all, unite to support and cover each other lovingly. (Caprio, page 98)

According to Jung, the unconscious yearning of humans from early times and valid today is for union of the polar masculine and feminine aspects. The human soul is the site where the polarities meet and slowly progress to unite in the personality.

In general, to achieve this inner unity, a man will require a woman and a woman will require a man. Yet, the union cannot be accomplished if one sexual aspect is enacted and the opposite sexual aspect unconsciously projected on the marital partner. The yearning requires persistent, unremitted attentiveness, and patience. Eventually, the union of polarities occurs over the span of a lifetime within the soul ignited by the yearning.

Honey Moon

The anima and animus lure and seduce the human to attention through the use of vivid erotic imagery. The bold, sensational, wanton sensuality and sexuality of the archetypal representations serve to awaken the person to the life of the soul.

The yearning for the union of the anima and the animus has long been spontaneously expressed cross culturally in the symbol of the marriage. Vivid images have been inscribed in such varied texts as the Cabala, the Iliad, and the Song of Songs; the marriage of Tifereth and Malchuth; Hera and Zeus, and the Bride and the Bride Groom portray the union of the feminine and the masculine. Vibrant logos depict the fusion of opposites: the Greek cross, rainbow, star of David, t'ai chi circle of yin and yang, tree, and unicorn. Terminology for this concord include *hieros gamos* (the sacred marriage), *mysterium conjunctionis* (the mystical marriage), and the marriage with the beloved.

This author believes that the honey moon is a specific archetypal image of the union of the anima and animus reflective in symbols and words which extend and expand those of the concept of marriage. The terminology used to describe the time immediately following the marriage ceremony tells of the excitation, provocation, and stimulation of the nuptial bed. For instance, the German word for honey moon, "Flitterwochen," literally means "a week of sequins and spangles" (*Langenscheidt's Universal Dictionary*, page 393). Stories told and examined in this analytic essay depict the amazement, astonishment, and surprise which electrify the union of opposites and then integrate into a creative, generative personality full of potentials.

The Bride Groom's Yearning and Role

The English word, "bride groom," is derived from the Latin word, "humus," which means earth (Neilson, page 334). The bride groom is the son of the earth who meets Venus, the Goddess of Generation.

The bride groom personifies the animus, the animating spirit. The word, "animus," is common in various Latin law phrases, indicating the legal sense of intention. Each of the bride grooms in the three myths told in this analytic essay have different stated intentions along with the unconscious yearning of unity of the life forces.

In the German fairy tale, "The Boy Who Set Out to Learn Fear," Mallet specifically tells the story referring to the hero as "the boy" until he is touched by the feminine and then he becomes "the young king." The honey moon is the developmental crisis in the boy's life which "turns him into a man."

In the Danish fairy tale, "King Lindworm," the bride groom is a wounded regressive who seeks wholeness. In the honey moon, he allows his bride to progressively eliminate his nine skins so that he can meet the feminine and be redeemed by her to authenticity.

In "Sir Gawain's Marriage," the bride groom is a knight in service to King Arthur's Court. He has successfully completed the tasks of a page in his exhibition of military skill, prowess, and generosity. In the presence of his bride, he removes his armor to accept the feminine.

The Bride's Yearning and Role

The English word, "bride," is a derivative of the Latin word, "Frutis," another name for Venus (Neilson, page 334), the Goddess of Generation (Walker, page 1043). The bride personifies the anima, the archetype of the heavenly ("an") mother ("ma") (Walker, page 37). The first experience that a male has with his mother constructs and produces the basic blueprint of his anima.

The second most profound experience the male has with his anima is with the bride. In the ancient art of pharmacy, the anima was the buoyant, changeable, volatile ingredient of drugs composed of natural animal and vegetable substances (Neilson, page 105). Likewise, the bride as an anima archetype entices and leads the bride groom to trek the voyage of risks and rewards toward a yet-to-be-learned inner knowing. The bride's yearning and role in the mythological honey moon is to alert and guide the bride groom to unity of the paradox, to life. The bride anima may appear as lovely or she may appear as ugly.

Although the bride's appearance is not described in "The Boy Who Set Out to Learn Fear" and "King Lindworm," the reader may deduce that they are attractive. In the first story, the princess is welcomed into the bedroom even when carrying a bucket of cold water and squirming fish. In the second story, the shepherd's daughter to save her life must be enticing to persuade King Lindworm to participate in a "simultaneous transformation." The bride anima, when cast as a seductive, voluptuous libertine, entices and leads the bride groom through sexually explicit fantasies and projections to awaken him to life. This may be exhibited in instinctual, biological sexual acts or it may be propelled into life-giving relationships of deep love.

When the bride anima appears as a loathsome lady as in "Sir Gawain's Marriage," she introduces the groom to the opposites of life in a striking fashion. This lady who appears as if her residence is hell, may, in fact, introduce man to hell. He may express this darkness of the soul outwardly through alcoholism, depression, disease, or suicide. If the bride groom meets and makes friends with the loathsome lady, he learns the laws of nature through viewing her portraits of opposite forces. He seizes the opportunity to act with sovereignty to his bride.

The bride is often tutored by an older and wiser woman, such as the chambermaid in "The Boy Who Set Out to Learn Fear" and the queen's garden counselor and the shepherd's daughter's old lady of the forest in "King Lindworm." The female sage holds and teaches the bride the intricate, advanced knowledge of the grand round of subsistence—from contracting the womb to ingressing the tomb; from rocking the cradle to firing the bier; from singing the lullaby to chanting the lamentations. The woman surrounds the surroundings, sustains the sustaining. She is the vital spark of the life force and the death rattle of the last breath.

The Grand Round

The unconscious pinings and yearnings of men, women, couples, kin, and communities rise in the sacred honey moon time when the veil is penetrated and the moon honey discovered. Some brides and bride grooms strive to meet life as if they reside forever within the consecrated honey moon continuum and nuptial bed foundation. E. E. Cummings writes of this honey moon exquisite with peril and yield.

> love's function is to fabricate unknownness
>
> (known being wishless; but love, all of wishing) . . .
>
> how lucky lovers are (whose selves abide
> under whatever shall discovered be)
> whose ignorant each breathing dares to hide
> more than most fabulous wisdom fears to see

(who laugh and cry) who dream, create and kill
while the whole moves; and every part stands still (page 446)

REFERENCES

Bulfinch, Thomas. *Bulfinch's Mythology*. New York: The Modern Library of Random House.

Campbell, Joseph. *The Hero with A Thousand Faces*. Second Edition. Princeton, New Jersey: Princeton University Press, 1968.

Caprio, Betsy. *The Woman Sealed in The Tower: A Psychological Approach to Feminine Spirituality*. Ramsey, New Jersey: Paulist Press, 1982.

Cummings, E.E. "Love's function is to fabricate unknownness" of *No Thanks. Complete Poems 1913–1962*. New York: Harcourt and Brace Jovanovich, 1972.

Dillard, Annie. *Living by Fiction*. New York: Harper Colophon, 1982.

Jeter, Kris. Unpublished doctoral dissertation. Denton, Texas: Texas Woman's University, 1973.

Jung, Carl G. *The Archetypes and the Collective Unconscious*. Second Edition. Translated by R.F.C. Hull. Princeton, New Jersey: Princeton University Press, 1969.

Langenscheidt's Universal Dictionary: English-German, German-English. New Edition. Berlin, Germany: Langenscheidt, 1976.

Mallet, Carl-Heinz. *Fairy Tales and Children: The Psychology of Children Revealed through Four of Grimm's Fairy Tales*. Translated by Joachim Neugroschel. New York: Schocken Books, 1984.

McBroom, Amanda. "The Rose" on *The Legend of the Rose* by Winafred Lucas and Sande Hershman. Beverly Hills, California: Roots and Wings, 1982.

Neilson, William Allan, Editor. *Webster's New International Dictionary of the English Language*. Second Edition. Unabridged. Springfield, Massachusetts: G. & C. Merriam Company, 1955.

Pratt, Annis. *Archetypal Patterns in Women's Fiction*. Bloomington, Indiana: Indiana University Press, 1981.

Sanford, John A. *The Invisible Partners: How The Male and Female in Each of Us Affects Our Relationships*. Ramsey, New Jersey: Paulist Press, 1980.

Taylor, Jonathan. "The Song of Yearning." *Anybody Can!* New York: The Possible Society Troubadors, 1985.

von Franz, Marie-Louise. *The Psychological Meaning of Redemption Motifs in Fairytales*. Toronto, Canada: Inner City Books, 1980.

Walker, Barbara G. *The Woman's Encyclopedia of Myths and Secrets*. New York: Harper and Row, 1983.

Whitmont, Edward C. *Return of the Goddess*. New York: The Crossroad Publishing Company, 1982.

BIBLIOGRAPHY

Fatherhood: A Library

Shirley M. H. Hanson
Frederick W. Bozett

Fatherhood is one of many roles that men perform in families that is undergoing rapid change. The majority of what is known about fathers/fathering/fatherhood has just been published only in the past decade. Before that, most of what was written or known could be located within several books and several dozen articles. Today, there is a prolific amount of literature available in journals of various disciplines, popular magazines and books for both professionals and the lay public. It is virtually impossible to keep abreast of the growing body of knowledge on this topic.

The purpose of this bibliography is to present an up-to-date reference list of the articles, books, and newsletters that best represents fatherhood in modern America. This source list is meant to be a users guide containing the classic and most current theoretical and empirical information available. It is what either a novice or a seasoned scholar would need in order to be current in the field. The authors used the topical outline from their recent book, *Dimensions of Fatherhood* (Hanson & Bozett, 1985). By soliciting the best references from the authors of this comprehensive book and several additional authors, there was assurance for completeness

Shirley M. H. Hanson, RN, PhD, FAAN, is Professor and Chairperson, Department of Family Nursing, The Oregon Health Sciences University, Portland, OR 97201. Frederick W. Bozett, RN, DNS, is Associate Professor, Graduate Program, College of Nursing, University of Oklahoma Health Sciences Center, Oklahoma City, OK 73190.

and timeliness of the citations listed. Each author contributed citations which best represented the majority of the important information available in their area of expertise on fatherhood.[1]

As one reviews the citations in each category, it is evident that the research and writings on various aspects on fatherhood are developing at different rates. For example, much research has been conducted on fathers and infants, whereas research on fathers and preschool children is sparse. The size of this bibliography was necessarily restricted so that the citations in no way represent all that is written about a given topic. However, it is the authors intent that one could read the citations listed and thus be alerted to the majority of what is known about the dimensions of fatherhood under investigation.

The bibliography presented is organized using the following outline. All books, articles and newsletters of a *general* nature are listed first; many of these books also contain chapters that are important to some of the specialized topics that follow.

I. Fatherhood: General Perspectives

1. General Books
2. Miscellaneous Chapters/Articles
3. Special Issues of Journals
4. Men's Journals and/or Newsletters
5. Other Father Bibliographies

II. Fatherhood: Historical, Legal, Theoretical, and Research Perspectives

1. Historical Perspectives
2. Legal Perspectives
3. Theoretical Perspectives

[1]The authors of this paper wish to express appreciation to the following people for their assistance in the compilation of this bibliography: Marc D. Baranowski, Robert Barret, Nijole, V. Benokraitis, Leonard Benson, Sherry T. Boyd, Gary Bowen, Robert Bradley, Jane K. Burgess, Audrey Wagner Elam, Greer Litton Fox, David Giveans, L. Colette Jones, David Lutwin, Dorothy H. Martin, Katharyn Antle May, Brent Miller, Dennis Orthner, Ross Parke, Steven Paul Perrin, Craig H. Roberts, Bryan E. Robinson, Michael Robinson, Jaopaul Roopnarine, E. Anthony Rotundo, Gary Sipperstein, Kay Pasley, Janice Swanson, and Lynda Henley Walters. Thanks are also extended to Portia Trotter and Merlene Lorenz-Cobb for their special secretarial assistance.

4. Research Perspectives

III. Fatherhood: The Family Life Span

1. Men and Family Planning
2. Transitions to Fatherhood
3. The Father in Pregnancy and Birth
4. Fathers and Infants
5. Fathers and School Age Children
6. Fathers and Adolescents
7. Fathers and Adult Children
8. Grandfatherhood

IV. Fatherhood: Social Contexts

1. Fathers in Dual-Earner Families
2. Househusband Fathers
3. Stepfathers
4. Military Fathers
5. Gay Fathers
6. Adolescent Fathers
7. Single Custodial Fathers
8. Non-Custodial Fathers

I. FATHERHOOD: GENERAL PERSPECTIVES

General Books

Adams, P. L., Milner, J. R. & Schrepf, N. A. (1984). *Fatherless children.* New York: John Wiley.

Anderson, C. P. (1983). *Father: The figure and the force.* New York: Warner Books.

Appleton, W. W. (1981). *Fathers and daughters: A father's powerful influence on a woman's life.* New York: Doubleday.

Benson, L. (1968). *Fatherhood: A sociological perspective.* New York: Random House.

Biller, H. (1971). *Father, child and sex roles.* Lexington, Mass.: D. C. Heath.

Biller, H. (1974). *Paternal deprivation.* Lexington, Mass.: D. C. Heath.

Biller, H. & Biller, D. (1975). *Father power.* New York: Doubleday.

Bittman, S. & Zalk, S. R. (1978). *Expectant fathers.* New York: Ballantine.

Cath, S. H., Gurwitt, A. R., & Ross, J. M. (Eds.). (1982). *Father and child: Developmental and clinical perspectives.* Boston: Little, Brown.

Colman, A. & Colman, L. (1981). *Earth father/Sky father*. Englewood Cliffs, NJ: Prentice-Hall.

Daley, E. A. (1978). *Father feelings*. New York: William & Company.

Dodson, F. (1974). *How to father*. New York: Signet Books.

Fields, S. (1983). *Like father, like daughter: How father shapes the woman his daughter becomes*. Boston: Little, Brown.

Grad, R., Bash, D., Guyer, R., Cevedo, Z., Trause, M. A., & Reukauf, D. (1981). *The father book: Pregnancy and beyond*. Washington, D.C.: Acropolis.

Green, M. (1976). *Fathering*. New York: McGraw-Hill.

Gresh, S. (1980). *Becoming father: A handbook for expectant fathers*. New York: Butterick.

Hamilton, M. L. (1977). *Father's influence on children*. Chicago: Nelson-Hall.

Herman, J. L. & Hirschman, L. (1981). *Father-daughter incest*. Cambridge, MA: Harvard University Press.

Johnson, S. (1983). *The one minute father*. NY: William Morrow.

Kahan, S. (1978). *The expectant father's survival kit*. New York: Monarch.

Klingman, D. G. & Kohl, R. (1984). *Fatherhood U.S.A.: The first national guide to programs, services and resources for and about fathers*. New York: Garland.

Kohn, J. B. & Kohn, W. K. (1978). *The widower*. Boston: Beacon Press.

Lamb, M. E. (Ed.). (1982). *Nontraditional families: Parenting and child development*. Hillsdale, NJ: Lawrence Erlbaum.

Lamb, M. E. (Ed.). (1976). *The role of the father in child development*. First edition. New York: John Wiley.

Lamb, M. E. (Ed.). (1981). *The role of the father in child development*. Second edition. New York: John Wiley.

Lockerbie, D. B. (1981). *Fatherlove*. Garden City, New York: Doubleday.

Lynn, D. B. (1974). *The father: His role in child development*. Monterey, California: Brooks/Cole.

Lynn, D. B. (1979). *Daughters and parents: Past, present and future*. Monterey, California: Brooks/Cole.

McKee, L. & O'Brien, M. (Eds.), (1981). *The father figure*. London: Tavistock.

Oakland, T. (1984). *Divorced father: Reconstructing a quality life*. New York: Human Sciences Press.

Parke, R. D. (1981). *Fathers*. Cambridge, MA: Harvard University Press.

Pederson, F. (1980). *The father-infant relationship: Observational studies in the family setting*. New York: Praeger.

Phillips, C. R. & Anzalone, J. T. (1982). *Fathering: Participation in labor and birth*. St. Louis: The C. V. Mosby.

Rabkin, P. A. (1980). *Fathers to daughters: The legal foundations of female emancipation*. London: Greenwood Press.

Rapoport, R., Rapoport, R. N., Strelitz, Z., & Kew, S. (1977). *Fathers, mothers, and society*. NY: Basic Books.

Robinson, B. E. & Barret, R. L. (1985). *Fatherhood*. NY: Guilford Press. (In Process).

Rosenthal, K. & Keshet, H. (1981). *Fathers without partners*. Totowa, NJ: Rowman and Littlefield.

Russell, G. (1983). *The changing role of fathers?* New York: University of Queensland Press.

Salk, L. (1982). *My father, my self: Intimate relationships*. New York: Putnam.

Salt, R. E. & Lewis, R. A. (1985). *Men in families.* Beverly Hills: Sage.

Sayers, R. (1983). *Fathering: It's not the same.* San Francisco: The Nurtury Family School.

Sifford, D. (1982). *Father and son.* Philadelphia: Bridgebooks.

Stanley, H. P. (1982). *The challenge of fatherhood in today's world.* New York: Abbey Press.

Steinberg, D. (1977). *Father journal: Five years of awakening to fatherhood.* NY: Times Change Press.

Stevens, J. H. & Mathews, M. (Eds.). (1978). *Mother/child, father/child relationship.* New York: The National Association for the Education of Young Children.

Sullivan, S. A. (1980). *The fathers almanac.* Garden City, New York: Doubleday.

Victor, I. & Winkler, W. A. (1977). *Fathers and custody.* New York: Hawthorn Books.

Yablonsky, L. (1982). *Fathers and sons.* New York: Simon & Schuster.

Miscellaneous Chapters/Articles

Aberg, M., Small, P., & Watson, J. A. (1977). Males, fathers, and husbands: Changing roles and reciprocal legal rights. *The Family Coordinator, 27,* 287–291.

Bradley, R. H. (1980). The renaissance of fathering. *Educational Horizons, 59,* 27–33.

Fein, A. (1978). Research on fathering: Social policy and an emergent perspective. *The Journal of Social Issues, 34,* 72–91.

Fishbein, E. (1981). Fatherhood and disturbances in mental health: A review. *Journal of Psychiatric Nursing and Mental Health, 19*(7), 24–27.

Lamb, M. E. (1979). Paternal influences and the father's role. *American Psychologist, 34,* 938–943.

Lamb, M. E. (1975). Fathers: Forgotten contributors to human development. *Human Development, 18,* 245–266.

Lamb, M. & Bronson, S. (1978). Fathers in the context of family influences: Past, present and future. *School Psychology Review, 9,* 336–353.

Macklin, E. (1980). Nontraditional family forms: A decade review. *Journal of Marriage and the Family, 32,* 367–376.

Parke, R. D. (1982). The father's role in family development. In M. Klaus and J. Kennell (Eds.), *Birth, Interaction, and Attachment.* Piscataway, NJ: Johnson and Johnson.

Parke, R. D. & Tinsley, B. R. (1984). Historical and contemporary perspectives on fathering. In K. A. McClusky and H. W. Reese (Eds.), *Life-span Development Psychology: Historical and Generational Effects in Life-span Human Development.* NY: Academic Press.

Pedersen, F. (1985). Research and the father: Where do we go from here? In S. Hanson and F. Bozett (Eds.), *Dimensions of Fatherhood.* Beverly Hills, CA: Sage.

Ross, J. M. (1979). Fathering: A review of some psychoanalytic contributions on paternity. *International Journal of Psychoanalysis, 60,* 317–327.

Russell, G. (1978). The father role and it's relationship to masculinity, femininity, and androgyny. *Child Development, 49,* 1174–1181.

Special Issues of Journals

Bozett, F. W. & Hanson, S. M. H. (1985). *Perspectives of fatherhood.* Special issue of *American Behavioral Scientist, 28*(6).

Lewis, R. A. & Pleck, J. H. (Eds.). (1979). Men's roles in the family. Special issue of *The Family Coordinator, 28*(4).

Walters, J. (Ed.). (1976). Fatherhood. Special issue of *The Family Coordinator, 25*(4).

Men's Journals and/or Newsletters

Nurturing News: A Quarterly Forum for Nurturing Men. David Giveans, Ed., 187 Caselli Avenue, San Francisco, CA 94114.

Legal Beagle: A Family Law Reform Newsletter. Peter Cyr, Ed., 69 Deering Street, Portland, ME 04101.

Fathergram. Fathergram, P.O. Box 2, Mobile, AL 36626.

Other Father Bibliographies

Boss, P. (1979). *The father's role in family systems: An annotated bibliography.* Madison, Wisconsin: Child and Family Studies Program, University of Wisconsin.

Grady, K. E., Brannon, R., & Pleck, J. H. (1979). *The male sex role: A selected and annotated bibliography.* Washington, D.C.: U.S. Government Printing Office (#79-790).

Price-Bonham, S. (1976). Bibliography of literature related to roles of fathers. *Family Coordinator, 25*(3), 489–512.

Price-Bonham, S., Pittman, J. F., & Welch, C. O. (1981). The father role: An update. *Infant Mental Health Journal, 2*(4), 264–289.

II. FATHERHOOD: HISTORICAL, LEGAL, THEORETICAL, AND RESEARCH PERSPECTIVES

Historical Perspectives

Bloom-Feshbach, J. (1981). Historical Perspectives on the father's role. In M. Lamb (Ed.), *The role of the father in child development.* (2nd ed). New York: John Wiley.

Cramer, R. (1980). *Images of the American father, 1790–1860.* Senior thesis, Brandeis University, 1980.

Demos, J. (1982). The Changing Faces of American Fatherhood: A New Exploration in Family History. In S. Cath, A. Gurwitt, & J. Ross (Eds.), *Father and Child: Developmental and Clinical Perspectives.* Boston: Little, Brown.

Ehrenreich, B. (1983). *The Hearts of Men.* New York: Anchor Press/Doubleday.

Filene, P. (1975). *Him/her/self: Sex roles in modern America.* New York: New American Library.

Fliegelman, J. (1982). *Prodigals and pilgrims: The American revolution against patriarchal authority, 1750–1800.* New York: Cambridge University Press.

Gerzon, M. (1982). *A choice of heroes: The changing face of American manhood.* Boston: Houghton Mifflin.

Greven, P. (1970). *Four generations: Population, land and family in colonial Andover, Massachusetts.* Ithaca: Cornell University Press.

Greven, P. (1977). *The protestant temperament: Patterns of childrearing, religious experience, and the self in early America.* New York: Alfred A. Knopf.

Gutman, H. (1976). *The black family in slavery and freedom, 1750–1925.* New York: Pantheon.

Komarovsky, M. (1940). *The unemployed man and his family.* New York: Dryden Press.

Lewis, J. (1983). *The pursuit of happiness.* New York: Cambridge University Press.

Lummis, T. (1982). The historical dimension of fatherhood: A case study 1890–1914. In L. McKee & M. O'Brien (Eds.). *The father figure.* New York: Tavistock.

Mintz, S. (1983). *A prison of expectations: The family in victorian culture.* New York: New York University Press.

Parke, R. D., & Tinsley, B. R. (1983). Fatherhood: Historical and contemporary perspectives. In K. A. McCluskey & H. W. Reese (Eds.), *Life span developmental psychology: Historical and cohort effects.* NY: Academic Press.

Rotundo, E. A. (1982). *Manhood in America: The northern middle class, 1770–1920.* Doctoral dissertation, Brandeis University, 1982.

Rotundo, E. A. (1985). Historical perspectives. In F. Bozett & S. Hanson (Eds.). Perspectives of Fatherhood. *American Behavioral Scientist, 28(6).*

Ryan, M. (1981). *Cradle of the middle class: The family in Oneida County, New York, 1780–1865.* New York: Cambridge University Press.

Smith, D. B. (1980). *Inside the great house: Planter family life in eighteenth-century Chesapeake society.* Ithaca: Cornell University Press.

Legal Perspectives

Bedwell, M. A. (1979). The Rights of Fathers of Non-Marital Children to Custody, Visitation and to Consent to Adoption. *University of California-Davis Law Review, 12,* 412–451.

Chambers, D. L. (1979). *Making Fathers Pay: The Enforcement of Child Support.* Chicago: University of Chicago Press.

Cotroneo, M. (1979). At the Intersection of Family Systems and Legal System: Child Custody Decisions in Context. *Connecticut Bar Journal, 53,* 349–355.

Developments in the Law—The Constitution and the Family, (1980). *Harvard Law Review, 93,* 1157–1383.

Foster, H. H., & D. J. Freed (1978). Life with Father: 1978, *Family Law Quarterly, 11,* 323, 326, 329, 341.

Johnson, A. (1976). Divorce, Alimony, Support and Custody: A Survey of Judges Attitudes in One State, *Family Law Reporter, 3,* 4003.

Jones, C. J. (1977–78). The Tender Years Doctrine: Survey and Analysis, *Journal of Family Law, 16,* 695–749.

Katz, L. (1979). The Maternal Preference and the Psychological Parent: Suggestions for Allocating the Burden of Proof in Custody Litigation, *Connecticut Bar Journal, 53,* 343–348.

Krause, H. D. (1981). *Child Support in America: The Legal Perspective.* Charlottesville, VA: The Michie Press.

Krause, H. D. (1982). A Review of the Progress Made in Child Support, Paternity, Illegitimacy, and Child Welfare, *Family Advocate, 5,* 12.

Leonard, M. F., & S. Provence (1979). The Development of Parent-Child Relationships and the Psychological Parent, *Connecticut Bar Journal, 53,* 320–329.

Levy, R. J. (1976). The Rights of Parents, *Brigham Young University Law Review,* 693–701.

Melli, M. S. (1982). The Changing View of Child Support. *Family Advocate, 5,* 16.

Mnookin, R. H. (1975). Child Custody Adjudication: Judicial Function in the Face of Indeterminancy, *Law and Contemporary Problems, 38,* 226.

Mnookin, R. H. (1978). *Child, Family and State: Problems and Materials on Children and the Law.* Boston: Little, Brown & Co.

Payne, A. T. (1977–78). The Law and the Problem Parent: Custody and Parental Rights of Homosexual, Mentally Retarded, Mentally Ill and Incarcerated Parents, *Journal of Family Law, 16,* 799–802.

Pearson, J., P. Munson, & N. Thoennes (1982). Legal Change and Child Custody Awards, *Journal of Social Issues, 3,* 6–8.

Redden, K. R. (1982). *Federal Regulation of Family Law.* Charlottesville, VA: The Michie Co.

Roth, A. (1977). The Tender Years Presumption in Child Custody Disputes, *Journal of Family Law, 15,* 423.

Schmidtman, K. A. (1976). The Demise of Parent-Child Tort Immunity, *Willamette Law Journal, 12,* 605–622.

Solomon, P. F. (1978). The Fathers' Revolution in Custody Cases, *Case and Comment, 84,* 11.

Speal, G. K. (1981). Who Shall Have Custody? A Case for the Equal Consideration of Fathers, *Law and Policy Quarterly, 3,* 408.

The Revolution in Family Law: 25 Years of New Directions, (1982). *Family Advocate, 5.*

Walters, L. H. & Elam, A. W. Legal perspectives. In F. Bozett & S. Hanson (Eds.). "Perspectives in Fatherhood." *American Behavioral Scientist, 28(6).*

Weitzman, L. J. & Dixon, R. B. (1979). Child Custody Awards: Legal Standards and Empirical Patterns for Child Custody, Support and Visitation After Divorce, *University of California-Davis Law Review, 12,* 473–521.

Weyrauch, W. O. and Katz, S. N. (1983). *American Family Law in Transition,* Washington, D.C.: Bureau of National Affairs, Inc.

Theoretical Perspectives

Benson, L. (1985). Theoretical perspectives. In F. Bozett and S. Hanson (Eds.), "Perspectives of fatherhood," *American Behavioral Scientist, 28(6).*

Broderick, C. (1971). Beyond the five conceptual frameworks: A decade of development in family theory. *Journal of Marriage and the Family, 33(1),* 139–159.

Burr, W. R. (1973). *Theory construction and the sociology of the family.* New York: John Wiley.

Burr, W. R., Hill, R., Nye, F. I., & Reiss, I. L. (1979). *Contemporary theories about the family,* Vol. I & II. New York: The Free Press.

Davids, L. (1972). Fatherhood and comparative social research. *International Journal of Comparative Sociology, 13*(3), 217–222.

Ekeh, R. (1974). *Social exchange theory.* Cambridge, MA: Harvard University Press.

Hays, W. C. (1977). Theorists and theoretical frameworks identified by family sociologists. *Journal of Marriage and the Family, 33*(1), 59–66.

Nye, F. I. & Berardo, F. M. (1981). *Emerging conceptual frameworks in family analysis.* New York: Praeger.

Rogers, R. H. (1973). *Family interaction and transaction: The developmental approach.* Englewood Cliffs, NJ: Prentice-Hall

Research Perspectives

Backett, K. (1982). *Mothers and fathers: Studies of negotiation of parental behavior.* New York: St. Martin's.

Barardo, Felix M. (1980). Decade preview: Some trends and directions for family research and theory in the 1980's. *Journal of Marriage and The Family, 42*(4), 723–728.

Boyd, S. (1981). Measurement of paternal attitude toward infant caretaking. *Children's Health Care, 10,* 66–67.

Boyd, S. (1985). Research perspectives. In F. Bozett & S. Hanson (Eds.), "Perspectives in Fatherhood." *American Behavioral Scientist, 28*(6).

Cook, T. & Campbell, D. (1979). *Quasi-experimentation: Design and analysis issues for field settings.* Chicago: Rand McNally.

Eron, L., Banta, T., Valder, L., & Laulicht, J. (1961). Comparison of data obtained from mothers and fathers on child rearing practices and their relation to child aggression. *Child Development, 32,* 457–472.

Gardner, P. (1943). A survey of the attitudes and activities of fathers. *The Journal of Genetic Psychology, 63,* 15–53.

Gilbert, L., Hanson, G. & Davis, B. (1982). Perceptions of parental role responsibilities: Differences between mothers and fathers. *Family Relations, 31,* 261–270.

Kaplan, A. (1964). *The Conduct of Inquiry: Methodology for Behavioral Science.* NY: Thomas Y. Crowell Company.

Klein, D., Jorgensen, S., & Miller, B. (1978). Research methods and development of reciprocity in families. In R. Lerner & G. Spaniers (Eds.), *Child Influences on Marital and Family Interaction.* NY: Academic Press.

Kotelchuck, M. (1976). The infant's relationship to the father: Experimental evidence. In M. Lamb (Ed.), *The Role of the Father in Child Development.* New York: John Wiley.

Lewin, M. (1979). *Understanding Psychological Research.* NY: John Wiley & Sons.

Parke, R. & O'Leary, S. (1975). A family interaction in the newborn period: Some findings, some observations, and some unresolved issues. In K. Riegel & J. Meacham (Eds.), *The Developing Individual in a Changing World* (Vol. 2). The Hague: Mouton.

Parke, R. & Sawin, D. (1980). The family in early infancy: Social and interactional and attitudinal analysis. In F. Pederson (Ed.), *The Father-Infant Relationship*. New York: Praeger.

Pederson, F. (1976). Does research on children reared in father-absent families yield information on father influences? *The Family Coordinator, 25*, 459–464.

Straus, M. A. & Brown, B. W. (1978). *Family measurement techniques: Abstracts of published instruments*, 1935–1974. Minneapolis: University of Minnesota Press.

Toney, L. (1983). The effects of holding the newborn at delivery on paternal bonding. *Nursing Research, 32*, 16–19.

Ventura, J. (1982). Parent coping behaviors, parent functioning, and infant temperament characteristics. *Nursing Research, 31*, 269–273.

Weaver, R. & Cranley, M. (1983). An exploration of paternal-fetal attachment behavior. *Nursing Research, 32*, 68–72.

III. FATHERHOOD: THE FAMILY LIFE SPAN

Men and Family Planning

Bozett, F. W. (1985). Male development and fathering throughout the life cycle. *American Behavioral Scientist, 28(6)*. Special edition entitled, "Perspectives on Fatherhood."

Chng, C. L. (1983). The male role in contraception: Implications for health education. *The Journal of School Health, 531*(3), 197–201.

Clark, M., Bean, F., Swicegood, G., & Ansbacher, R. (1979). The decision for male versus female sterilization. *The Family Coordinator, 28*, 250–254.

Delamater, J. & MacCorquodale, P. (1978). Premarital contraceptive use: A test of two models. *Journal of Marriage and the Family, 40*(2), 235–247.

Diller, L. & Hembree, W. (1977). Male contraception and family planning: A social and historical review. *Fertility and Sterility, 28*(12), 1271–1279.

Finkel, J. & Finkel, D. (1975). Sexual and contraceptive knowledge, attitudes and behaviors of male adolescents. *Family Planning Perspectives, 7*(6), 256–260.

Fox, G. L. (1977). Sex-role attitudes as predictors of contraceptive use among unmarried university students. *Sex Roles, 3*(3), 265–283.

Hansson, R., Jones, W., & Chernovetz, M. (1979). Contraceptive knowledge: Antecedents and implications. *The Family Coordinator, 28*(1), 29–34.

Hornick, J., Doran, L., & Crawford, S. (1979). Premarital contraceptive usage among male and female adolescents. *The Family Coordinator, 28*(2), 181–190.

Johnson, J. H. (1983). Vasectomy—An international appraisal. *Family Planning Perspectives, 15*(1), 45–48.

Misra, B. D. (1967). Correlates of males' attitudes toward family planning. In D. Bogue (Ed.), *Sociological contributions to family planning research*. Chicago: Community and Family Study Center, University of Chicago.

Mullen, P., Reynolds, R., Cignetti, P., & Dornan, D. (1973). A vasectomy education program: Implications from survey data. *The Family Coordinator, 22*(3), 331–338.

Redford, M., Duncan, G., & Prager, D. (Eds.). (1974). *The condom: Increasing utilization in the United States*. San Francisco: San Francisco Press.

Scales, P., Elelis, R., & Levitz, N. (1977). Male involvement in contraceptive decisionmaking: The role of birth control counselors. *Journal of Community Health, 3*, 54–60.

Spillane, W. H. & Ryser, P. E. (1975). *Male fertility survey: Fertility knowledge, attitudes, and practices of married men.* Cambridge, MA: Ballinger.

Stokes, B. (1980). *Men and family planning.* (Worldwatch Paper No. 41). Washington, D.C.: Worldwatch Institute, December.

Stycos, J. M. (1981). A critique of focus group and survey research: The machismo case. *Studies in Family Planning, 12*(12), 450–456.

Swanson, J. M. (1980). "Knowledge, knowledge, who's got the knowledge": The male contraceptive career. *Journal of Sex Education and Therapy, 6*(2), 51–57.

Swanson, J. M. (1985). Men and family planning. In S. Hanson & F. Bozett (Eds.), *Dimensions of Fatherhood.* Beverly Hills, CA: Sage.

Swanson, J. M. & Forrest, K. (1984). *Men's reproductive health.* New York: Springer.

World Health Organization Task Force on Psychosocial Research in Family Planning (1980). Acceptability of drugs for male fertility regulation: A prospectus and some preliminary data. *Contraception, 21*(2), 121–134.

Zelnik, M., & Kantner, J. (1980). Sexual activity, contraceptive use and pregnancy among metropolitan-area teenagers: 1971–1979. *Family Planning Perspectives, 12*(5), 230–237.

Transitions to Fatherhood

Belsky, J. (1981). Early human experience: A family perspective. *Developmental Psychology, 17*, 3–23.

Belsky, J., Spanier, G., & Rovine, M. (1983). Stability and change in marriage across the transition to parenthood. *Journal of Marriage and the Family, 45*, 567–577.

Bozett, F. W. (1985). Male development and fathering throughout the life cycle. *American Behavioral Scientist, 28*(6). Special edition entitled "Perspectives on Fatherhood."

Fein, R. A. (1976). Men's entrance to parenthood. *Family Coordinator, 25*, 341–348.

Frodi, A., Lamb, M., Leavitt, L., Donovan, W., Neff, C., & Sherry, D. (1978). Fathers' and mothers' responses to the faces and cries of normal and premature infants. *Developmental Psychology, 14*, 490–498.

Lamb, M. (1978). Influence of child on marital quality and family interaction during the prenatal, perinatal, and infancy periods. In R. Lerner & G. Spanier (Eds.), *Child influence on marital and family interaction.* New York: Academic Press.

LaRossa, R. & LaRossa, M. (1981). *Transition to Parenthood: How infants change families.* Beverly Hills, CA: Sage.

Miller, B. C. & Bowen S. L. (1982). Father-to-newborn attachment behavior in relation to parental class and presence at delivery. *Family Relations, 31*, 71–78.

Miller, B. C. & Myers-Walls, J. A. (1983). Stresses of parenting. In H. McCubbin and C. Figley (Eds.), *Stress and the Family.* New York: Brunner/Mazel.

Miller, B. C. & Sollie, D. L. (1980). Normal stresses during the transition to parenthood. *Family Relations, 29*, 459–465.

Roopnarine, J. & Miller, B. (1985). Transitions to fatherhood. In S. Hanson and F. Bozett (Eds.), *Dimensions of Fatherhood*. Beverly Hills, CA: Sage.

Rossi, A. S. (1968). Transition to parenthood. *Journal of Marriage and the Family, 30*, 26–39.

Russell, C. (1974). Transition to parenthood: Problems and gratifications. *Journal of Marriage and the Family, 36*, 294–301.

Ryder, R. (1973). Longitudinal data relating marriage satisfaction and having a child. *Journal of Marriage and the Family, 35*, 604–607.

Sollie, D. L. & Miller, B. C. (1980). The transition to parenthood as a critical time for rebuilding family strengths. In N. Stinnett, B. Chesser, J. DeFrain, & P. Knaub (Eds.), *Family Strengths: Positive Models for Family Life*. Lincoln, NE: University of Nebraska Press.

Wente, A. & Crockenberg, S. (1976). Transition to fatherhood: Lamaze preparation, adjustment, difficulty and the husband-wife relationship. *The Family Coordinator, 27*, 351–357.

The Father in Pregnancy and Birth

Bowen, S. and Miller, B. (1980). Paternal attachment behavior at labor and delivery and preparenthood classes: A pilot study. *Nursing Research, 29*(5), 307–311.

Bozett, F. W. (1985). Male development and fathering throughout the life cycle. *American Behavioral Scientist, 28*(6). Special edition entitled "Perspectives on Fatherhood."

Cain, R., Pedersen, F., Zaslow, M., and Kramer, E. (1984). Effects of the fathers' presence or absence during a cesarean birth. *Birth, 11*(1), 10–15.

Cronenwett, L. & Kunst-Wilson, W. (1981). Stress, social support and the transition to fatherhood. *Nursing Research, 30*(4), 196–201.

Fein, R. (1976). Men's entrance into parenthood. *Family Coordinator, 25*, 341–347.

Fishbein, E. (1981). Fatherhood and disturbances in mental health: A review. *Journal of Psychiatric Nursing and Mental Health Services, 19*(7), 24–27.

Fishbein, E. (1981). The couvade: A review. *Journal of Obstetric, Gynecologic and Neonatal Nursing, 5*, 356–359.

Greenberg, M., and Morris, N. (1974). Engrossment: The newborn's impact on his father. *American Journal of Orthopsychiatry, 44*, 520–534.

Leibenberg, B. (1973). Expectant fathers, In P. Shereshefsky and L. Yarrow (Eds.), *Psychological aspects of the first pregnancy and early postnatal adaptation*. New York: Raven Press.

Lipkin, M., & Lamb, G. (1982). The couvade syndrome: An epidemiologic study. *Annals of Internal Medicine, 96*, 509–511.

MacLaughlin, S. & Taubenheim, A. (1983). A comparison of prepared and unprepared first-time fathers' needs during the childbirth experience. *Journal of Nurse Midwifery, 28*(4), 9–16.

May, K. (1980). A typology of detachment/involvement styles adopted during pregnancy by first-time expectant fathers. *Western Journal of Nursing Research, 2*(2), 445–453.

May, K. (1982). Three phases in the development of father involvement in pregnancy. *Nursing Research, 31*(6), 337–342.

May, K. & Perrin, S. (1985). Prelude: Pregnancy and birth. In S. Hanson and F. Bozett (Eds.), *Dimensions of Fatherhood*. Beverly Hills, CA: Sage.

May, K. & Sollid, D. (1984). Unanticipated cesarean birth from the father's perspective. *Birth, 11*(2), 87–95.

Nicholson, J., Gist, N., Klein, R., and Standley, K. (1983). Outcomes of father involvement in pregnancy and birth. *Birth, 10*(1), 5–9.

Palkowitz, R. (1982). Fathers' birth attendance, early extended contact, and father-infant interaction at five months postpartum. *Birth, 9*(3), 173–177.

Petersen, G., Mehl, L., & Leiderman, H. (1977). The role of some birth related variables in father attachment. *American Journal of Orthopsychiatry, 49*(2), 330–338.

Phillips, C. & Anzalone, J. (1982). *Fathering: Participation in labor and birth*, St. Louis: C.V. Mosby.

Richman, J. & Goldthorp, W. (1978). Fatherhood: The social construction of pregnancy and birth. In S. Kitzinger & J. David (Eds.), *The Place of Birth*. Oxford, England: Oxford University Press.

Toney, L. (1983). The effects of holding the newborn at delivery on paternal bonding. *Nursing Research, 32*(1), 16–19.

Weaver, R. & Cranley, M. (1983). An exploration of paternal-fetal attachment behavior. *Nursing Research, 32*(2), 68–72.

Fathers and Infants

Bozett, F. W. (1985). Male development and fathering throughout the life cycle. *American Behavioral Scientist, 28*(6). Special edition entitled, "Perspectives on Fatherhood."

Chibucos, T. R., & Kail, P. R. (1981). Longitudinal examination of father-infant interaction and infant-father attachment. *Merrill-Palmer Quarterly, 27*(2), 81–96.

Clarke-Stewart, K. A. (1978). And daddy makes three: The father's impact on mother and young child. *Child Development, 49*(2), 466–478.

Cordell, A. L., Parke, R. D., & Sawin, D. G. (1980). Fathers' views on fatherhood, with special reference to infancy. *Family Relations: Journal of Applied Family and Child Studies, 29*, 331–338.

Field, T. (1978). Interaction behaviors of primary versus secondary caretaker fathers. *Developmental Psychology, 14*, 183–184.

Frodi, A. M. (1980). Paternal-baby responsiveness and involvement. *Infant Mental Health Journal, 1*(3), 150–160.

Greenberg, M., & Morris, N. (1974). Engrossment: The newborn's impact upon the father. *American Journal of Orthopsychiatry, 44*, 520–531.

Jones, C. (1981). Father to infant attachment: Effects of early contact and characteristics of the infant. *Research in Nursing and Health, 4*, 193–200.

Jones, C. (1985). Relationships during the first year of life. In S. Hanson & F. Bozett (Eds.), *Dimensions of Fatherhood*. Beverly Hills, CA: Sage.

Jones, C. & Parks, P. (1983). Mother, father, and examiner-reported temperament across the first year of life. *Research in Nursing and Health, 6*(4), 183–189.

Lamb, M., Chase-Lansdale, L., & Owen, M. T. (1979). The changing American family and its implications for infant social development: The sample case of maternal employment. In M. Lewis & L. A. Rosenblum (Eds.), *The child and its family*. NY: Plenum.

Lamb, M. E. (1977). Father-infant and mother-infant interaction in the first year of life. *Child Development, 48*, 167–181.

Lamb, M. E. (1977). The development of mother-infant and father-infant attachments in the second year of life. *Developmental Psychology, 13*, 637–648.

Lamb, M. E. (1982). Paternal influences on early socio-emotional development. *Journal of Child Psychology & Psychiatry & Allied Disciplines, 23*(2), 185–190.

McDonald, D. L. (1978). Paternal behavior at first contact with the newborn in a birth environment without intrusions. *Birth and the Family Journal, 5*(3), 123–132.

Pannabecker, B. J., Emde, R. N., & Austin, B. C. (1982). The effect of early extended contact on father-newborn interaction. *The Journal of Genetic Psychology, 141*, 7–17.

Parke, R. D. (1981). Father-infant interaction in a family perspective. In P. Berman (Ed.), *Women: A developmental perspective*. Washington, D.C.: United States Government Printing Office.

Parke, R. D. (1979). Perspectives on father-infant interaction. In J. D. Osofsky (Ed.), *Handbook of infant development*. New York: John Wiley.

Parke, R. D., Grossman, K., & Tinsley, B. R. (1981). Father-mother-infant interaction in the newborn period: A German-American comparison. In T. Field (Ed.), *Culture and early interactions*. Hillsdale, N.J.: Erlbaum.

Parke, R. D., & Tinsley, B. R. (1981). The father's role in infancy: Determinants of involvement in caregiving and play. In M. Lamb (Ed.), *The role of the father in child development* (2nd edition). New York: John Wiley.

Parke, R. D., & Suomi, S. J. (1981). Adult male-infant relationships: Human and nonhuman primate evidence. In K. Immelmann, G. Barlow, M. Main, and L. Petrinovitch (Eds.), *Behavioral Development: The Bielefeld Interdisciplinary Project*. New York: Cambridge University Press.

Pedersen, F. A. (Ed.). *The father-infant relationship: Observational studies in a family setting*. New York: Praeger, 1980.

Power, T. G. (1981). Sex typing in infancy: The role of the father. *Infant Mental Health Journal, 2*(4), 226–240.

Power, T. G., & Parke, R. D. (1983). Patterns of mother and father play with their 8-month-old infant: A multiple analyses approach. *Infant Behavior and Development, 6*, 453–459.

Rodhan, M. (1982). The behavior of human male adults at their first contact with a newborn. *Infant Behavior & Development, 5*(2), 121–130.

Snow, M. E., Jacklin, C. N., & Maccoby, E. E. (1983). Sex-of child differences in father-child interaction at one year of age. *Child Development, 54*, 227–232.

Toney, L. (1983). The effects of holding the newborn at delivery on paternal bonding. *Nursing Research, 32*(1), 16–19.

Yogman, M. W. (1982). Development of the father-infant relationship. In H. E. Fitzgerald, B. M. Lester, & M. W. Yogman (Eds.), *Theory and Research in Behavioral Pediatrics*. New York: Plenum.

Fathers and School Age Children

Bartz, K. (1978). Selected childrearing tasks and problems of mothers and fathers. *Family Coordinator, 27,* 209–214.

Bozett, F. W. (1985). Male development and fathering throughout the life cycle. *American Behavioral Scientist, 28*(6). Special edition entitled, "Perspectives on Fatherhood."

Eversoll, D. (1979). A two generational view of fathering. *Family Coordinator, 28,* 503–508.

Friedman, H. (1980). The father's parenting experience in divorce. *American Journal of Psychiatry, 137,* 1177–1182.

Hanson, S. (1981). Single custodial fathers and the parent-child relationship. *Nursing Research, 30,* 202–204.

Heath, D. (1976). Competent fathers: Their personalities and marriages. *Human Development, 19,* 26–39.

Henderson, J. (1980). On fathering: The nature of functions of the father role: II, conceptualizations of fathering. *Canadian Journal of Psychiatry, 25,* 413–431.

Hock, E., McKenry, P., Hock, M., Triolo, S. & Stewart, L. (1980). Child's school entry: A stressful event in the lives of fathers. *Family Relations, 29,* 467–472.

Keshet, H. & Rosenthal, K. (1978). Single parent fathers: A new study. *Children Today, 7,* 13–17.

Kestenberg, J. (1970). The effect on parents of the child's transition into and out of latency. In E. Anthony & T. Benedeck (Eds.), *Parenthood: Its psychology and psychopathology.* Boston: Little, Brown.

Levant, R. & Doyle, G. (1983). An evaluation of a parent education program for fathers of school-aged children. *Family Relations, 32,* 29–38.

Lewis, M. & Weinraub, M. (1974). Sex of parent x sex of child: socioemotional development. In R. Friedman, R. Richart & R. Vande Wiele (Eds.), *Sex differences in behavior.* New York: Wiley.

Mobley, E. (1975). Ego ideal themes in fatherhood. *Smith College Studies in Social Work, 45,* 230–252.

Price-Bonham, S. & Addison, S. (1978). Families and mentally retarded children: Emphasis on the father. *Family Coordinator, 28,* 221–230.

Radin, N. & Sagi, A. (1982). Childrearing fathers in intact families, II: Israel and the USA. *Merrill-Palmer Quarterly, 28,* 111–136.

Russell, G. (1982). Shared-caregiving families: An Australian study. In M. Lamb (Ed.), *Nontraditional families: Parenting and child development.* Hillsdale, NJ: Lawrence Erlbaum.

Fathers and Adolescents

Baranowski, M. D. (1983). Adolescents' attempted influence on parental behaviors. *Adolescence, 13*(52), 585–604.

Bayley, N. & Schaefer, E. (1964). Correlations of maternal and child behaviors with the development of mental abilities: Data from the Berkeley growth study. *Monographs of the society for Research in Child Development, 29,* (Serial No. 97).

Bozett, F. W. (1985). Male development and fathering throughout the life cycle.

American Behavioral Scientist, 28(6). Special edition entitled, "Perspectives on Fatherhood."

Bronfenbrenner, U. (1961). Some familial antecedents of responsibility and leadership in adolescents. In L. Petrullo & B. M. Boss (Eds.), *Leadership and interpersonal behavior.* New York: Holt Rinehart and Winston.

Cohen, J. (1979). Male roles in mid-life. *Family Coordinator, 28*(4), 465–471.

Erikson, E. (1959). Identity and the life cycle. *Psychological Issues, 1,* 50–100.

Fisher, B. & Berdie, J. (1978). Adolescent abuse and neglect: Issues of incidence, intervention and service delivery. *Child Abuse and Neglect, 2,* 173–192.

Fleck, R., Fuller, C., Malin, S., Miller, D., & Acheson, K. (1980). Father psychological absence and heterosexual behavior, personal adjustment and sex-typing in adolescent girls. *Adolescence, 15*(6), 849–860.

Grando, R. & Ginsberg, B. (1976). Communication in the father-son relationship: The parent-adolescent relationship development program. *The Family Coordinator, 25*(4), 465–572.

Heilbrun, A. B. Jr. (1976). Identification with the father and sex-role development of the daughter. *The Family Coordinator,* October, *25*(4), 411–416.

Hepburn, E. (1981). The father's role in sexual socialization of adolescent females in an upper-middle class population. *Journal of Early Adolescence, 1*(1), 53–59.

Herman, W. W. (1973). Fathers: What are you? Who are you? *Adolescence, 8*(29), 139–144.

Hunter, F. T., & Youniss, J. (1982). Changes in functions of three relations during adolescence. *Developmental Psychology, 18*(6), 806–811.

Kahl, J. (1953). Educational and occupational aspirations of "common man" boys. *American Educational Review, 23,* 186–203.

Martin, D. (1980). Expressiveness in the father-adolescent daughter relationship measured by their perceptions and desires. In N. Stinnett, B. Chesser, J. DeFrain & P. Knaub (Eds.), *Family strengths: Positive models for family life.* Lincoln: University of Nebraska Press.

McDonald, G. W. (1982). Parental power perceptions in the family. *Youth and Society, 14*(1), 3–31.

McKenry, P. (1979). Adolescent pregnancy: A review of the literature. *Family Coordinator, 28,* 17–28.

Millen, L. & Roll, S. (1977). Adolescent males' ratings of being understood by fathers, best friends and significant others. *Psychological Reports, 50*(3, pt. 2), 1079–1082.

Montemayor, R. (1982). The relationship between parent-adolescent conflict and the amount of time adolescents spend alone with parents and peers. *Child Development, 53*(6), 1512–1519.

Roll, S. & Miller, L. (1978). Adolescent males' feeling of being understood by their fathers as revealed through clinical interviews. *Adolescence, 13*(49), 83–94.

Wright, H., & Keple, W. (1981). Friends and parents of a sample of high school juniors: An explanatory study of relationship intensity and interpersonal rewards. *Journal of Marriage & the Family, 43*(3), 559–570.

Fathers and Adult Children

Bozett, F. W. (1985). Male development and fathering throughout the life cycle. *American Behavioral Scientist, 28*(6). Special edition entitled "Perspectives on Fatherhood."

Caplow, T., Bahr, H. M., Chadwick, B. A., Hill, R., and Williamson, M. H. (1982). *Middletown families: Fifty years of change and continuity*. Minneapolis: University of Minnesota Press.

Chudacoff, H. P., and Hareven, T. K. (1979). From the empty nest to family dissolution: Life course transitions into old age. *Journal of Family History, 3*, 69–83.

Circirelli, V. G. (1981). *Helping elderly parents*. Boston: Auburn House.

Deutscher, I. (1964). The quality of postparental life: Definitions of the situation. *Journal of Marriage and the Family, 26*, 52–59.

Deutscher, I. (1969). From parental to postparental life: Exploring shifting expectations. *Sociological Symposium, 3*, 47–60.

Eichorn, D. H., Clausen, J. A., Haan, N., Nonzik, M. P., & Mussen, P. H. (Eds.). (1981). *Present and past in middle life*. New York: Academic Press.

Farrell, M. P., & Rosenberg, S. D. (1981). *Men at Midlife*. Boston: Auburn House.

Hawkins, E. (1978). Effects of empty nest transition on self-report of psychological and physical well-being. *Journal of Marriage and the Family, 40*, 549–556.

Levinson, D. J. (1978). *The seasons of a man's life*. New York: Knopf.

Lewis, R. A. (1978). Transitions in middle age and aging families: A bibliography from 1940 to 1977. *Family Coordinator, 27*, 457–76.

Lewis, R. A., Freneau, P. J. & Roberts, C. L. (1979). Fathers and the post-parental transition. *Family Coordinator, 26*, 514–520.

Lowenthal, M. F., & Chiriboga, D. A. (1971). Transition to the empty nest. *Archives of General Psychiatry, 26*, 8–14.

Lowenthal, M. F., Thurnher, M., Chiriboga, D., & Associates (1975). *Four Stages of Life: A Comparative Study of Women and Men Facing Transitions*. San Francisco: Jossey-Bass.

Maas, H. S. & Kuypers, J. A. (1974). *From Thirty to Seventy*. San Francisco: Jossey-Bass.

Neugarten, B. L. (1976). *Middle age and aging*. Chicago: University of Chicago Press.

Roberts, C. L. & Lewis, R. A. (1981). The empty nest syndrome. In J. G. Howells (Ed.), *Modern perspectives in the psychiatry of middle age*. New York: Brunner/Mazel.

Rossi, A. A. (1980). Aging and parenthood in the middle years. In P. B. Baltes and O. G. Brim, Jr. (Eds.), *Life-span development and behavior* (Vol. 3). New York: Academic Press.

Streib, G. F., and Beck, R. W. (1980). Older families, a decade review. *Journal of Marriage and the Family, 42*, 937–956.

Troll, L., and Bengtson, V. (1979). Generations in the family. In W. R. Burr, R. Hill, F. I. Nye, and I. L. Reiss (Eds.), *Contemporary theories about the family: Research-based theories* (Vol. 1). New York: The Free Press.

Troll, L. E., Miller, S. J., and Atchley, R. C. (1979). *Families in later life*. Belmont, CA: Wadswoorth.

Grandfatherhood

Baranowski, M. H. (1985). Men as grandfathers. In S. Hanson & F. Bozett (Eds.), *Dimensions of Fatherhood*. Beverly Hills, CA: Sage.

Bozett, F. W. (1985). Male development and fathering throughout the life cycle. *American Behavioral Scientist, 28*(6). Special edition entitled "Perspectives on Fatherhood."

Cath, S. H. (1982). Vicissitudes of grandfatherhood: A miracle of revitalization? In S. H. Cath, A. R. Gurwitt & J. M. Ross (Eds.), *Father and child: Developmental and clinical perspectives*. Boston: Little, Brown.

Kahana, E., & Kahana, B. (1971). Theoretical and research perspectives on grandparenthood. *Aging and Human Development, 2*, 261–268.

Kivnick, H. Q. (1982). Grandparenthood: An overview of meaning and mental health. *The Gerontologist, 22*(1), 59–66.

Kivnick, H. Q. Grandparents and family relations. (1984). In W. H. Quinn & G. A. Hughston (Eds.), *Independent aging: Family and social systems perspectives*. Rockville, MD: Aspen Systems.

Kivnick, H. Q. (1982). *The meaning of grandparenthood*. Ann Arbor, Mich: UMI Research Press.

Neugarten, B., & Weinstein, K. (1964). The changing American grandparent. *Journal of Marriage and the Family, 26*, 199–204.

Robertson, J. F. (1976). Significance of grandparents: Perceptions of young adult grandchildren. *The Gerontologist, 16*(2), 137–140.

Sprey, J., & Matthews, S. H. (1982). Contemporary grandparenthood: A systemic transition. *The Annals of the American Academy of Political and Social Science, 464*, 91–103.

Troll, L. E. Grandparenting. (1980). In L. W. Poon (Ed.), *Aging in the 1980s: Psychological issues*. Washington, D.C.: American Psychological Association.

Troll, L. E. (1983). Grandparents: The family watchdogs. In T. H. Brubaker (Ed.), *Family relationships in later life*. Beverly Hills, CA: Sage.

Wilson, K. B., & DeShane, M. R. (1982). The legal rights of grandparents: A preliminary discussion. *The Gerontologist, 22*(1), 67–71.

IV. FATHERHOOD: SOCIAL CONTEXTS

Fathers in Dual-Earner Families

Aldous, J. (Ed.) (1982). *Two paychecks: Life in dual-earner families*. Beverly Hills: Sage.

Bebbington, A. C. (1973). The function of stress in the establishment of a dual-career family. *Journal of Marriage and the Family, 35*, 530–537.

Benokraitis, N. (1985). Fathers in the dual-earner family. In S. Hanson & F. Bozett (Eds.), *Dimensions of fatherhood*. Beverly Hills, CA: Sage.

Bird, C. (1979). *The two-paycheck marriage*. New York: Rawson, Wade Publishers.

Bryson, J. B. & R. Bryson (Eds.) (1978). *Dual-career couples.* New York: Human Sciences Press.

Ferber, M. & Huber, J. (1979). Husbands, wives, and careers. *Journal of Marriage and the Family, 41,* 315–325.

Gerstel, N. R. (1977). The feasibility of commuter marriage. In P. J. Stein, J. Richman, & N. Hannon (Eds.), *The family: functions, conflicts and symbols.* Reading, MA: Addison-Wesley.

Hanson, S. M. H. (1985). Fatherhood: Contextual Variations. In F. W. Bozett & S. M. H. Hanson (Eds.), *American Behavioral Scientist, 28*(6). Special edition entitled "Perspectives on Fatherhood."

Hayghe, H. (1981). Husbands and wives as earners: An analysis of family data. *Monthly Labor Review, 104,* 46–53.

Heckman, N. A., Bryson, R. & Bryson, J. B. (1977). Problems of professional couples: A content analysis. *Journal of Marriage and the Family, 39,* 323–330.

Hiller, D. & Philliber, W. W. (1982). Predicting marital and career success among dual worker couples. *Journal of Marriage and the Family, 44,* 53–62.

Holahan, C. K. & Gilbert, L. A. (1979). Conflict between major life roles: Women and men in dual career couples. Human Relations, *32,* 451–467.

Holmstrom, L. L. (1972). *The two career family.* Cambridge, MA: Schenckman.

Hood, J. & Golden S. (1979). Beating time/making time: The impact of work scheduling on men's family roles. *The Family Coordinator, 28,* 575–582.

Kamerman, C. B. & Hayes, C. D. (Eds.). (1982). *Families that work: Children in a changing world.* Washington, D.C.: National Academic Press.

Papanek, H. (1973). Men, women and work: Reflections on the two-person career. *American Journal of Sociology, 78,* 852–872.

Peterson, S., Richardson, J. M., & Kreuter, G. B. (Eds.). (1978). *The two-career family: Issues and alternatives.* Washington, D.C.: University Press of America.

Rapoport, R. & Rapoport, R. N. (1976). *Dual-career families reexamined.* New York: Harper and Row.

Rapoport, R. & Rapoport, R. N. (1969). The dual career family. *Human Relations, 22,* 3–30.

Walker, K. (1970). Time spent by husbands in household work. *Family Economics Review, 4,* 8–11.

Ybarra, L. (1982). When wives work: The impact on the Chicano family. *Journal of Marriage and the Family, 44,* 169–178.

Househusband Fathers

Beer, W. R. (1983). *Househusbands: Men and housework in American families.* New York: Praeger.

Berk, S. F. (1979). Husbands at home: Organization of the husband's household day. In K. W. Feinstein (Ed.), *Working Women and Families.* Beverly Hills, CA: Sage.

Hanson, S. M. H. (1985). Fatherhood: Contextual Variations. In F. W. Bozett and S. M. H. Hanson (Eds.), *American Behavioral Scientist, 28*(6). Special edition entitled "Perspectives on Fatherhood."

Hunt, J. G. & Hunt, L. L. (1982). The dualities of careers and families. New integrations or new polarizations? *Social Problems, 29*(5), 499–510.

Lutwin, D. & Sipersten, G. (1985). *Househusband fathers*. In S. Hanson and F. Bozett (Eds.), *Dimensions of Fatherhood*. Beverly Hills, CA: Sage.

Pruitt, K. D. (1983). Infants of primary nurturing fathers. *The Psychoanalytic Study of the Child, 38*, 257–277.

Radin, N. (1982). Primary caregiving and role-sharing fathers. In M. E. Lamb (Ed.), *Nontraditional Families: Parenting and Child Development*. Hillsdale, NJ: Lawrence Erlbaum.

Russell, G. (1983). *The changing role of fathers?* New York: University of Queensland Press.

Stepfathers

Albrecht, S. L. (1979). Correlates of marital happiness among the remarried. *Journal of Marriage and the Family, 41*, 857–867.

Clingempeel, W. G. (1981). Quasi-kin relationships and marital quality. *Journal of Personality and Social Psychology, 41*, 890–901.

Duberman, L. (1975). *The reconstituted family: A study of remarried couples and their children*. Chicago: Nelson-Hall.

Esses, L., & Campbell, R. (1984). Challenges in researching the remarried. *Family Relations, 33*, 415–424.

Ganong, L. & Coleman, M. (1984). Effects of remarriage on children: A review of the empirical literature. *Family Relations, 33*, 389–406.

Giles-Sims, J. (1984). The stepparent role: Expectations, behavior, sanctions. *Journal of Family Issues, 5*, 116–130.

Hanson, S. M. H. (1985). Fatherhood: Contextual Variations. In F. W. Bozett & S. M. H. Hanson (Eds.), *American Behavioral Scientist, 28*(6). Special edition entitled ''Perspectives on Fatherhood.''

Ihinger-Tallman, M. (1984). Epilogue: Special issue on remarriage and stepparenting. *Family Relations, 33*, 483–487.

Knaub, P. K., Hanna, S. L., & Stinnett, N. (1984). Strengths of remarried families. *Journal of Divorce, 7*, 41–55.

Lutz, P. (1983). The stepfamily: An adolescent perspective. *Family Relations, 32*, 367–376.

Papernow, P. The stepfamily cycle: An experiential model of stepfamily development. *Family Relations, 33*, 355–363.

Rallings, E. M. (1976). The special role of the stepfather. *The Family Coordinator, 25*, 445–450.

Robinson, B. (1984). The contemporary American stepfather. *Family Relations, 33*, 381–388.

Sager, C. J., Brown, H. S., Crohn, H., Engel, T., Rodstein, E., & Walker, E. (1983). *Treating the remarried family*. New York: Brunner/Mazel.

Stern, P. N. (1978). Stepfather families: Integration around child discipline. *Issues in Mental Health Nursing, 1*, 49–56.

Troph, E. D. (1984). An exploratory examination of the effect of remarriage on child support and personal contacts. *Journal of Divorce, 7*(3), 57–73.

Military Fathers

Boss, P. (1980). The relationship of psychological father presence, wife's personal qualities and wife/family dysfunction in families of missing fathers. *Journal of Marriage and the Family, 42*(3), pp. 541–549.

Bowen, G. L. (in press). Families in blue. Insights from Air Force Families. *Social Case Work.*

Bowen, G. L. (1981). Family patterns of U.S. military personnel. In J. S. Parry and K. L. Parkinson (Eds.), *Proceedings of the National Association of Social Workers Pre-Conference on Social Work Services for Military Families.* Springfield, VA.: Military Family Resource Center.

Bowen, G. L. (in press). Inter-cultural marriage in the U.S. military: A comparative analysis. *International Journal of Sociology of the Family.*

Bowen, G. L. (1984). Quality of Air Force family life. *Air University Review, 35*(2), 77–84.

Bowen, G. L. & Orthner, D. K. (1983). Sex-role congruency and marital quality. *Journal of Marriage and the Family, 45*(1), 223–230.

Faris, J. H. (1981). The all-volunteer force: Recruitment from military families. *Armed Forces and Society, 1*(4), 545–559.

Hanson, S. M. H. (1985). Fatherhood: Contextual Variations. In F. W. Bozett & S. M. H. Hanson (Eds.), *American Behavioral Scientist, 28*(6). Special edition entitled "Perspectives on Fatherhood."

Kim, Bok-Lim, C. (1981). *Women in the shadows: A handbook for service providers working with Asian wives of U.S. military personnel.* La Jolla, CA.: National Committee Concerned with Asian Wives of U.S. Servicemen.

Lanier, D. (1978). Child abuse and neglect among military families. In E. Hunter and D. J. Nice (Eds.), *Children of military families: A part and yet apart.* Washington, D.C.: U.S. Government Printing Office.

Orthner, D. K. (1980). *Families in blue.* Greensboro, N.C.: Family Development Press.

Orthner, D. K., & Bowen, G. L. (1982). Attitudes toward family enrichment and support programs among Air Force families. *Family Relations, 31*(3), 415–424.

Orthner, D. K., & Bowen, G. L. (1982). *Families in blue: Insights from families in the Pacific.* Greensboro, N.C.: Family Development Press.

Orthner, D. K., & Bowen, G. L. (1985). Fathers in the military. In S. Hanson & F. Bozett (Eds.), *Dimensions of Fatherhood.* Beverly Hills, CA: Sage.

Orthner, D. K., & Brown, R. (1978). Single parent fathers: Implications for the military family. In E. Hunter & D. Nice (Eds.), *Military families: Adaptation to change.* New York: Praeger.

Shaw, J. (1978). The adolescent experience and the military family. In E. Hunter and D. Nice (Eds.), *Children of military families.* Washington, D.C.: U.S. Government Printing Office.

Szoc, R. (1982). *Family factors critical to the retention of Navy personnel: Final report.* Washington, D.C.: Westinghouse Public Applied Systems.

Gay Fathers

Bell, A. P., & Weinberg, M. S. (1978). *Homosexualities: A study of diversity among men & women.* New York: Simon and Schuster.

Bozett, F. W. (1985). Gay men as fathers. In S. M. H. Hanson and F. W. Bozett (Eds.), *Dimensions of Fatherhood*. Beverly Hills, CA: Sage.

Bozett, F. W. (1981). Gay fathers: Evolution of the gay-father identity. *American Journal of Orthopsychiatry, 51*(3), 552–559.

Bozett, F. W. (1980). Gay fathers: How and why they disclose their homosexuality to their children. *Family Relations, 29*(2), 173–179.

Bozett, F. W. (1981). Gay fathers: Identity conflict resolution through integrative sanctioning. *Alternative Lifestyles, 4*(1) 90–107.

Bozett, F. W. (1984). Parenting concerns of gay fathers. *Topics in Clinical Nursing, 6*(3), 60–71.

Bozett, F. W. (1982). Heterogenous couples in heterosexual marriages: Gay men and straight women. *Journal of Marital and Family Therapy, 8*(1), 81–89.

Dank, B. M. (1971). Coming out in the gay world. *Psychiatry, 34*(2), 180–197.

Fadiman, A. (1983, May). The double closet. *Life*, pp. 76–78; 82–84; 86; 92; 96; 100.

Gay Fathers. (1981). Toronto, Canada: Gay Fathers of Toronto.

Hanson, S. M. H. (1985). Fatherhood: Contextual Variations. In F. W. Bozett & S. M. H. Hanson (Eds.), *American Behavioral Scientist, 28*(6). Special edition entitled "Perspectives on Fatherhood."

Maddox, B. (1982). *Married and gay*. New York: Harcourt Brace Jovanovich.

Mager, D. (1975). Faggot father. In K. Jay & A. Young (Eds.), *After you're out*. New York: Links.

Miller, B. (1978). Adult sexual resocialization. *Alternative Lifestyles, 1*(2), 1978.

Miller, B. (1979). Gay fathers and their children. *The Family Coordinator, 28*(4), 544–552.

Miller, B. (1979). Unpromised paternity: The life-styles of gay fathers. In M. P. Levine (Ed.), *Gay Men: The Sociology of Male Homosexuality*. New York: Harper & Row.

Robinson, B. E. (1985). Gay fathers. In B. E. Robinson & R. L. Barret (Eds.), *Fatherhood*. New York: The Guilford Press.

Robinson, B. E., & Skeen, P. (1982). Sex-role orientation of gay fathers versus gay nonfathers. *Perceptual and Motor Skills, 55*, 1055–1059.

Ross, M. W. (1983). *The married homosexual man: A psychological study*. London: Routledge and Kegan Paul.

Skeen, P., & Robinson, B. (1984). Family backgrounds of gay fathers: A descriptive study. *Psychological Reports, 54*, 999–1005.

Voeller, B., & Walters, J. (1978). Gay fathers. *The Family Coordinator, 27*, 149–157.

Adolescent Fathers

Barret, R. L., & Robinson, B. E. (1981). Teenage fathers: A profile. *The Personnel and Guidance Journal, 60*, 226–228.

Barret, R. L., & Robinson, B. E. A descriptive study of teenage expectant fathers. (1982). *Family Relations: Journal of Applied Family and Child Studies, 31*, 349–352.

Barret, R. L., & Robinson, B. E. (1982). Teenage fathers: Neglected too long. *Social Work, 27*, 484–488.

Barret, R. L., & Robinson, B. E. (1985). The adolescent father. In S. Hanson & F. Bozett (Eds.), *Dimensions of Fatherhood*. Beverly Hills, CA: Sage.

Card, J. J., & Wise, L. L. (1978). Teenage mothers and teenage fathers: The impact of early childbearing on the parents' personal and professional lives. *Family Planning Perspectives, 10*, 199–205.

Earls, F., & Siegel, B. (1980). Precocious fathers. *American Journal of Orthopsychiatry, 50*, 469–480.

Furstenberg, F. F. (1980). Teenage parenthood and family support. *Dimensions, 9*, 49–54.

Furstenberg, F. F., Lincoln, R., & Menken, J. (Eds.). (1980). *Perspectives on teenage sexuality, pregnancy, and childbearing*. Philadelphia: University of Pennsylvania Press.

Furstenberg, F. F. & Talvitie, K. G. (1980). Children's names and paternal claims: Bonds between unmarried fathers and their children. *Journal of Family Issues, 1*, 31–57.

Hanson, S. M. H. (1985). Fatherhood: Contextual Variations. In F. W. Bozett & S. M. H. Hanson (Eds.), *American Behavioral Scientist, 28*(6). Special edition entitled "Perspectives on Fatherhood."

Hendricks, L. E. (1980). Unwed adolescent fathers: Problems they face and their sources of social support. *Adolescence, 15*, 861–869.

Johnson, L. B. & Staples, R. E. (1979). Family planning and the young minority male: A pilot project. *The Family Coordinator, 28*, 535–543.

Leashore, B. R. (1979). Human services and the unmarried father: The "forgotten half." *The Family Coordinator, 28*, 529–534.

Pannor, R., Massarik, F., & Evans, B. (1981). *The unmarried father: New helping approaches for unmarried young parents*. New York: Springer.

Parke, R. D., Power, T. G. & Fisher, T. (1980). The adolescent father's impact on the mother and child. *Journal of Social Issues, 36*, 88–106.

Robinson, B. E., & Barret, R. L. (1982). Issues and problems related to the research of teenage fathers: A critical analysis. *Journal of School Health, 52*, 596–600.

Robinson, B. E., Barret, R. L. & Skeen, P. (1983). Locus of control of unwed adolescent fathers versus adolescent nonfathers. *Perceptual and Motor Skills, 56*, 397–398.

Rothstein, A. A. (1978). Adolescent males, fatherhood, and abortion. *Journal of Youth and Adolescence, 7*, 203–214.

Russ-Eft, D., Spreger, M., & Beever, H. (1979). Antecedents of adolescent parenthood and consequences at age 30. *Family Coordinator, 28*, 173–179.

Shostak, A. B. (1979). Abortion as fatherhood lost: Problems and reforms. *Family Coordinator, 28*, 569–574.

Single Custodial Fathers

Ambert, A. M. (1982). Differences in children's behavior toward custodial mothers and custodial fathers. *Journal of Marriage and the Family, 44*, 73–85.

Bartz, K. W. & Witcher, W. C. (1978). When father gets custody. *Children Today, 7*, 2–6.

Burgess, J. K. (1970). The single parent family: A social and sociological problem. *The Family Coordinator, 19*, 137–144.

Burgess, K. & Kohn, W. (1978). *The Widower*. Boston: Beacon Press.

Chang, P. & Deinard, D. (1982). Single father caretakers: Demographic characteristics and adjustment process. *American Journal of Orthopsychiatry, 52*, 236–243.

Defrain, J. & Eirick, R. (1981). Coping as divorced parents: A comparative study of fathers and mothers. *Family Relations, 30*, 265–274.

George, V. & Wilding, P. (1972). *Motherless Families*. London: Routledge and Kegan Paul.

Gersick, K. E. (1979). Fathers by choice: Divorced men who receive custody of their children. In George Levinger and Oliver Noels (Eds.), *Separation and Divorce*. New York: Basic Books.

Grief, G. L. (1982). Dads raising kids. *Single Parent, 25*, 19–23.

Grief, G. L. (1985). *Single Fathers*. Lexington, MA: Lexington Books.

Hanson, S. M. H. (1981). Single custodial fathers and the parent-child relationships. *Nursing Research, 30*, 202–204.

Hanson, S. M. H. (1985). Fatherhood: Contextual Variations. In F. W. Bozett & S. M. H. Hanson (Eds.), *American Behavioral Scientist, 28*(6). Special edition entitled "Perspectives on Fatherhood."

Hanson, S. M. H. & Sporakowski (Eds.) (1986). Single parent families. Special issue of *Family Relations*. (In process).

Hanson, S. M. H. (1985). Father/child relationships: Beyond *Kramer versus Kramer*. *Marriage and Family Review, 9(3/4)*, 135–150.

Hanson, S. M. H. (1985). Parent-Child relationships in single-father families. In R. E. Salt & R. A. Lewis, *Men in Families*. Beverly Hills: Sage.

Hanson, S. M. H. (1985) Single fathers with custody: A synthesis of the literature. In B. Schlesinger's (Ed.), *The One-Parent Family: Perspectives and annotated bibliography*. Toronto: University of Toronto Press.

Hanson, S. M. H. (1985). Single custodial fathers. In S. Hanson & F. Bozett (Eds.), *Dimensions of Fatherhood*. Beverly Hills, CA: Sage.

Lewis, K. (1978). Single-father families: Who they are and how they fare. *Child Welfare, 57*, 643–651.

Lewis, A. & Pleck, J. H. (1979). (Eds.). Men's roles in the family. Special issue of *The Family Coordinator, 28*(4), 429–462.

McFadden, M. (1974). *Bachelor fatherhood: How to raise and enjoy your children as a single parent*. New York: Charter Communications.

Orthner, D. & Lewis, K. (1979). Evidence of single father competence in childrearing. *Family Law Quarterly, 8*, 27–48.

Roman, M. & Haddad, W. (1978). *The disposable parent: The case for custody*. New York: Holt, Rinehart and Winston.

Rosenthal, K. M. & Keshet, H. F. (1981). *Fathers without partners: A study of fathers and the family after marital separation*. Totowa, NJ: Rowman and Littlefield.

Santrock, J. W. & Warshak, R. (1979). Father custody and social development in boys and girls. *The Journal of Social Issues, 35*, 112–125.

Schlesinger, B. (1984). *The one-parent family: Perspectives and annotated bibliography*. Toronto, Canada: University of Toronto Press, 5th edition.

Smith, R. M. & Smith, C. W. (1981). Child-rearing and single-parent fathers. *Family Relations, 30*, 411–417.

Todres, R. (1978). Runaway wives: An increasing North-American phenomenon. *The Family Coordinator, 27,* 17–21.

Victor, I. & Winkler, W. A. (1977). *Fathers and custody.* New York: Hawthorn Books.

Walters, J. (Ed.). (1976). Fatherhood. Special issue of *The Family Coordinator, 25*(4), 335–520.

Washington Chapter of U.S. Divorce Reform (1978). *What you always wanted to know about divorce but were afraid to ask: A guide to divorce for the man (or woman) seeking child custody in a divorce or who wishes to have a joint custody arrangement.* P.O. Box 11, Auburn, Washington.

Non-Custodial Fathers

Abarbanel, A. (1979). Shared parenting after separation and divorce: A study of joint custody. *American Journal of Orthopsychiatry, 49*(2), 320–329.

Ahrons, C. R. (1980). Joint custody arrangements in the postdivorce family. *Journal of Divorce, 3*(3), 139–205.

Chambers, D. L. (1977). Men who know they are watched: Some benefits and costs of failing for nonpayment of support. *Michigan Law Review, 75,* 900–940.

Cherlin, A., Griffith, J., & McCarthy, J. (1983). A note on maritally-disrupted men's reports of child support in the June 1980 Current Population Survey. *Demography, 20*(3), 385–390.

Grief, J. B. (1979). Fathers, children and joint custody. *American Journal of Orthopsychiatry, 49*(2), 311–319.

Hanson, S. M. H. (1985). Fatherhood: Contextual Variations. In F. W. Bozett & S. M. H. Hanson (Eds.), *American Behavioral Scientist, 28*(6). Special edition entitled "Perspectives on Fatherhood."

Hetherington, E. M., Cox, M., & Cox, R. (1976). Divorced fathers. *The Family Coordinator, 4,* 417–428.

Hetherington, E. M., Cox, M., & Cox, R. (1979). Play and social interaction in children following divorce. *The Journal of Social Issues, 35*(4), 26–49.

Hetherington, E. M., Cox, M., & Cox, R. (1978). The aftermath of divorce. In J. H. Stevens & M. Matthews (Eds.), *Mother/Child, Father/Child Relationships.* Washington, D.C.: National Association for the Education of Young Children.

Keshet, H. F., & Rosenthal, K. M. (1978). Fathering after marital separation, *Social Work, 23*(1), 11–18.

Moreland, J., & Schwebel, A. I. (1978). A gender role transcendent perspective on fathering. *The Counseling Psychologist, 9*(4), 45–52.

Santrock, J. W., & Warshak, R. A. (1979). Father custody and social development in boys and girls. *The Journal of Social Issues, 35*(4), 112–125.

Warshak, R. A., & Santrock, J. W. (1983). Children of divorce: Impact of custody disposition on social development. From E. J. Callahan and K. A. McCluskey (Eds.), *Life-Span Developmental Psychology: Non-Normative Life Events.* New York: Academic Press.

Today's Spectrum of Fathering Examined Through Film

David L. Giveans

Film is an excellent medium for the introduction or reinforcement of a new concept. Perhaps because viewers' reactions are protected from detection by a darkened room or because film is two dimensional, viewers are less intimidated or threatened by the subject and/or message than when they are directly confronted by persons making similar statements. As an increasing amount of material has been published on men's issues and fathering, e.g., books, journals, articles, so also has there been a steady production of fine films on egalitarian parenting, fathering and men's issues in general.

In 1979, *Kramer vs Kramer*[1] exploded on the commercial silver screen shattering forever the traditional Hollywood Celluoid interpretation of fathers, mothers and family life. Four years prior to this, however, filmmakers Josh Hanig and Will Roberts produced the brilliant and now classic documentary film, *Men's Lives*.[2] For those of us who saw it during the first few years after production, who cannot forget the profound, haunting effect this film had on its

David L. Giveans has taught on the early childhood, elementary and college levels. His early childhood experience has been as both a teacher and directing person. He is an author and lecturer advocating non-sexist education and men in nurturing roles and edits the nationally distributed newsletter, *Nurturing News: A Quarterly Forum for Nurturing Men*, published since 1979. For further information on his work write: 187 Caselli Avenue, San Francisco, CA 94114, Tel (415) 861-0847.

audiences. I have not seen it for several years but its images are still indelibly etched upon my mind. Although perhaps a bit dated in vocabulary and other minor points, its message—unfortunately—still to a greater degree accurately assesses the still prevailing Middle American attitudes of the mid-1980's.

As a humanist and educator advocating men in nurturing roles, I am pleased to offer for consideration eleven films representing issues and thoughts on men in fathering roles ranging from boys in their early childhood years to men in their senior years. As I prepared this filmography, I previewed about twenty films on the subject. I do not wish to imply that the films I have selected are necessarily the best on the subject nor is it my intent to judge one film technically over another. I feel the selected films offer a stimulating cross section of material and I am confident they will provide meaningful viewing experiences as well as generate subsequent consideration of the new breed of fathers slowly surfacing in American society. Pandora's box has been sprung! The word is out! Fathering is definitely in!

The films I have chosen for consideration are:

> *Nicholas and the Baby*—Centre Productions, Inc.
> *William's Doll*—Phoenix Films
> *Oh, Boy! Babies!*—Simon & Schuster Communications
> *Teenage Fathers*—Children's Home Society of California
> *Heroes and Strangers*—New Day Films
> *Pregnant Fathers*—Joseph Anzalone Foundation
> *Fathers*—ASPO/Lamaze
> *2 AM Feeding*—New Day Films
> *New Relations: A Film About Fathers and Sons*—Fanlight
>   Productions
> *Men in Early Childhood Education*—Davidson Films
> *Portrait of Grandpa Doc*—Phoenix Films

I firmly believe that if we are to "bring up" nurturing fathers (as we have always "brought up" nurturing mothers) then we must provide children—especially boys—with nurturing experiences from their early childhood years onward. After all, what better place to plant the seeds of human liberation than in the minds of our young children.[3] Early childhood specialist, Jennifer Birckmeyer suggests that children learn to be adults by watching adults.[4] Therefore, if we encourage boys and girls to interchange roles and be aware of each other's natural nurturing characteristics and at the same time provide them with role models of adults who respect each other as individual persons and who work together in unison as parents, our society will take a giant step forward toward humankind.

The films I have selected are briefly discussed—drawing upon the thoughts expressed in their various film fliers and guides along with my own thoughts—in a sequence beginning with a film about a pre-school boy and ending with a film about a grandfather. These films are equally as important for consideration by all professionals, e.g., educators, researchers, social scientists, famologists, mental health specialists and all lay persons who have or have not yet considered changes in their lifestyles. Individually and collectively these films have a sensitive, human message focusing on male interaction with other males, his mate and his children which needs to be heard again and again and again.

I would like to point out that I have used all of these films in college classrooms, at parent meetings or at educational and parenting conferences and have repeatedly observed with profound joy the reactions they generate. Many of the films are accompanied by study sheets or guides and I strongly recommend that for optimum viewing, the films be previewed and studied in advance of presentation. I find it effective to stimulate a discussion concerning the topic, e.g., boys playing with dolls, fathers' changing attitudes, prior to a screening taking care not to directly answer the questions generated. In most cases the films will substantiate the pre-screening discussions and learning will be far more meaningful than if the films were seen without an introductory discussion.

In closing, individually the films are a joyous viewing experience and collectively they will electrify to the fullest a new found understanding of fathering. Without any doubt they will dispel a statement attributed to Margaret Mead, "Fathers are a biological necessity but a social accident."

NICHOLAS AND THE BABY. Produced by Victress Hitchcock, 1981. *Distributed by Centre Productions, Inc., 1800 30th Street, Suite 207, Boulder, CO 80301, Tel: (800) 824-1166. Color, 23 mins., 16mm and video. 20 pp study guide with references.*

As indicated in the opening comments of this filmography, in order that we bring up fathers from their earliest years, we need to present young boys with opportunities to interact with infants and other young children. We also need to expose young boys (and girls) to role models of nurturing fathers.

Nicholas and the Baby is a warm, charming film narrated by four year old Nicholas. It follows the pregnancy of Nicholas' mother and father. With patient love and understanding shared by his parents, this young four year old never feels isolated from the birth of his new sister. It is an excellent film to introduce parents to the perceptions and questions of children as well as introducing children ages four to 12 to the birth of a sibling.

Nicholas talks a great deal about his unborn sibling and some times acts out his resentment that his mother is not able to interact with him as much as she did before her pregnancy. He visits the doctor with his mother and listens to the embryo's heart beat. He talks with his father about how important it is to take care of children recognizing that it is hard work. He is also assured to know that he will always be four years older.

As the delivery time draws near, Nicholas' father picks him up from his day care center. Upon learning that the birth is imminent, he joyously exclaims, "Oh, boy I get to have my baby now!" On the way to the hospital he becomes quite insecure and wants to be with his mother. At the hospital he is happy to see his mother in the birthing room. Feeling his mother's stomach, he calls out to the unborn baby, "Get out!" He also talks with the female doctor about the birth and so as not to be isolated from the family spends the night at the hospital with a family friend.

The birth is sensitively filmed and with proper parent approval and parent teacher reinforcement before screening it is appropriate for preschoolers to see. The length of the film does not affect their attention span. After viewing the film, one four year old girl said, "I like the part where the baby popped out."

During the birth, (Nicholas is not present) the sharing of the parents is clearly evident and viewers become intimately part of the immediate bonding experienced by mother, father and infant. After the birth Nicholas is brought to see his infant sister and gently kisses her. The family enjoys a birthday celebration singing happy birthday to the newborn child.

The film concludes with the return of the entire family to their home. Nicholas carrying a stuffed animal in his Snugli as his mother carries the infant in her Snugli. All harmoniously resume family life once again with Nicholas very confident of his special place in the family.

WILLIAM'S DOLL. Produced by Roberto C. Chiesa, 1981. *Distributed by Phoenix Films, 468 Park Avenue South, New York, NY 10016, Tel: (212) 684-5910. Color, 18 mins., 16mm and video. One page study sheet.*

This is a tremendously valuable docudrama to help break down many stereotypes concerning elementary school boys and their accepted play activities; about fathers who learn to rethink their traditional parenting attitudes and about grandfathers who serve as a nurturing link between their own fathering experiences to the future fathering roles of their grandchildren.

American society has a tragic, homophobic attitude regarding boys participating in nurturing roles—especially doll play. Dr. Lee Salk wrote:

> I think it is normal for little boys to want to play with dolls and for little girls to want to play with toy cars . . . A boy's desire to play with dolls is parental rather than effeminate, and it should help him to be a good father.[5]

William's Doll based on the 1972 classic children's book by the same name[6] is important for all persons striving towards developing a more open environment in which young children may flourish. Its message is threefold: (1) doll play enables a boy to prepare for future fathering; (2) adult men (fathers) often forget the nurturing activities they once themselves participated in and (3) seniors (male and female) often seem much more in tune with the real needs of children and are far more accepting.

William displays great affection for his father (who appears to be a single father) and has a poster in his bedroom, "I love you, Dad." He has lots of traditional toys and loves to play baseball and basketball. He also loves to touch little babies or to combine truck and doll play with his neighboring girl playmate. When William suggests to his father that he would really like a doll for his birthday, he is firmly informed that dolls are for girls.

William's paternal grandfather comes to visit him on his birthday. It is obvious that he basks in the warmth of his "Gramps" and that the older man enjoys the affection of young William. Somewhat hesitantly William tells his grandfather that inspite of his father's objection, he would love a doll. Without hesitation, Gramps takes his grandson to buy a doll—conveying assurance and acceptance of William's selection. William's father is very upset, "But why does he need a doll?" The senior father patiently explains, "So he will grow up to be a father like you." In a touching scene, Gramps recounts how very attached his son was to a Raggedy Andy doll a long time ago.

After Gramps departs there exists a much deeper, unsuppressed affection between father and son. William continues to love playing with his doll taking it for rides in his dump truck. When his friends come along and want him to play baseball, he easily puts down his doll and runs off with them.

OH, BOY! BABIES! Produced by Bruce and Carole Hart, 1982, *Distributed by Simon and Schuster Communications, 108 Wilmot Road, Deerfield, Il 60015, Tel (800) 323-5343. Color, 29 mins., 16mm and video. 2 pp study sheet.*

Although young boys may have an opportunity to explore their natural interests as pre-schoolers, they are usually skillfully restricted by societal expectations as they move through elementary school. *Oh, Boy! Babies!* is a delightfully important consciousness raising film substantiating that elementary boys—given the opportunity and support—can and will recognize their natural, nurturing characteristics.

The film begins with a guidance counsellor introducing an elective course in infant care as a good idea for sixth graders. He suggests, "Learning to take care of babies will turn you guys on to the best part of yourselves."

This film is very natural presenting an actual group of sixth grade boys learning to care for infants. It realistically depicts how some boys are more willing than others to participate in diapering, bathing and feeding infants.

The female infant care class teacher is very patient with her class and explains how important the boys' participation is. Viewers are delighted with charming scenes of boys struggling to diaper, to feed not always receptive mouths, to take in their stride a sudden jet stream of urine or to delight in simply holding a baby communicating through loving eye contact.

One boy is quite antagonistic towards the class manifesting his dicomfort by making fun of the other participants. Slowly, however through the supportive encouragement of his parents, the teacher, his classmates and most importantly the babies, he begins to react positively to the class.

Over the duration of the course, the boys hold meaningful discussions with their teacher concerning their interactions with the babies, a father's role with infants and older children and their own future potential fathering roles. As the boys observe a mother breast feeding, one asks, "Doesn't the father feel sort of left out?" A boy whose own father has left his home asks, "How could a father walk out and miss all of this?" The class profoundly questions, "If boys and men have this 'nurturing thing,' how could they run off to work or leave them (the babies)?"

The concluding scene of the class' graduation ceremony clearly establishes how attached all the boys have become to the infants—not to mention confident concerning their abilities to care for young children. Equally as important, through interaction with the infants, the boys have learned a great deal about each other as persons.

TEENAGE FATHERS. Produced by Taylor Hackford, 1979. *Distributed by Children's Home Society of California, 2727 W. 6th Street, Los Angeles, CA 90057, Tel (213) 389-6730. Color, 30 mins., 16mm and video, 16 pp study guide.*

Teenage Fathers, a 1979 Academy Award Best Live Action Short Film, is a provocative, moving docudrama realistically and honestly presenting the attitudes, apprehensions and turmoil experienced by an unwed teenage couple, their respective parents and friends. It is a composite story professionally acted based on case studies and interviews with 71 young men involved in pregnancy as unmarried teenagers.

The film was produced to stimulate discussion about young people involved in an unplanned pregnancy and to facilitate communication between teenagers with respect to their responsibilities for parenthood. Another purpose for this film is to encourage communication between teenagers and their parents regarding sexuality and finally it was produced to develop an understanding of the needs and rights of mothers, fathers and children.

John is a 17 year old who suddenly discovers his girlfriend, Kim, 15, is pregnant. He is initially shocked and his parents even more so. His male contemporaries discuss their thoughts about sexuality, their responsibilities, abortion, adoption and potential fathering experiences. They all feel they are too young to accept total fathering responsibilities.

John's parents and Kim's mother present their view. John's parents feel Kim and John are too young to parent and that sex education should not be taught in schools, but that boys should be held accountable for the "adult act." Kim's mother can't understand why Kim "went wrong" since her two other daughters did not. She holds John directly responsible and indicates that Kim feels that raising a child is like playing with dolls.

The social worker is an effective intermediary as the young couple participate in a tug of war concerning their emotions and the future of the unborn child. Neither wish to get married. John seems more mature in his approach to the problem and he feels guilt concerning his financial responsibilities. Kim, on the other hand vacillates between keeping the child and adoption. When the child is born, John sees his son for the first time. He becomes angry as he learns that the baby will be put up for adoption. Tragically, the social worker informs him, he has absolutely no say or rights in the decision.

HEROES AND STRANGERS. Produced by Lorna Rasmussen and Tony Herzia, 1984, *Distributed by New Day Films, 22 Riverview Drive, Wayne, New Jersey 07470-3191, Tel (201) 633-0212, Color, 29 mins., 16mm and video. No study guide.*

Heroes and Strangers is a poignantly moving film more than likely relevant to ninety-five percent of its viewing audience. The film vividly stimulates professionals and lay persons alike to recall their own childhood relationships with their fathers. In most cases few ever have known the person inside the man called Father.

> Father: Counselor, protector, teacher and friend. These are the images we grew up with and if our own realities didn't measure up we hid the truth and we pretended it didn't matter. But it does matter—it matters enough to risk looking honestly at our relationships with our fathers.

> When I was growing up, the image of father for me was "Father Knows Best." I would look at "Father Knows Best" and think that is what a father is supposed to be like. My father was the antithesis of "Father Knows Best." He was the one who did not know anything that was going on in the family.

These retrospective, opening comments by the narrating man and woman in their twenties reinforce Virginia Satir's statement, "Fathers have been traditionally left out of the emotional life of the family. What a price we paid for that . . . [7]

In order to "find" their fathers, these two young people returned to their childhood homes to visit their fathers. The male's parents are still married and the female's parents divorced.

Through narrative, still photos of traditional fathers, television clips of fathering in the 1950's and direct discussions, viewers learn of these two fathers. Both men were under tremendous pressure to provide for their families. One father worked three jobs to support his family and had no time to be with his children. The other father was a traveling salesperson and would only be home on weekends. Both young people wanted love and recognition from their fathers and felt varying degrees of anger that they had not received it.

The young man and woman put forth great effort to know their father. The male indicates at first he was uncomfortable with his father not knowing what to talk about. Viewers see the young man walking with his father in the fields and the young woman talking with her father in the woods. The male decides to stop talking and listen to what his father wanted to talk about. When the female learned that her father really did care about her she became curious as to why he did not express affection. Both people discover that as they move out of anger towards their father they begin to remember the things both men did for them. As the film concludes, both part from their fathers with a new found understanding of the men they had never known.

PREGNANT FATHERS. Produced by Stanford University, 1977. *Distributed by Joseph T. Anzalone Foundation, PO Box 5206, Santa Cruz, CA 95063, Tel (408) 423-2600, Color, 27 mins., 16mm and video. 4 pp study sheet.*

The concept of "pregnant fathers" is still not part of society's working vocabulary yet it is vitally significant for consideration by the medical profession, famologists, sociologists—not to mention first-time and experienced parents. The male's paternal role has been traditionally limited to impregnation and financial source—leaving all other attention to the mother. Father traditionally has been recognized as important in his children's lives (especially boys) when it was necessary to role model masculinity.

Pregnant Fathers graphically portrays the profound importance of a father experiencing pregnancy and the support and love he offers his spouse during the prenatal and postpartum periods. This film follows a well prepared father who is actively involved in the pregnancy, labor and birth as he explores the significance to him of the birth of his child. The film's study sheet indicates the film was produced to: (1) stimulate thought on the changing role of men in today's society, (2) encourage men to participate in emotional, social and cognitive preparation for birth and parenthood, (3) provide professionals in childbirth education, maternity nursing and general education with a more complete understanding of the needs of expectant fathers, (4) explore meaningful participation for a father in the birth process and (5) motivate men to consider their potential to be nurturing fathers.

The film follows an actual couple through a prenatal class, the acceptance that fathering is a developmental process, how a man's own father influences his son's fathering. A father's needs in labor are explored and the sharing experience of the couple as labor progresses. If one is not convinced of a father's total involvement before the birth, the birth scene will eliminate any doubts as the couple share support, love and the joy of birth and immediate bonding of mother, father and child. The film concludes with the couple returning home with their new infant. An older male sibling holds the newborn and the proud new parents discuss the new life that has entered their family.

Pregnant Fathers encourages its viewers and society in general that it is time to take a new look at men—not as coaches or support systems in labor but as fathers with needs of their own. The film assures its viewers that fathers are nurturing, caring, involved, supportive, important and love—just as mothers have always been.

FATHERS. Produced by Durrin Films, Inc. 1980. *Distributed by ASPO/Lamaze, 1840 Wilson Blvd., Arlington, VA 22201, Tel (800) 368-4404, Color, 26 mins., 16mm* only, *No study guide.*

Fathers takes place in the lives and homes of contemporary American men. These men share their innermost feelings about childbirth and parenthood. The result is a warm, revealing and sometimes astonishing film portrait of men breaking down the barriers to love, affection, and satisfaction in their own lives. Narrated by developmental psychologist, Henry Biller, the film offers glimpses into the lives of an expectant father, a first-time father and experienced fathers as they interact with children ranging from an infant to an elementary school boy—including a disabled preschooler.

Biller, a pioneer in family psychology drawing upon his at the time of the film 15 years of experience with fathers and families, encourages men to open up possibilities of fathering and stresses that one is a father for his entire life. He also indicates, "It is sad when the only thing a father can do for a child is to provide money for them." He also reinforces that good fathering contributes to a better relationship with a wife.

Through direct filming and narration, viewers meet four Caucasian fathers interacting with their children. Initially viewers witness an intimate conversation between a first-time father and an expectant father. The expectant father wants a boy because he feels he would be more comfortable participating in "boy things," such as going to basketball games. He is not completely firm about his future parenting role. As he talks he observes his first-time father friend loving his child. "Not to show affection for a child is 'unnatural.'" The expectant father is involved in natural child birth classes and is eager for "some action." The couple is followed through labor and birth. The loving support the husband offers his wife during the birth is very obvious. The expressions of love for each other is extremely heartwarming at the birth. Upon seeing and holding his newborn girl he concedes that she might like to go to basketball games as well. Bonding is evident.

The film also presents other fathers interacting with their children as they discuss their roles. One father has taken leave from a teaching position to be home as a full time caregiver and delights in gently bathing and talking with his child. Yet another father has resigned a high pressured government position in order to be more involved at home with his two children: an elementary school boy and a pre-school girl who is disabled. This father talks frankly about the special love and attention Molly requires. The father also talks with his son when he complains that Molly disrupts his play activities. The boy is reminded that the family all need to be especially patient with Molly as she develops. Another father and son enjoy a deck sweeping activity and settle down to enjoy a beer and juice respectively. The message is the same from all of these men. Involvement with their children is very precious to them and makes each man a far better person.

2 AM FEEDING. Produced by Kristine Samuelson. 1983, *Distrib-uted by New Day Films, 22 Riverview Drive, Wayne, New Jersey 07470-3191, Tel (201) 633-0212, Color, 24 mins., 16mm and video. No study guide.*

2 AM Feeding is a multi-cultural, realistic and upbeat examina-tion of parenting experiences during the post partum months. It examines in a straightforward manner a broad spectrum of concerns of both the mother and father including nursing, fatigue, mother's recovery, fathering and single parenthood from a mother's point of view.

Through humorous, frank and warm scenes of both mothers and fathers interacting with their babies, in interviews, and segments extracted from parent support group discussions important insights are gained regarding "life after birth" for new parents.

Father is equally evident in this film not only as a supporting mate to his spouse, but as a parent in his own right. In addition to charming scenes and still photographs of men interacting with their newborns, e.g., giving a bottle in a rocking chair and putting a baby to bed, fathers express concerns relative to finding it difficult to tolerate babies crying constantly, the slow return of sex life for couples after birth—finding excuses not to have sexual relations, differences on how a child should be raised—based upon their own upbringing. During a rap session fathers discuss how strongly they feel about their roles as fathers and the differences mothers were to sons rather than fathers. One father states he does not think so much of being a father as he does a parent. What matters to another father is that his child can come to him for love and fun. He wants his child to know him and that he is not "the big, bad guy," but that he is soft, warm and loving and that his child is more than welcome to share these qualities with him. Other fathers discuss how they want to be at home more and that the pressures of family life pull them away from their occupations. One father exclaims that having a baby offers him wonderful excuses for discussions with strangers.

The film presents mothers talking about their own concerns. They discuss fathers' fantasies about going to work and not being with the child while the mother can be home and "play all day" with the baby. Mothers also poignantly present their feelings concerning leaving their babies to return to work.

NEW RELATIONS: A FILM ABOUT FATHERS AND SONS. Produced by Ben Achtenberg, 1980. *Distributed by Fanlight Productions, 47 Halifax Street, Boston, MA 02130, Tel (617) 524-0980, Color, 34 mins., 16mm and video, No study guide.*

New Relations: A Film About Fathers and Sons is a tremendously valuable film emphasizing the complex and profound life changes accompanying the birth of a first child. Its message is particularly relevant and representative of mid-30's parents since its origin stems from the organic experiences of filmmaker Achtenberg and his wife, Emily. The film provides useful insight into a new father's interaction both with his wife and infant son—clearly emphasizing both the pains and rewards of nurturing fathering and mothering. The sensitivity of this film offers for consideration realistic problems parents experience today, e.g., changing sex roles and parenting styles, the effects of isolation from extended family role models, contrasting images of masculinity over three decades, today's childcare options and conflicts experienced by parents regarding careers and family roles.

Through narrative commentary, direct scenes, still photographs and 1950's home movies, *New Relations* carefully addresses a major transition in adult development—the process of parenthood. This autobiographical film begins at the filmmaker's son's first birthday. Viewers learn of Achtenberg's recollection of his readiness to father and his preparation for natural childbirth and the subsequent disappointment by a necessitated Cesarean birth. Pregnant fathers as well as first-time fathers (and no doubt seasoned fathers as well) will find this film supportive as Achtenberg discusses his post partum depression, e.g., jealousy concerning wife's extended nursing, qualitative differences in the baby's relationship with mother and father, "He turns to his mother when he is hurt," differences in caregiving—including discipline and development—not to mention possible resurfacing of previous marital problems.

Viewers also share discussions between Achtenberg and his father concerning a three generation difference in fathering styles and communication. The film project enabled both fathers to communicate with each other more effectively and naturally. One men's group decided the film, "Helped us break through a whole new level in discussing our relationships with our own fathers." The senior Achtenbergs discuss with Ben and Emily contrasting parenting roles in the 50's and now. Insight is offered concerning what fathers in the 50's—out pursuing the American dream—missed with their children and how they can recapture it now through their grandchildren and their adult sons. The film clearly underscores how mothers of the 50's shouldered the major responsibility for raising their children.

At the conclusion of the film Achtenberg shares the following:

> If having a child has placed a lot of strain on us as a couple, being parents has also brought us closer together in a lot of ways . . . Like my father I guess I am not very comfortable talking about my feelings. The last two years have not been exactly easy for me. . . . I have gained more joy and contentment from being a parent than from anything else I have ever done. And I like myself better than I used to.

MEN IN EARLY CHILDHOOD EDUCATION. Produced by David L. Giveans, 1982. *Distributed by Davidson Films, 231 "E" Street, Davis, CA 95616 Tel (916) 753-9604, color, 24 mins., 16mm and video, 3 pp study sheet with references.*

Men in Early Childhood Education provides the long overdue "missing link" to documentary films focusing on the field of early childhood education. It presents a new perspective to many viewers—the role of psychological fathers[8] in the development of young children. This multi-cultural, intergenerational film offers men and women talking about and working with young children in a broad spectrum of activities. It presents an overview of joys, frustrations and rewards men experience as they enter the traditionally female world of professional nurturing. The film is a consciousness raising presentation offering support to men already in the field, to fathers of young children and to young men considering career options. It also serves as a gentle advocate of the natural, nurturing characteristics of men and the importance of men and women working together to role model to children a realistic view of the world outside their classrooms. The film is particularly timely to help offset the surging fear of suspected child molestation and homophobic attitudes pertaining to men who have chosen to work with young children.

This film presents for consideration the low professional status both men and women experience in the field of early childhood education not to mention their unprofessional salaries. It reinforces the necessity of presenting to children comparisons of men as they always have been provided with comparisons of women. Men of various ages discuss the difficulties they have experienced stepping out of traditional societal expectations of what "male work" is all about and they poignantly discuss their feelings of isolation experienced as a minority group in the field.[9]

Men in Early Childhood Education emphasizes the necessity of eliminating the division of labor in an early childhood learning environment freeing both men and women to do what is needed—rather than to adhere to traditional societal dictates of what men do and what women do. Gender does not need to limit the roles men and women play in our society.

In his closing narration, Giveans, who has had several years of experience as a day care teacher, offers a statement more than likely echoed by many other male teachers around the nation: "The most rewarding aspect of my career in early childhood education is the time spent learning and sharing with young children. . . . within minutes of my arrival at school, I am swept into their amazing world."

Perhaps the strongest and most convincing feature of the film are the charming scenes of men interacting with children in a wide spectrum of activities, e.g., marching in a circus parade, changing a toddler's diaper, enjoying a nature walk, sawing, dramatic play dress up and baking muffins. The adage, "One picture is worth a thousand words," was never truer than in the concluding montage of men nurturing children. These scenes present a profound awareness of how children enthusiastically respond to male interaction and the natural gentleness men possess.

PORTRAIT OF GRANDPA DOC. Produced by Diane Baker, 1977, *Distributed by Phoenix Films, 468 Park Avenue South, New York, NY 10016. Tel (212) 684-10016, color, 28 mins., 16mm and video. No study sheet available.*

Our mobile society has generally isolated nuclear family members from their extended family. *Portrait of Grandpa Doc* touchingly reminds viewers of the importance of intergenerational sharing and the rich resources available to children in their grandparents—in this case, a grandfather and his grandson.

This is a docudrama with a professional cast headed by Melvin Douglas, Ann Seymour and Bruce Davison. Douglas brilliantly portrays Grandpa Doc who upon first sight becomes real to viewers conjuring up images and memories of special times spent with grandmothers and grandfathers. It is a particularly significant film in that it dramatically emphasizes the wisdom, love, joy, patience and genuine acceptance seniors are so willing to share. Resources which are unfortunately generally overlooked by our fast-paced society.

Greg Hunter is a young artist preparing for his first one-person showing of paintings. One of the works to be included will be a portrait of his maternal grandfather who died several years earlier. The young artist struggles to capture on canvas the gentle man who shared so much with him as he was growing. To refresh his memory, Greg looks through old family albums and watches 8mm home movies. These films offer nostalgic glimpses of a family (minus the father who was no doubt off working) passing idyllic days at a seaside cottage.

As Greg works, he reflects upon his grandfather who was a sensitive, patient, fun loving supportive friend to the developing boy. Grandpa Doc encouraged him to dream and to build his sandcastles by the sea. He consoled him when Greg's peers teased him because he played with puppets; and he basked in the joy of walking arm and arm with this wise man. Grandpa Doc was the first to recognize his grandson's artistic talent by giving him his first commission saying, "I see the seeds in what you will become."

Greg's mother, who was not always so supportive or aware of his individual interests and budding talent as a child, travels to Los Angeles to attend the art show. She is amazed and touched by the sensitivity of his painting and the vivid remembrances he has captured on canvas of their summers by the sea. Greg's portrait of Grandpa Doc is truly an emotional experience for her. She sees her son in a new light and through this portrait mother and son lovingly communicate as Grandpa Doc lives on vividly in their memories.

REFERENCES

1. *Kramer vs Kramer*, 1979, is the film adaptation of Avery Corman's 1977 book by the same title (Random House, NY). The film was written and directed by Robert Benton and starred Dustin Hoffman, Meryl Streep and Justin Henry. The film was awarded an Academy Award for the Best Picture of the Year in 1980.

2. *Men's Lives*, produced and directed by Josh Hanig and Will Roberts in 1975. The film was awarded an Academy Award for the Best Student Documentary in 1975, as well as receiving several other awards at various film festivals. Distributed by New Day Films, 93 Mill Street, Athens, Ohio 45701, Tel (614) 592-1600, color, 43 mins., 16mm and video, study guide available.

3. Giveans, D.L., One Man's Opinion: Why Do We Need Men Working With Young Children? *First Teacher, 1*, 11, 2.

4. Quoted in: Miner, R., Do Fathers Make Good Mothers? *Family Weekly*, June 15, 1980, p. 6.

5. Spock, Benjamin, *Baby and Child Care*. New York, Pocket Books, 1976 (revised), pp. 42 & 47.

6. Zolotow, Charlotte, *William's Doll*. New York, Harper & Row, 1972.

7. Quoted in: Film brochure for *Heroes and Strangers*, Community Media Productions, 412 W. Fairmount Avenue, State College, PA 16801.

8. *Psychological Fathers* are men who respond to and are responsible for the forming of a child's future. To father, one need not be biologically linked to the child. Good fathering expresses a caring human being who nurtures the love of life, the preservation of human values and who is warm and worthy of a child's trust. Examples of psychological fathers other than male teachers are: family friends, school volunteers, foster grandparents, PAL volunteers, Big Brothers, Boy Scout leaders, etc.

9. According to the 1983 Bureau of Labor statistics of the total male teachers employed in education 1.8% work in nursery through kindergarten, 1.0% work in daycare and 0.1% provide home day care.

GLOSSARY OF MAJOR TERMS

Androgyny: The blending of both traditional masculine and feminine traits into an individual's personality, e.g., a person having qualities of both males and females, e.g., being "strong" yet "tender."

Appointive (hierarchical) System: A ruling body of clergy organized into rank, each subordinate to the one above. Operationally, it refers to a system of decision-making by bishop and cabinet (comprised of superintendents) regarding the assignment of clergy to their respective pastoral position.

Ascription (or status ascription): The expectations of another that are based on group characteristics, such as age, sex, kinship, race, i.e., expectations based on characteristics that a person cannot control. (The opposite of "ascription" is "achievement," things a person does that the person can control, such as getting an education, or doing a job.)

Associative: Casual, friendly relations between people who find themselves in the same neighborhood, office, etc.; lacking the commitment necessary to endure beyond the context where the relationships were formed.

Avoidance: This is a psychological defense mechanism which consists of refusal to encounter situations or activities which are anxiety provoking.

Best interest of the child: Current legal doctrine arguing that custody of the child should go to the person who is in the child's best interest.

Borderline personality: This is a personality disorder in which there is instability in a variety of areas including interpersonal behavior, mood, and self-image.

Child custody: Immediate charge and control over a child, as e.g., performed by a parent.

Child nurturers: People who are in the business or avocation of providing love, support, and care for young children.

Child support: Monetary payments to a child, e.g., monthly payments to a child's custodian by a non-custodial parent.

Child support: Money given by a parent to support children after the parents' divorce. By practice this has been more often required of the non-custodial parent (usually the father).

Cohabitation: Living together without marriage but under marriage-like conditions.

Cohort: Individuals born in the same time period whose timing of critical life transitions in their family careers can often be determined through archival records such as U.S. Census data.

Cognitive dissonance: The tensions a person experiences and may try to resolve, because the person holds contradictory perceptions, e.g., "all people are equal," vs. "my sex is superior to the other sex."

Commitment: A pledge or intention to do something in the future, or a state of being obligated or emotionally impelled to do something.

Concurrent therapy: A form of marital therapy in which each partner is treated individually and simultaneously by the same therapist as contrasted to conjoint therapy wherein both partners are treated together by the same therapist in joint sessions.

Countertransference: The conscious or unconscious response of a therapist to a patient, determined by the therapist's own needs.

Cross-over effects: Effects of one spouse's work schedule on the other spouse's family life.

Cross-sex jobs: Jobs which persons of either gender enter that are typically performed by members of the opposite sex.

Custodial parent: Mother or father who has legal responsibility for his/her child(ren).

Custody: Refers to the guardianship status of children. Custody may be mandated by the state (legal custody) or occur by natural informal circumstances.

Joint: Custody over a child by more than one person, usually the two parents.

Legal: Custody as defined by law or as decided upon by a court (in contrast to physical custody).

Physical: Custody in "true life" (in contrast to legal custody); in some countries a court can define custody in a special case so as to be the intended physical custody.

Sole: Custody over a child by one person only, usually one of the parents.

Delusion: A false belief which arises without appropriate external stimulation, as maintained despite evidence to the contrary, and is not one which is ordinarily accepted by other members of one's culture.

Delusional jealousy: This is a delusion that one's sexual partner is unfaithful.

Denial: This is a psychological defense mechanism employed in an attempt to disavow the existence of unpleasant reality.

Dialectic: A struggle of contradictions or opposites, such as Karl Marx's idea of dialectical materialism, where the social structure is believed to arise from the economic structure (class position creates consciousness).

Divorce: The legal dissolution of a marriage (which does not end by the death of one of the spouses); sometimes the separation of a cohabitation is (technically wrongly) called divorce; sometimes the term divorce is used to include legal or physical separation and annulment.

Dyadic power: The relative advantage or power of the man or the woman in marriage. ("dyads" are pairs or groups of two).

Equalitarian marriage: An egalitarian relationship between a husband and wife where there is an equal sharing of authority, tasks and responsibilities.

Expressive roles: Bundles of social expectations which involve love, nurturance, moral support, and trust; non-judgmental and accepting.

Externalization: A step in the social construction of reality; the actions of people which produce a culture or system or set of rules.

Family work: Housework and childcare; this term contrasts with *paid work*; paid work, family work, and volunteer work are the principal forms of work.

Female-dominated workworld: Jobs that are filled predominantly by women such as nursing and child care.

Flextime: An alternative work schedule in which full-time workers can select their starting and ending time, within limits set by the employer.

Four-day week: A work schedule involving four consecutive ten-hour days each week.

Friendship network: A target person's set of friends.

Fully developed friendship: One in which members have passed through stages in which they successfully deal with anxieties about the escalation of commitment, anxieties about leadership and decision-making, and anxieties about intimacy. Having passed through these stages the friendship group is characterized by shared values, open communication, and the capacities to nurture its members, resolve conflicts, obtain and exchange resources, set priorities, and achieve collective goals.

Healthy families: Family systems that are in a state of physical, mental and social well-being.

Homogeneity of friendship network: The degree of similarity of social characteristics of members of a friendship network.

Husband-wife wage ratio: The ratio of the husband's hourly wage to the wife's hourly wage.

Instrumental roles: Bundles of expectations centered in tasks and specific goals, where performance is measured and judged, such as in one's occupation, decision-making, and organized activity.

Internalization: The final step in the social construction of reality, wherein one incorporates an externalized, objectivated world into one's psyche.

Intimacy between friends: Disclosure of personal information about the self (hopes, fears, past history, current problems, future plans, etc).

Itinerancy: A system of rotating clergy in the United Methodist Church.

Joint custody: Parents sharing the responsibility and decision making in regard to the care of children. Joint custody generally connotes a legal agreement but it may occur through an informal co-parenting arrangement. Joint custody implies but does not necessarily result in shared living arrangements for the children.

Legitimation: A system of meanings to explain and justify institutions or sets of rules or political systems; the definition of a system as "correct" or "natural" or "right".

Male caregivers: Men who provide care for preschool children, such as in child-care centers or nursery schools.

Male sex role identity: A theory which argues that for men to become psychologically mature they must acquire or have the sex-appropriate traits, attitudes, and interests that psychologically validate or affirm their biological sex.

Mediation: Separating or separated individuals working together with a neutral person to attempt to resolve or settle issues such as support, custody, and property division. It contrasts with the more traditional adversarial approach to marital separation and divorce.

Multiplex relationships: Relationships in which persons relate to each other in more than one role; for example, a relationship in which the same person interacts as a co-worker, a member of the same church, a neighbor, and a friend.

Network density: The connectedness of a friendship network; the degree to which a target person's friends know and interact with one another.

Nonstandard work schedules: Work schedules that depart from the standard pattern of regular daytime work on weekdays only.

Nurturing roles: Roles which require expressive behaviors that traditionally have been characterized as feminine by our society, such as child-care.

Objectivation: A step in the social construction of reality, wherein the social world, though humanly created, seems to take on an existence of its own, independent of its human creators.

Paranoid schizophrenia: A type of schizophrenia dominated by persecutory delusions, grandiose delusions, delusional jealousy, or hallucinations with persecutory or grandiose content.

Paternity: In law, the determination or finding of the one who is the legal father of a child born out of wedlock.

Paternity leave: A paid or unpaid leave from the job, of short or long duration, for fathers whose wives have recently given birth.

Patriarchy: Literally, a community where the father is the supreme authority; the term denotes rule by male elites over women and children, and non-elite men.

Passive-dependency: A personality type characterized by helplessness, indecisiveness, and a tendency to cling to others.

Passive-aggressive: A situation in which the patient shows his aggressive feelings in passive ways, such as obstructionism, pouting, and stubbornness.

Preschool teachers: Classroom teachers of children between the ages of birth to five.

Putative father: Father of a child born out of wedlock.

Receptive: A friendship in which one member is primarily a giver (usually higher status) and the other is a receiver. The receiver idealizes the giver, and the giver identifies with and vicariously participates in the experiences of the receiver.

Reciprocal: A friendship that involves strong commitment between persons who relate to each other as equals, and who value each other's personalities.

Role: A group of norms that defines the rights, obligations and privileges of a person who occupies a particular status.

Role behaviors: The ways a specific person plays a role corresponding to a status.

Role expectations: Norms, rules and patterns for behavior.

Role-making: The process of creating or innovating new norms for a role.

Role-overlap: Similar roles played in common by two or more people.

Satisfaction: The quality or state of being fulfilled in want or need. In a global sense it refers to being contented and pleased with one's state of being.

Sex bias: Prejudicial beliefs about people based upon their maleness or femaleness.

Sex of custodial parent: Refers to whether a single parent is male or female. Single parents are separated, divorced, widowed or never married men or women with sole or joint custody raising dependent children in fatherless/motherless homes.

Sex ratios: The number of males per 100 females; stated in males' numbers, e.g., "103" means 103 men per 100 women.

Sex-role attitudes: Beliefs that are held in regard to what is appropriate behaviors for males and females.

Sex-role conflict: On-the-job difficulty that centers around one's expected role as defined by his sex and his actual role as he perceives it.

Sex role-reversal: Roles traditionally played by one sex being played by the other sex.

Sex-role stereotypes: Beliefs that it is only natural and fitting for males and females to adhere to traditional sex-role patterns.

Sexist: A blind allegiance or simple-minded devotion to one's own sex, which may result in behaving toward persons of the opposite sex in stereotypical ways.

Sex-role prescriptions: Rules of proper behavior for a male or female who play a role as defined by cultural standards.

Single custodial fathers: Male parents who have physical custody of their minor children acquired through separation, divorce, adoption or widowhood.

Single parent families: Families in which one parent has the primary responsibility for care of the child(ren). They occur as a result of adoption, separation, divorce, widowhood or a never-married status.

Social construction of reality: The description of how a culture is created by human actions; there is no ''objective'' culture existing independently of its human creators.

Social support: Exchange of concrete goods or services (aid), emotional support (affect), and validation of each other's self-concepts, perceptions, and world views (affirmation).

Socialization: The process of becoming a human being and a part of a specific social group.

Sole custody: One parent assuming the primary responsibility for the care of children. Sole custody can occur by legal or informal circumstances. The other parent may or may not have visitation privileges.

Super-dads: Fathers who attempt to excel equally as fathers, husbands and wage-earners.

Tender years doctrine: Legal doctrine that young children should remain in the mother's custody. This doctrine was used extensively in American courts until recent years.

Termination of parental rights: A legal decision to take decision-making responsibility away from one or, in rare situations, both parent(s).

Theodicy: A justification of the existence of evil, by showing that evil is part of the divine plan; evil becomes the test of belief and believers, to prove faithfulness to God.

Time diary-studies: The recording of role behaviors by respondents during 24 hour periods to quantify behavior played in various roles.

Work-family interference: Worker's perception of conflict between his/her work and family life.